D1671639

Planning your coherent
11–16 geography curriculum:
a design toolkit

David Gardner

Geographical
Association

Acknowledgements

Source information for each figure is included at the end of each figure caption.

Every effort has been made to identify and contact the original sources of copyright material. If there have been any inadvertent breaches of copyright we apologise and will make any necessary amendments at the first opportunity.

© The Geographical Association, 2021

This book is copyright under the Berne Convention. All rights are reserved. Apart from any fair dealing for the purpose of private study, research, criticism or review, as permitted under the Copyright, Designs and Patents Act 1988, no part of this publication may be reproduced, stored in a retrieval system, or transmitted in any form or by any means, electronic, electrical, chemical, mechanical, optical, photocopying, recording or otherwise, without the prior written permission of the copyright owner. Enquiries should be addressed to the Geographical Association. The authors have licensed the Geographical Association to allow members to reproduce material for their own internal school/ departmental use, provided that the authors hold the copyright. The views expressed in this publication are those of the authors and do not necessarily represent those of the Geographical Association.

ISBN 978-1-84377-480-8 (print)
ISBN 978-1-84377-531-7 (digital eBook)
First published 2021
Impression number 10 9 8 7 6 5 4 3 2 1
Published by the Geographical Association, 160 Solly Street, Sheffield S1 4BF
Company number 07139068
Website: www.geography.org.uk
E-mail: info@geography.org.uk
The Geographical Association is a registered charity: no 1135148

Cover image: © Anna Frajtova/Shutterstock.com
Copy edited by Fran Royle
Designed and typeset by Ledgard Jepson Ltd
Printed and bound in UK by TJ Books Limited, Padstow

Access the online resources

We have created a password-protected web page where you can find the activities, ongoing support, resources and downloadable versions of many of the figures in this book. Items that are available to download are indicated by this symbol: ⬇

In addition, you will find a wealth of support:

- Links will take you direct to relevant information on the GA and other websites.
- Downloadable templates and tables that you can use in school.
- The complete versions of the case studies from Chapter 8.

To access the web page, please type the following URL into the address bar in your browser: **www.geography.org.uk/planningyourcurriculum**.

You will be asked to enter a password. The unique password for this book is **DGPG21**.

Please note that you cannot get to this page through searching or via the GA website.

David Gardner taught geography in comprehensive schools in Leicester and Scarborough, before moving to the Qualifications and Curriculum Authority as a Curriculum Advisor and National Lead for geography. He has worked with teachers all over the world on curriculum and assessment development. During his time, at QCA, David developed the 2007 National Curriculum for geography, the GCSE and A level geography subject criteria, and accredited the resultant specifications as part of the 2007 New Secondary Curriculum Review. Since 2011 he has worked in teacher education as a PGCE lecturer, as well as with Schools Direct and Teach First at Goldsmiths, University College London Institute of Education and the Open University. David is an active member of the Geographical Association. He was chair of the GA's Education Group from 2011 to 2016 and became chair of the GA's Assessment and Examinations Special Interest Group in 2021. He edited *Assessing progress in your Key Stage 3 geography curriculum*, published by the Geographical Association in 2015. He is the author of a number of successful geography textbooks and teacher guides including the GA Award-winning *Progress in Geography*, and followed by *Progress in Geography Skills*, for Hodder Education. He has also led a wide range of professional development for secondary teachers focusing, in particular, on curriculum design and assessment. David is now a freelance education consultant, and a consultant to the GA.

Acknowledgments

I would like to thank David Lambert, Alan Kinder and Elaine Anderson, for their invaluable advice and support in writing this book.

I would like to thank, with love, my wife Pat, for her ongoing patience, support and understanding, through what became my daily obsession in writing this book.

It was a particular pleasure to work with a group of excellent geography teachers and leaders who have added an array of curriculum stories, presenting their impressive approaches to curriculum design in Chapter 8 of this book. Their hard work and skills provide a compelling picture of curriculum design in action, which significantly enhances this book. They are:

- Caiti Walter, until 2021 Deputy Head of Geography, Graveney School

- Andy Freer, Head of Humanities, Trinity Academy Grammar

- Daniel Whittall, Geography Subject Lead and Head of Year 13, Trinity Sixth Form Academy

- Kirsty Holder, Senior Leader responsible for implementation of the ECF and ITT, Fortismere School

- Lizzie Butler, Lead Geography Consultant for the Harris Federation

- Aidan Hesslewood, Head of Geography, Spalding Grammar School.

Foreword

It is a great privilege to be invited to write the foreword to this hugely informative and practical book.

As David Gardner shows, the idea of curriculum is a big one, and a very precious one – perhaps the only truly defining *educational* concept in the whole business of education. Curriculum is *the* educational concept, and no other profession needs to bother with it. The National Curriculum, on the other hand, is simply a few words on a page – significant words of course, but no more than that. The fact that the National Curriculum is now no longer the lawful requirement of many secondary schools (because it does not apply to academies and free schools) is tantamount to official recognition of this fact.

This book fully recognises the significance of curriculum thinking, particularly in relation to official documents such as the National Curriculum itself, but others too such as examination specifications. The book pays due regard to Ofsted's relatively recent conversion to curriculum thinking – and its recognising the central importance of coherent curriculum design, planning and enactment in schools. But the book also manages to go far beyond any instrumental 'checklist' in order to prepare us for when the inspector calls. As David points out, 'The curriculum problem (i.e. resolving the question of what to teach and how to sequence it) can never be satisfactorily addressed by a step-by-step technical template. The problem is just too complex to be solved with a recipe. Moreover, such a step-by-step model is unlikely to encourage the kind of creativity that is needed from teachers to produce effective, imaginative and engaging curricula.' (p. 24)

I like that. The ambition is electrifying. For instance, the '... curriculum is not a physical thing, but rather a series of interactions between teachers, students and the knowledge to be imparted. The curriculum is more a human, rather than a technical, process. In other words, curriculum is far messier and more dynamic than the clean, 'scientific' process implied by 'rational curriculum planning.' (p. 23)

This sentiment is of enormous importance and explains the long-term commitment by geography educationists in Britain (and internationally) to look beyond stultifying standards and competences – i.e. the words on the page. And instead, seek more human ways to express the significance of engaging with geographical knowledge and ideas – whether through 'thinking geographically', or 'GeoCapabilities' or through the GA's own manifesto *A Different View* or critical thinking in geography.

In convincingly straddling the needs of Ofsted with a more theoretically nuanced grasp of decades of work in the literature focussed on the 'curriculum problem', David shows he is possibly uniquely placed to write this book. He has taught for many years in state secondary schools. He is an acclaimed school textbook author. He has been a long-time volunteer in the Geographical Association (GA), and for a period had a national leadership role as geography subject officer for the Qualifications and Curriculum Authority (QCA) until its disbandment in 2010. Since then, he has served as a university tutor in teacher education and training and has run professional development courses for serving teachers. His breadth of knowledge is extraordinary, therefore, and it is a considerable feat that he has managed to synthesise and summarise such an enormous amount of source material and experience. I would go as far as to say that he has picked a way through a labyrinth of seemingly contradictory material – and in so doing reconcile several issues that sit uncomfortably within the famed chasm that divides theory and practice.

Thus, for some readers, accommodating and assimilating traditions of 'rational curriculum planning' and associated ideas of sequencing and progression, together with open-ended critical thinking and calls for decolonising the curriculum and at the same time accommodating geography as powerful knowledge with the attendant 'Future 3' curriculum scenarios ... may all seem too much. But not so. For this book manages to help us see across all of this and more besides. It is not, after all, a manual or handbook, but a *toolkit*.

We can select from this book the tools that we need at any one time, and then return when our focus changes or our priorities shift – as will inevitably happen. As David does not shy away from telling us: the job of curriculum design and enactment is never 'finished.' These processes are both the product and the source of professional development and growth, and this book should serve well those who possess it, for years to come.

One of the unique qualities of this book is its continual inter-weaving of theory and practice, and practice and theory. There is no one way of doing this. Good practice doesn't just flow from good theory, just as a bit of theory is unlikely to 'fix' poor practice. But there is both thought and practice from which we can draw, make sense of and use. The detailed case studies selected for the book are, therefore, of enormous importance. And especially, great thanks to the teachers who have supplied them! Identifying and writing case studies in a form that can be understood and recognised by readers is no easy matter. But they really work here.

We read diverse solutions to the curriculum problem. We learn from experienced geography curriculum makers, who are not just content with ticking boxes but want to use the subject in school to help young people understand the Earth as the home of humankind – who want students to grasp the Earth as an object of disciplined thought and imagination. Furthermore, it is great to read the different ways teachers interpret what it means to 'think geographically', how they organise and sequence this, how they build in means to evaluate their success (as well as the achievement of their students). It is inspiring to see how these teachers are willing to share their work openly and especially their commitment to geography as a dynamic, contestable and yet rigorous subject which can deepen students' grasp of change, diversity, risk, dispute (etc) when it comes to the worlds in which we live on planet Earth.

Having been 'on the scene' for quite a few years now (I started teaching geography in a comprehensive school in 1974) I have maintained a strong desire to keep geography at the centre of my work as an educationist. This is not always easy. For example, promotions in school can easily take you away, if not from the classroom exactly, from the day-to-day engagement with school geography:

its form and function, its quality and even its popularity at options time. It therefore takes conscious effort to maintain one's personal fidelity to the idea of geography in education. Some of the case study writers know exactly what I mean by this! And I admire the way David Gardner has achieved this too, throughout the long and winding road of his career.

Such 'passion and commitment' should not have to come at a price. Furthermore, such enthusiasm for the subject should not result in blind spots or tunnel-vision (sometimes the price of long-term loyalty). Having reached the end of this book, with its reminders of the importance of vision, big picture aims and indeed critical evaluation, I am reassured. This isn't a book that fetishizes the potential bureaucracy of 'coherent planning'. There are plenty of grids, lists, figures and tables but the point is always the bigger purpose that these serve. And neither does this book grotesquely over intellectualise the curriculum problem. Instead, we are simply encouraged to engage with each other's curriculum stories – which is where the GA comes in. The GA offers avenues and forums for such sharing. This book contributes much to enabling this to happen with a common language and set of tools.

So, when it comes to questions of quality in curriculum it is a professional matter; the profession needs to own it, not Ofsted or any other external agency. And when it comes to urgent matters that face the world of geography education, for instance, how adequately to deal with issues of race and racism in the geography curriculum or questions concerning energy futures or how (or even whether) to teach 'development', this book serves us well – because it explicitly states that the mission, the vision, the educational purposes of teaching geography ... this is all in our hands. Dan Whittall points this out elegantly in his own mission statement and if, like me, you like to read books and newspapers from back to front, then go to page 155 and have a look.

David Lambert

Honorary Professor of Geography Education, UCL Institute of Education

Chief Executive of the Geographical Association 2002–12

August 2021

Context
and theory

CHAPTER 1

Curriculum: concept and context

This introductory chapter hopes to establish an understanding of the concept of curriculum, and how this has evolved over the last 40 years. In England, this has been a period characterised by frequent and wide-ranging curriculum reform.

It is fitting to begin a book about curriculum in geography and its design by considering the ground-breaking work of Norman Graves in *Curriculum Planning in Geography* (1979). Before becoming Professor of Geography Education at the University of London Institute of Education, he had taught at various state secondary schools in England. His book on curriculum planning is still a useful foundation for curriculum discussion. Graves pointed out that in order to understand the present situation regarding curriculum, it is useful to look first at what has happened in the past: 'it must be understood that not only have ideas about curriculum planning changed, but so has the terminology, the whole context of schooling and the subject of geography.' (p. 2)

This has certainly been the case in the 40 years since. In England, for example, national curricula and GCSEs have been introduced and modified several times. The National Strategies professional development programme from 1998 to 2011 transformed the way schools approached teaching and learning. Schools have become far more accountable, with the creation and development of Ofsted, and the annual publication of so-called 'school league tables', both introduced in 1992. More recently a growing number of schools have been transformed into academies, and do not have to follow the National Curriculum (NC). Over these years the world, and the way geography perceives it, have also been transformed. Many practising teachers have experienced some or all of these changes; many more are only now entering the profession. Each of these changes has left a legacy, creating a complicated, and at times confusing, matrix and context for curriculum change.

Graves believed that our thinking is shaped by our formative experiences, and we can ascribe a meaning to a concept, such as curriculum, which is no longer relevant; also, that different people can use the word curriculum in different senses, or there are people who don't consider it at all. As Ofsted Chief Inspector Amanda Spielman says: 'One of the areas that I think we sometimes lose sight of is the real substance of education. Not the exam grades or the progress scores, important though they are, but instead the real meat of what is taught in our schools and colleges: the curriculum. ... Yet all too often that objective, the real substance of education, is getting lost in our schools. I question how often leaders really ask, "What is the body of knowledge that we want to give to young people?" As one head, Stuart Lock, put it during a typically insightful thread of tweets: "Most schools don't think about curriculum enough, and when they think they do, they actually mean qualifications or the timetable."' (Spielman, 2017)

This chapter will hopefully help place your own experiences and understanding of the school curriculum within the context of this widespread reform, to determine your starting point for responding to Ofsted's 2019 Education Inspection Framework (EIF), with its curriculum focus. It may also help you to fully appreciate the implications for curriculum design of the 2014 NC, new GCSEs and Ofsted's new perspective on curriculum, which is embedded into the EIF.

What is the curriculum?

At this stage it would make sense to consider what we mean by curriculum, and how ideas about it have evolved over the last 40 years. Graves (1979, pp. 12–13) identified four meanings in a school context:

1. In a general sense, to indicate the broad scope of activities that go on in a school, with certain types of learning occurring in different subjects.

2. To indicate the content of a particular subject that is to be taught. Content refers to the ideas, concepts, principles, facts and skills which may be taught.

3. To indicate the process whereby aims, objectives, content, teaching strategies and evaluation

interact in the school – the dynamic aspect of the curriculum in action.

4. To describe what is planned to happen in a school within a particular subject. In a planned geography curriculum this could be set out in a document that shows the aims of a course, what the content consists of, what teaching units, with their objectives and teaching strategies, and how the course is to be evaluated.

In the 1980s, before the introduction of a national curriculum in England and Wales, Her Majesty's Inspectorate (HMI) supported schools and LEAs in formulating curriculum policies via 17 *Curriculum Matters* discussion booklets. These documents were a vital component of the thinking that ultimately created the first NC. *The Curriculum from 5 to 16* (Department of Education and Science (DES), 1985), the second in the series, offered a much broader definition of a school's curriculum:

'A school's curriculum consists of all those activities designed or encouraged within its organisational framework to promote the intellectual, personal, social and physical development of its pupils. It includes not only the formal programme of lessons, but also the "informal" programme of so-called extracurricular activities as well as all those features which produce the school's "ethos", such as the quality of relationships, the concern for equality of opportunity, the values exemplified in the way the school sets about its task and the way in which it is organised and managed. Teaching and learning styles strongly influence the curriculum and in practice they cannot be separated from it. Since pupils learn from all these things, it needs to be ensured that all are consistent in supporting the school's intentions.' (DES, 1985, p. 7)

The guidance went on to argue that there are some essential skills, aspects and issues which are not necessarily contained within subjects, but which need to be included in the curriculum:

- environmental education
- health education
- information technology
- political education
- education in economic understanding
- preparation of young people for the world of work.

These wider themes in part led to the development of cross-curricular skills, themes and dimensions that became a non-statutory component of the first NC, and which returned more prominently in the 2007 revision (see Figure 1.2).

Lambert and Hopkin (2014) captured the essence of curriculum, and its distinctive contribution to stimulating learning, by stressing the significance of curriculum as opposed to pedagogy: 'Conceptually, we distinguish curriculum as being concerned with the overriding question of *what* to teach the young. This is a difficult and profound question. It is conceptually distinct from the question of *how* to teach – although we readily and eagerly concede that *in practice* the two may be very closely intertwined.' (p. 2)

Curriculum – a contested concept

The concept of curriculum in schools was to become more contested with the Education Reform Act in 1988. This Act marked a significant increase in centralised government control over education, and in particular the curriculum. It led to the formation of the NC, as well as GCSEs and new A levels, underpinned by defined subject criteria, and in the 2014 versions specified subject content (DfE, 2014). In the 1980s geographers found themselves having to defend the place of geography in the emerging NC, as the DES favoured a peripheral role for it. The Geographical Association (GA) led a campaign to protect the subject, publishing *A Case for Geography* (Bailey and Binns, 1987), which promoted the essential skills, attitudes and values that geography contributes to the whole curriculum. By 1991 the place of geography had been successfully secured in the NC, albeit with an overly prescriptive programme of study, giving teachers little choice but to 'deliver' the vast content to students (DES, 1991). Successive reviews of the geography NC (GNC) sought to reduce the overloaded content of the 1991 version, as well as reflect the developing ideas of society, and the political ideas of successive governments. Eleanor Rawling's important text *Changing the Subject: The impact of national policy on school geography, 1980–2000* (Rawling, 2001) explains in depth how political influences on the national educational system had significant consequences for the geography curriculum. Key elements of this are summarised and updated in Figure 1.1 (on page 10).

Year	1991 (4yrs)	1995 (4yrs)	1999 (8yrs)	2007 (7yrs)	2014
Government	Conservative	Conservative	Labour	Labour	Conservative-led coalition
What was/ is it like?	Very detailed – five attainment targets 114 statements of attainment at KS3. Prescriptive PoS – outlined countries to be studied.	'Dearing Review' to slim down the content of NC subjects. Introduced level descriptions to replace statements of attainment to clarify student outcomes.	Content rearranged, highlighting geographical enquiry and skills, and also big ideas/concepts – places, patterns and processes, environmental change and sustainable development.	Content significantly reduced. PoS emphasised key concepts – place, space, scale, interdependence, environmental interaction, physical and human processes, cultural understanding and diversity, and key processes; geographical enquiry and skills.	Focus on core knowledge – locational and place knowledge, physical and human geography and geography skills and fieldwork. Level descriptions abolished as the progression framework. Multi-academy trusts (MATs) do not have to follow the NC.
Good features	The fact that geography included in NC raised status of subject.	Reduced content, re-sorted into skills, places and themes. Highlighted the importance of investigation (enquiry).	Clarified skills, big ideas and strengthened the aims and rationale of geography, with importance statement, and KS statement.	The underlying framework of concepts and skills clearly stated, as were the aims and rationale.	Core knowledge is provided as a simple list, underpinned by three aims to develop contextual knowledge of location of significant places, understanding processes forming key physical and human features, competence in geographical skills.
Problems	Content heavy and unworkable. It became a curriculum of delivery.	Failed to: ■ distinguish concepts from content ■ define geographical enquiry ■ clarify the role of the teacher.	Teachers and publishers focused more on content, a legacy of the first two versions of GNC. Lack of clarity in how concepts, skills, content and level descriptions work together. The NC documents also provided guidance about important cross-curricular approaches.	Very little content provided. Guidance was required to help teachers understand the new structure of the PoS – importance statement, key concepts, key processes, range and content, curriculum opportunities.	Reference to concepts and geographical enquiry are largely omitted. The progression framework of level descriptions used in schools since 1995 abolished with no system or suggestion of how to replace it. Schools given the responsibility to develop their own systems to gauge pupil progress. NC no longer compulsory for all schools; weakens its significance.

Figure 1.1: The geography National Curriculum at key stage 3, 1991–2014: a comparison (adapted from Rawling 2007, Figure 1, page 6).

Year	1991 (4yrs)	1995 (4yrs)	1999 (8yrs)	2007 (7yrs)	2014
Government	Conservative	Conservative	Labour	Labour	Conservative-led coalition
Consequences	Provided template for successive versions with framework of locational/place knowledge, knowledge and understanding, and skills.

Little scope for curriculum development in school – led to coverage of large amount of content.

Created a legacy of delivery approach, characterised in *Key Geography* textbook series. | Still emphasised content rather than concepts and skills, did little to reduce the focus on delivery rather than curriculum development.

Introduction of level descriptions provided a progression framework separate to the curriculum, further reducing the potential of coherent curriculum planning. | To help schools better understand how the elements of the NC work together. QCA (2000) published a guidance scheme of work for each subject. This also emphasised cross-curricular approaches, and general teaching requirements. Publishers developed textbooks covering all 24 unit plans in the SoW, conflating the content of the curriculum.

National Strategies launched in 1997 developed elaborate training packages for schools, focusing on approaches to these general requirements – pedagogy, AfL, thinking skills, literacy, numeracy and ICT across the curriculum. These initiatives further deflected teachers from what to teach to focus more on how to teach. | This curriculum review focussed on whole statutory aims, with a whole-school approach to curriculum design considering the role of Personal Learning and Thinking Skills, cross-curricular dimensions, the 'Every Child Matters' agenda as well as subjects. Subjects were only a component of a bigger picture of the curriculum, with curriculum design focusing on making links between subjects, and other aspects of the curriculum. This led to schools questioning the role of subjects in schools. | Schools had developed the use of data based on level descriptions to measure school effectiveness. Once abolished schools tended to focus on developing new assessment and progression frameworks, rather than developing the KS3 curriculum. |

Figure 1.1 (continued): The geography National Curriculum at key stage 3, 1991–2014: a comparison (adapted from Rawling 2007, Figure 1, page 6).

Throughout its development the GNC has failed to clearly identify the role of teachers as curriculum makers or architects. The 2014 National Curriculum (DfE, 2013) represents the fourth major revision in 23 years. Biddulph (2017) summed up the problem facing schools: 'It seemed that the curriculum had become a battleground for competing, and often incompatible, educational agendas' (p. 33). Any discussion about the *what* to teach highlighted by Lambert and Hopkin (2014) has been dominated for over 30 years by the changing content and ideology of the NC.

The 2007 Secondary Curriculum Review (QCA, 2007) provides an example of how political ideology influenced the geography curriculum. In 1997 a new Labour government demonstrated a commitment to refocusing on education with an emphasis on social inclusion, supporting all children to achieve their potential: the 'Every Child Matters' agenda (HMSO, 2003). Thirteen years of continuous Labour government led to two versions of the NC, in 1999 and 2007, coupled with the National Strategies training programme, introduced in 1998. According to the Department for Education

(DfE, 2011a) National Strategies were designed to 'to drive improvements in standards through a focused programme of managing changes in the way that ... subjects are taught in classrooms' (p. 2). In practice, these developments diverted the attention of schools away from curriculum and subjects to focus on pedagogy and 'assessment for learning' with an emphasis on whole-school and cross-curricular approaches.

In 2007 the Government published its Education White Paper 'The children's plan' (Department for Children, Schools and Families (DCSF), 2007). The Secondary Curriculum Review was a key aspect of this plan, with the central aim of developing a coherent 11–19 curriculum to help all young people become successful learners, confident individuals and responsible citizens. This was part of a wide set of 11–19 reforms including a new NC key stage 3, Diplomas, new A levels and GCSEs. These were designed to provide schools with greater flexibility to tailor learning to their learners' needs. There was less prescribed content in the new key stage 3 programmes of study, which focused more on the key concepts and processes that were thought to underlie each subject. In explaining 'What has Changed and Why?' (2007) the Qualifications and Curriculum Authority (QCA) described an inclusive view of curriculum, not dissimilar to that described by Graves some 40 years previously: 'The new curriculum is much more than a set of content to cover: it is the entire planned learning experience, including lessons, events, the routines of the school, the extended school day and activities that take place out of school.' (p. 4)

The common format for each subject's programme of study was designed to contribute to greater coherence, making it easier to see links between subjects. Several subjects shared key concepts and processes, highlighting the potential for cross-curricular links. QCA reintroduced the thinking of the HMI from 1986 (p. 9) and the cross-curricular guidance of the first NC, bringing back dimensions such as healthy lifestyles, enterprise, the global dimension and sustainable development that cross subject boundaries.

This review also placed a strong emphasis on the development of skills for life and work. A framework for personal, learning and thinking skills (PLTs) – under the six headings of independent enquirers, creative thinkers, team workers, self-managers, effective participators and reflective learners – was introduced into the curriculum.

For the first time in a curriculum review, a comprehensive programme of training, practical support and guidance, funded by government and led by QCA, was put in place to help schools implement this new curriculum. In particular, new guidance was developed to show schools how the whole curriculum contributed to learners' personal development and the achievement of the 'Every Child Matters' agenda. The Qualifications and Curriculum Development Agency (QCDA) published a new NC website and guidance booklets to support the curriculum design process. At its heart were three curriculum questions:

- What are we trying to achieve?
- How do we organise learning?
- How well are we achieving our aims?

It presented a definition of a school's curriculum as 'the entire planned learning experience', consisting of everything that promotes learners' intellectual, personal, social and physical development.

QCDA designed a big picture of the secondary curriculum (Figure 1.2) as a tool to demonstrate how the three curriculum questions interacted. See also Chapter 2: Powerful Knowledge pages 27–8 which places this review in a model of 'Futures thinking'.

This big picture of the curriculum caused concern in the geography and other subject communities, as it seemed to demote subjects to a row of boxes – and fairly low down in the 'stratigraphy' of the process. Rawling (2007, p. 10) felt the diagram better represented the items QCDA was dealing with: 'it is more like an administrator's checklist than a serious aid to curriculum planning ... subjects don't appear until well down the page after layer on layer of national initiatives and recommendations.'

Lambert and Morgan (2010) concluded '... we have suggested that contemporary education policies are underpinned by two main drivers. These are preparation for life in a global knowledge economy, and the goals of a cohesive and happy society. Schools and teachers are to play their part in meeting these goals, and school subjects such as geography are to be welcomed to the extent that they contribute to these goals ... In such circumstances, curriculum

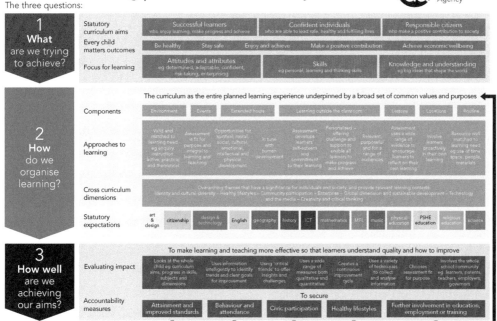

Figure 1.2:
A big picture of
the secondary
curriculum.
Source: QCDA,
2010.

planning in school geography is unlikely to be based on a strong and principled analysis of the way the subject can contribute to an understanding of the making and remaking of society and nature.' (pp. 35–6) In other words, the curriculum question of what to teach seemed to have been removed from the subject communities – who were now subservient to the 'big picture' (the aims of which were not necessarily educational *per se*, but economic, social and political).

The GA was sufficiently concerned to once again fight the subject's corner, as it had done in 1987. *A different view: a manifesto from the Geographical Association* (GA, 2009) reaffirmed geography's place in the curriculum and the role of teachers as 'autonomous professionals driven by educational goals and purposes: that is, they are the curriculum makers and the subject leaders ... Designing a curriculum is not just a technical matter, specifying objectives and a course of study to meet them. It is a moral concern, and should reflect what we think we should be teaching. This is why we believe the curriculum should be deeply influenced by confident, autonomous teachers.' (p. 27)

Impact of increased centralised government control on school geography

Roberts (2018) helpfully summarises the impact of central government policy-making on geography education: 'Since 1993, teachers have been faced with frequent changes to the curriculum and a pervasive accountability culture. This has restricted rather than enhanced geographical education, and has limited the scope for teachers to make their own professional judgements. Students' experience of geography has become more controlled through standardised lessons, a focus on examinations and fewer opportunities for individual investigations. After 25 years of policies aimed at improving education, the majority of students experience a truncated geographical education often taught by non-specialists.' (p. 107)

This is a rather damning indictment of over 25 years of centralisation. Roberts clearly lays the blame at the door of accountability and frequent curriculum change. These have led to the complicated matrix of confusion and misunderstanding that permeates the education system.

Mitchell (2020) takes a socio-economic lens to broader contexts determining conditions prevalent in schools, which he calls 'hyper-socialisation': 'Hyper-socialisation describes the intensification of teachers' curriculum work and how teachers cope (when the demands exceed their personal curriculum making resources) by 'contracting out' curriculum making to others, particularly through internet reliance. This intensification is driven by late capitalist society, which tries to hold a contradiction of seeing the individual (including the student) simultaneously as a narcissistic consumer and competitive producer' (p. 7). His research in four schools discovered that 'at times ... school policies, which [teachers] are required to follow, are driven by Ofsted anxiety.' (p. 154)

Investigating how subject teachers are enacting the curriculum in changing times, Mitchell found that 'all the heads of department portray a keen desire to change and develop the geography curriculum. However, evidence shows much curriculum inertia – topics, lessons and materials, which remain for many years' (p. 158). He links this inertia to accountability – 'teachers portray change as risk' – and points out that even when department planning meetings do discuss the curriculum from a strategic perspective 'the process is one of making adjustments to the existing curriculum plans rather than "wholesale" re-writing' (p. 158). He believes that 'the pressures of assessment and accountability and the priority of high-stakes examination courses (GCSE and A Level) conspire against spending time making substantial changes to the KS3 curriculum' (pp. 158–9).

The findings of four years leading CPD, working with over 100 teachers to develop approaches to assessment without levels and planning at key stage 3, were summarised by Gardner (2016). When planning for progress, school geography departments often lack strategic thinking and vision. A new teacher or head of department inherits an existing key stage 3 curriculum and uses it and the associated resources without question. At the time of a national curriculum review, time constraints mean teachers tend to look at the new content and tweak the existing plan, rather than seeing the review as an opportunity to plan strategically. Over successive reviews, the key stage plan can become less of a plan and more a collection of disconnected topics.

If key stage 3 geography is inert, it runs the risk of hindering student progress, creating a lack of coherence in the 11–16 curriculum. These factors are all legacies of 25 years of change that have diverted schools from the vital aspect of a teacher's job – determining what to teach – in the pursuit of data collection to map school effectiveness and good Ofsted grades. Dylan Wiliam (2013) makes a further point of significance: 'All over the country, teachers and leaders assumed that curriculum was a non-issue, because the government had decided what the curriculum should be. Of course, teachers did try to design effective and engaging lessons, but too often this was treated as a straightforward process of 'delivering' the national curriculum.' (p. 10)

Drawing on the 2008 and 2011 Ofsted geography reports (Ofsted, 2008; 2011) Biddulph (2017) identified significant issues that emerged in secondary schools (Figure 1.3) as a result of teachers' attention being diverted from decisions about what to teach.

National Curriculum 2014 – an opportunity for curriculum design?

In 2010, the election of a Conservative-led coalition government quickly led to yet more significant change in education, including a refocus on 'traditional subjects' with a core of essential knowledge. The White Paper *The Importance of Teaching* (DfE, 2010) set down the direction of travel and identified a number of clear issues. The new government believed that the previous two curriculum reviews, under Labour, had strayed too far into guidance on **how** to teach, rather than **what** to teach, and that this had led to overloading schools and confusion as to what the statutory NC actually required: '... at present the National Curriculum includes too much that is not essential knowledge, and there is too much prescription about how to teach' (pt. 10, p. 10). It proposed a new approach to the National Curriculum, specifying a tighter, more rigorous, model of the knowledge which every child should expect to master in core subjects at every key stage (pt. 11, p. 11).

It also challenged how the whole school curriculum had evolved. 'The National Curriculum was never meant to be the whole school curriculum – the totality of what goes on in any school. It was

Issue identified	Reason
Lack of subject specialists teaching geography (especially at key stage 3).	Greater accountability for attainment at GCSE and A level meant that subject specialists prioritised teaching examination classes.
Sustained lack of subject-based professional development for many geography teachers.	CPD agenda dominated by 'other' educational agendas (e.g. Every Child Matters) at the expense of subject-focused professional development, leading to what Ofsted described as a curriculum of 'neglect' (2008, p. 23). The 2006–11 Action Plan for Geography and the awarding bodies became key subject-specific CPD providers.
Too rigid an adherence to the national strategies guidance (objectives-led teaching, three-part lessons).	Period of intense local authority support and pedagogical 'tool kits' to meet the expectations of the national strategies. Perceptions that the Ofsted inspection process required prescribed lesson formats led to formulaic lesson structures.
Too much attention on the *how* of teaching and learning and not enough consideration of the *what*. Teaching and learning, particularly in year 7, often linked to general skills-based initiatives.	Increased emphasis on 'learning to learn' and learning skills, framing how geography teachers approached subject teaching. Easing the transition between primary and secondary school led to a range of generic curriculum initiatives, at the expense of subjects such as geography and history.
Curriculum decisions at key stage 3 were driven by developments at key stage 4 and A level.	Key stage 3 seen as a 'seed-bed' for GCSE and possibly A level, leading to a certain degree of content repetition at each key stage.
Reduced time for geography in key stage 3.	The gradual reduction in time to teach geography, in favour of more generic curricula or in order to provide addition curriculum time for subjects such as English, maths and science.
Poorly planned and taught integrated units of work in the humanities.	Schools with a history of 'humanities' provision often retained a humanities structure at key stage 3, resulting in many non-specialists teaching geography.

Figure 1.3: The state of geography in secondary schools in England. **Source:** Jones, M. (ed) (2017, p. 34).

explicitly meant to be limited in scope yet in practice has come to dominate.' (4.2, p. 40). It went on to propose that the NC should be 'a benchmark not a straitjacket, a body of knowledge against which achievement can be measured' (4.2, p. 40) and that schools should have greater flexibility, 'which affirms the importance of teaching and creates scope for teachers to inspire.' (4.3, p. 40)

The White Paper stated that 'The National Curriculum should set out clearly the core knowledge and understanding that all children should be expected to acquire in the course of their schooling. It must embody their cultural and scientific inheritance, the best that our past and present generations have to pass on to the next. But it must not try to cover every conceivable area of human learning or endeavour, must not become a vehicle for impos-ing passing political fads on our children and must not squeeze out all other learning.' (4.7, p. 40).

Much of this government thinking appeared to align with the concerns expressed by the geography education community about the 2007 NC review, although there was some trepidation about the influence of the idea of 'core knowledge', derived from American commentator E.D. Hirsch (1987; 2003).

In tune with the government's vision for reform, a panel of experts chaired by Tim Oates, Director of Assessment Research and Development at Cambridge Assessment, was appointed to provide advice on the construction and content of a new National Curriculum. It proposed the abolition of level descriptions:

'... all assessment and other processes should bring people back to the content of the curriculum (and the extent to which it has been taught and learned), instead of focusing on abstracted and arbitrary expressions of the curriculum such as 'levels' ... There must be great care to avoid the problems of the past regarding development of highly cumbersome and bureaucratic assessment and reporting arrangements. However, we believe that constant assessment to levels is itself over-burdensome, obscures the genuine strengths and weaknesses in a pupil's attainment, obscures parental understanding of the areas in which they might best support' (DfE, 2011b, p. 50). (The significance of this change for curriculum design is explored more fully in Chapter 3, pages 43–52.)

The resulting National Curriculum for England was launched in September 2014, and applied to maintained schools in England – so technically *not* to academies or free schools. However, Ofsted uses the NC as a benchmark in terms of curriculum ambition, breadth and depth.

The government's desire to return the school curriculum to a 'more rigorous model of ... knowledge' (4.8, p. 42) is clearly evident with the introduction of the English Baccalaureate (EBacc) as a measure of school performance. Geography is one of only two humanities subjects included in the EBacc, and this had the immediate impact of significantly increasing the numbers of students taking geography at GCSE (after years of decline). Another significant change was the development, for the first time, of prescribed content for GCSE and A level. This again reinforces the idea of 'knowledge' as the main driver. In previous post-14 curriculum reviews, the government provided a framework of GCSE and A level subject criteria – broad guiding principles, such as the proportion of physical geography to be included in the awarding bodies' specifications. This gave awarding bodies significant freedom to develop different approaches in their specifications. Flexibility was significantly reduced in the new GCSE and A level subject content documents; in order to gain accreditation from Ofqual all awarding bodies have to comply with prescribed content requirements.

Schools were now required to respond to a radical change of approach and thinking about education. This change is encapsulated in the different wording of the stem used in the 2007 and 2014 NC documents:

- 2007 – 'Pupils should be able to ...'
- 2014 – 'Pupils should be taught to ...'

Schools had to adapt to these changes at speed and without the support of organisations such as QCDA which had been abolished. They were confronted with competing and possibly conflicting priorities and despite the encouraging pronouncements of the White Paper, an accountability culture of testing, league tables and Ofsted inspections prevailed. In the early years of the 2014 NC, schools and teachers focussed their time and energy on preparing for more rigorous, linear GCSEs and A levels and replacing levels with a variety of approaches, mainly linked to using data collection and management systems to maintain student tracking and gauge school effectiveness. The key stage 3 curriculum, the '**what to teach**', was still often neglected, efforts instead being devoted to developing new ways to measure student progress for data-hungry software.

Hesslewood (2017) expressed his exasperation that an 'assessment for management' rather than 'assessment for learning' scenario still prevailed: 'The frustrating irony is that removing levels in 2014 has created lots of hot air and new labels that are just as useless and confusing as the old. The centrality of *geographical thinking* in assessment is paramount, yet seems to be utterly lost in most of the assessment systems acclaimed in the education press. This is because decisions about assessment (and therefore 'tracking progress') are often made in the interests of senior leaders under the constant threat of inspection, to enable the collection of more and more data.' (p. 25)

ACTIVITY 1.1

Examine the changes that have taken place in each iteration of the GNC shown in Figure 1.1 (pp. 10–11) together with the issues identified by Ofsted summarised in Figure 1.3. Reflect on your existing key stage 3 curriculum, and consider how far it and your approach to curriculum making have been influenced by these changes.

Conclusion

This chapter has attempted to provide a sketch of 40 years of curriculum change and their impact on schools. A consideration of curriculum thinking in the context of working in a hyper-socialised environment, represents an important starting point when embarking on this potential new era of curriculum enactment.

The White Paper *The Importance of Teaching* (DfE, 2010) includes a very significant and bold statement which offers hope for the future: 'Teachers, not bureaucrats or Ministers, know best how to teach – how to convey knowledge effectively and how to unlock understanding. In order to bring the curriculum to life, teachers need the space to create lessons which engage their pupils, and children need the time to develop their ability to retain and apply knowledge.' (4.8, pp. 41–2). Ofsted has now picked up the challenge with a new Education Inspection Framework (EIF) that places the curriculum firmly at the centre of their approach to inspecting.

In its Annual Report 2018–19 (Ofsted, 2020) Ofsted echoes the views of Margaret Roberts: 'In our first phase of curriculum research back in 2017, we found that school leaders were focused on increasing performance measures, too often to the detriment of much else. Teaching to the test, narrowing the curriculum, off-rolling and qualification-gaming have become all too common. We do acknowledge the role that strongly data-driven accountability, including our own inspection frameworks, has played in distracting us collectively from the real substance of education, at the centre of which is the curriculum.' (p. 8)

Launching this report on 21 January 2020, Amanda Spielman commented on the impact of the new EIF on approaches to curriculum and its design in schools. 'While it's too early to draw any meaningful conclusions, we are seeing a shift in emphasis. Curriculum discussion is most definitely – and rightly – back on the agenda for leadership teams ... I'm approached at almost every event I attend by people telling me how rewarding it is to be going back to the fundamentals of education; thinking through what they teach and how best to teach it.' (Spielman, 2020)

The two factors identified by Roberts (2018) that have led to 'a truncated geography education' – accountability and frequent curriculum reform – seem now to be aligned to acknowledge the importance of curriculum enactment by teachers in schools. This can unleash new ways of thinking and working in schools, and most importantly, lead to students progressing their capability to perceive the world and thinking geographically.

References

All websites last accessed 27/07/2021.

Bailey, P. and Binns, T. (1987) *A Case for Geography: A Response to The Secretary Of State For Education From Members Of The Geographical Association*. Sheffield: GA.

Biddulph, M. (2017) 'What do we mean by curriculum?' in Jones, M. (ed) *The Handbook of Secondary Geography*. Sheffield: Geographical Association. pp. 30–39.

DCSF (2007) *The children's plan: building brighter futures*. Available at www.gov.uk/government/publications/the-childrens-plan

DES (1985) 'The curriculum from 5 to 16', *HMI Series: Curriculum Matters No. 2*. Available at www.educationengland.org.uk/documents/hmi-curricmatters/curriculum.html

DES (1991) *Geography in the National Curriculum (England)*. London: HMSO.

DfE (2010) *The Importance of Teaching: The Schools White Paper 2010*. London: The Stationery Office. Available at https://assets.publishing.service.gov.uk/government/uploads/system/uploads/attachment_data/file/175429/CM-7980.pdf

DfE (2011a) *The national strategies 1997 to 2011: Summary of the legacy and effectiveness of the former national strategies*. Available at www.gov.uk/government/publications/the-national-strategies-1997-to-2011

DfE (2011b) *The Framework for the National Curriculum: A report by the Expert Panel for the National Curriculum Review*. Available at https://assets.publishing.service.gov.uk/government/uploads/system/uploads/attachment_data/file/175439/NCR-Expert_Panel_Report.pdf

DfE (2013) *Geography: programmes of study: key stage 3*. Available at https://assets.publishing.service.gov.uk/government/uploads/system/uploads/attachment_data/file/239087/SECONDARY_national_curriculum_-_Geography.pdf

Gardner, D. (2016) 'Planning for progress in geography', *Teaching Geography*, 41, 2, pp. 54–5

Geographical Association (2009) *A Different View: A Manifesto from the Geographical Association*. Sheffield: GA. Available at www.geography.org.uk/GA-Manifesto-for-geography

Graves, N. (1979) *Curriculum Planning in Geography*. London: Heinemann Educational.

HMSO (2003) *Every Child Matters*. Available at https://assets.publishing.service.gov.uk/government/uploads/system/uploads/attachment_data/file/272064/5860.pdf

Hesslewood, A. (2017) 'Geography against learning?', *Teaching Geography*, 42, 1, pp. 23–5.

Hirsch, E. D. (1987) *Cultural Literacy: What every Amerncan needs to know*. Boston, MA: Houghton-Mifflin Co.

Hirsch, E. D. (2007) *The Knowledge Deficit*. Boston, MA: Houghton-Mifflin Co.

Jones, M. (ed) (2017) *The Handbook of Secondary Geography*. Sheffield: Geographical Association.

Lambert, D. and Morgan, J. (2010) *Teaching Geography 11–18: A conceptual approach*. Maidenhead: The Open University.

Lambert, D. and Hopkin, J. (2014) 'A possibilist analysis of the geography national curriculum in England', *International Research in Geographical and Environmental Education*, 23, 1, pp. 64–78

Mitchell, D. (2020) *Hyper-Socialised: How Teachers Enact the Geography Curriculum in Late Capitalism*. London: Routledge.

Ofsted (2008) *Geography in schools: Changing practice*. Available at https://www.geography.org.uk/download/ofsted%20report%20good%20practice%20in%20schools%20-%20changing%20practice%202008.pdf

Ofsted (2011) *Geography: Learning to make a world of difference*. Available at www.gov.uk/government/publications/geography-learning-to-make-a-world-of-difference

Ofsted (2019) *The education inspection framework*. Available at https://www.gov.uk/government/publications/education-inspection-framework/education-inspection-framework

Ofsted (2020) *Ofsted Annual Report 2018/19: education, children's services and skills*. Available at https://assets.publishing.service.gov.uk/government/uploads/system/uploads/attachment_data/file/859422/Annual_Report_of_Her_Majesty_s_Chief_Inspector_of_Education__Children_s_Services_and_Skills_201819.pdf

QCA (2000) Schemes of work. Available at https://www.qca.org.uk/232.html

QCA (2007a) *National Curriculum guidance*. Available at https://webarchive.nationalarchives.gov.uk/20080620095439/http://www.qca.org.uk/qca_13575.aspx

QCA (2007b) *National Curriculum: What's changed and why?* Available at https://webarchive.nationalarchives.gov.uk/20080610180401/http://curriculum.qca.org.uk/key-stages-3-and-4/developing-your-curriculum/what_has_changed_and_why/index.aspx

Rawling, E. (2001) *Changing the Subject: The impact of national policy on school geography 1980–2000*. Sheffield: GA.

Rawling, E. (2007) *Planning Your Key Stage 3 Geography Curriculum*. Sheffield: GA.

Roberts, M. (2018) 'Secondary school geography: twenty-five years of centralisation', *Teaching Geography*, 43, 3, pp.105–8.

Spielman, A. (2017) *Enriching the fabric of education*. Speech at the Festival of Education. Available at www.gov.uk/government/speeches/amanda-spielmans-speech-at-the-festival-of-education

Wiliam, D. (2013) *Principled curriculum design*. London: Specialist Schools and Academies Trust.

Emerging opportunities to plan a coherent geography curriculum?

'Whereas geography's place in the National Curriculum for England has been achieved ... what has not yet been achieved ...is the... geography the Geographical Association Manifesto began to advocate in 2009.... This is a curriculum made by teachers, and which takes its cue as much from the subject discipline as from the official programme of study ... this may mean that teachers will need to better understand bodies of knowledge, the subject disciplines – and how they can be used in educational settings.' (Lambert and Hopkin, 2014, pp. 75–6)

This introductory quote makes an ambitious claim for the fully-formed professional role of teachers to include a large measure of responsibility for the curriculum. As we saw in Chapter 1, it is in line with what Ofsted is now advocating (Ofsted, 2019, p. 15). This chapter examines ideas about curriculum controls and coherence, curriculum planning models and the proposition of curriculum making. It will also examine powerful disciplinary knowledge – the GeoCapabilities approach – and the possibility of what has become known as a 'Future 3' geography curriculum. This chapter also considers how the curriculum research undertaken by Ofsted to determine the 2019 Education Inspection Framework (Ofsted, 2019) relates to Future 3 curriculum thinking.

Norman Graves (1979, pp. 18–19) determined that the 'curriculum problem' geography teachers must address in their curriculum planning operates at five levels:

1. How 'the total curriculum' is to be planned in secondary schools.

2. Deciding what kind of geography to teach; considering changes in the nature of the subject at a research level; but also deciding on the aims of school geography.

3. How to structure a course in a way that ensures progression in understanding. For Graves, this enables the teacher to 'effectively help to stretch some young minds without putting others off ... a course needs to be structured in a way that takes cognizance of what is known about the processes of mental maturation'.

4. How to devise the learning experiences to 'enable the students to learn certain skills and ideas that dovetail into the overall geography course'.

5. How to make this planning flexible so that it can be modified in the light of feedback.

Such considerations express the dynamic process of curriculum planning, which have not changed over time. However, as we saw in Chapter 1, what have changed are the controls in the education system, which have diverted many teachers' attention away from their key role as the curriculum makers – that is, to create curriculum coherence.

Curriculum coherence

Curriculum coherence operates at a variety of scales in the education system: national level, school level and the classroom level. All three have a significant impact on students' learning; however, it is at the classroom level where it has the greatest impact.

At a national level, Tim Oates in his report 'Could do better' (Oates, 2010) identified curriculum coherence as one of the characteristics of high-performing countries. As Oates explained, 'The term "coherence" does not carry the meaning typically associated with a "broad and balanced curriculum" but is a highly precise technical term: a national curriculum should have content arranged in an order that is securely based in evidence associated with age-related progression'. He further explained that 'A system is regarded as "coherent" when the national curriculum content, textbooks, teaching content, pedagogy, assessment and drivers and incentives all are aligned and reinforce one another' (Oates, 2010, p. 5). Oates identifies 13 control factors, which he states 'exist in complex relations and balances' (Figure 2.1, overleaf). Oates argues that high-performing education systems tend to have strong 'curriculum coherence', which he suggests has been lacking in the UK. A framework of levels, for example, presented as a separate structure to the curriculum, leading to a misalignment of assessment and curriculum in schools.

At a school level, leadership teams have tended to focus on student data built on a foundation of levels to determine school effectiveness, rather than curriculum. Curriculum planning at a school level is more a task of organising the timetable. This has been indicative of schools' response to a misalignment of several curriculum controls in the system, such as accountability and inspection, as well as curriculum and assessment. As Ofsted discovered in Phase 1 of its research into curriculum in schools (Ofsted, 2017a), there was very little debate or reflection about the curriculum in schools; when asked about it, school leaders were more likely to talk about the timetable. There was also evidence of a weak theoretical understanding of curriculum, leading to misunderstandings about the purpose of key stage 3 and the new GCSE assessment criteria. Curriculum narrowing at key stage 3 was a consequence of these misunderstandings.

Wiliam (2013) believes that discussion about curriculum has been neglected in schools, because the government has specified what schools were required to teach, so further discussion of curriculum was not required. Wiliam points out that 'the national curriculum is not really a curriculum at all'. He sees the real curriculum as the enacted curriculum or achieved curriculum, in other words the lived daily experience of students in the classroom, and believes that insufficient attention is paid to enacting the curriculum in school. As a result, it is not allocated enough professional time and tends to be done in an ad-hoc manner. The curriculum, therefore, lacks coherence. Wiliam argues that 'attention to the issue of curriculum has the potential to be one of the most powerful levers for improving the performance of the system' (p. 6).

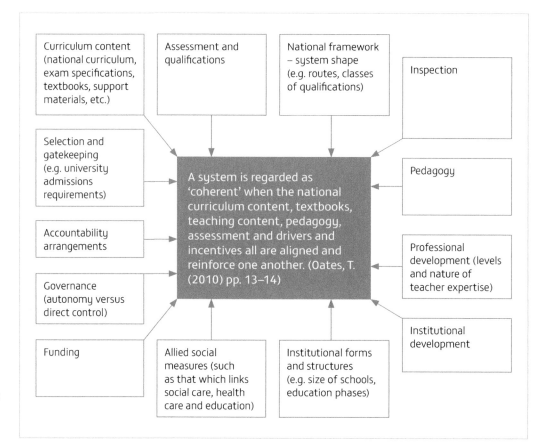

Figure 2.1: Control factors on the education system. **Source:** Adapted from Oates, 2010

Planning your coherent 11–16 geography curriculum: a design toolkit

It is at the classroom level that curriculum coherence has the greatest impact on students' progress. Myatt (2018) believes that when a curriculum lacks coherence, it is harder to teach and harder for students to locate and place any new knowledge. She explains: 'We are a pattern-seeking species. We look to make sense and order from the world around us. The plethora of information and stimuli become overwhelming if each is encountered without a context in which to place it … coherence comes from the Latin to stick together, and when we think about the curriculum coherently, it becomes much simpler to teach and for pupils to understand'. She believes teachers need to consider the big ideas that underpin each subject discipline. She acknowledges that under time pressure teachers can be tempted to go straight to the detail of what is to be taught – the list of content in the NC or the GCSE specification. She maintains that in the long term this can lead to wasting time, as the key ideas and concepts are not shared with students, 'denying them the chance to get the material to stick together'. She believes that the aims and purpose of the NC and GCSE are vital starting points to create a coherent curriculum (Myatt, p. 23).

Charles Rawding (2015) has applied this idea of curriculum coherence to geography education. He maintains that a curriculum document (whether an examination specification or the NC) in itself does not result in coherence. 'In a worst-case scenario, pupils could complete their geography education considering geography to be simply a long list of case studies from around the world.' He believes that what is needed is what Bruner (1996) called 'an interpretive narrative'.' He explains this as the contextualization of what is being studied so that geographical thinking, themes and skills are being continuously developed. It is really important that students see linkages between these progressive elements of their curriculum. Rawding states that 'Curriculum coherence is determined by the elements of connectivity within the curriculum and by the existence of clear threads of geographical thinking that run through the lesson sequences' (pp. 76-7). Mary Biddulph (2017) also highlights the need for curriculum coherence: 'It is impossible to engage in any meaningful curriculum decision-making until you attend to aims and rationale; without some sense of what you are trying to

achieve educationally and why, your geography curriculum will lack purpose' (Biddulph, p. 35). Hesslewood (2017) clearly states 'geography teachers need to emphasise the importance and *purpose* of geography to their students, not just as a discipline that helps provide solutions to global problems … students need a clearer idea of what geography is, and how to *become better geographers*, not just how to move from one "level of progress" to another, however articulated' (p. 25). Ideas about developing curriculum coherence will be developed in the guidance section of this book – Chapter 4, Curriculum Intent – and are further illustrated in the school case studies in Chapter 8.

Curriculum planning models

As Oates points out, it is the role of the teacher or geography department to contextualise the NC or GCSE specification, through a process of curriculum design to create a planned curriculum. So how do teachers approach this? Long ago, Margaret Roberts (1997) showed that the way teachers approach curriculum planning is influenced by the models of planning they have encountered. In other words, they necessarily draw from some kind of theory, even though this might sometimes be implicit. As a result, the planned and taught curriculum generally reflects one of the following curriculum models:

- the curriculum transmission model – with a body of knowledge to be transmitted or simply delivered

- the objectives-led model – a curriculum as the vehicle to achieve certain outcomes for students (product)

- the process-praxis model – a curriculum in which students and teachers are 'engaged' with the content. This is a very dynamic view of the curriculum, in which the contents are reviewed frequently.

Biddulph (2017) explains that these models '… are not frameworks, grids or tables to complete; they are ideas, principles and value positions to debate. Each model has significant implications for the kind of curriculum you plan and the kind of geography you teach'. Biddulph (2014) even suggests that the evolution of the geography NC can be understood and critiqued using these models.

In the early 1990s, the very heavy content load of the first GNC assumed a delivery model of knowledge. In the 2000s the generic skills-based curricula (with a much lighter statutory content load) required the frequent measurement of learning outcomes, assuming an objectives-led model. The language of the 2014 GNC (DfE, 2013), on the surface, seemed to be a return to a core knowledge focus, worryingly mirroring the 1991 curriculum.

There is, however, a difference in vision about the purpose and nature of knowledge between the subject community and the government. And this is where 'theory' comes in. For what Roberts found was that teachers' approach to curriculum could override whatever the 'statutory order' said or implied. The transmission model was not inevitable in 1990, and it is not today. The 2014 GNC brief, yet precise, outline of the 'core of essential knowledge' in geography offers an enormous opportunity for teachers to engage with active curriculum making – a process-praxis model. These three curriculum models can be loosely linked to the 'three Futures' analysis – the knowledge component of the curriculum, first identified by Young and Muller (2010), developed further by Young and Lambert (2014) and used extensively in the GeoCapabilities project (see also Biddulph, Lambert and Balderstone, 2015) (see pp. 27–8 in this chapter). A Future 3 curriculum – a curriculum of engagement – is achieved through a dynamic process-praxis approach to curriculum making.

The curriculum transmission model

This is often referred to as a 'traditional' approach to teaching; the stereotypical view of Victorian schools and classrooms. Biddulph (2014) describes this model as '... traditional, conservative and teacher-centred; students are positioned as passive recipients of authoritative, given knowledge.' (p. 6)

There are clear links to this transmission model in the way some schools approach curriculum planning today – equating a curriculum with the NC document or GCSE specification. Priority is given to the series of content headings with guidance notes that set out the areas that are to be 'delivered'. However, the NC or GCSE specification does not necessarily indicate the relative importance of its topics, or the order in which they are to be studied, or why they should be studied in the first place. In many schools, teachers use the GCSE specification

as the curriculum, a key argument being that the structure of the specification is mirrored in the structure of the examination papers – an approach to teaching that is only really concerned with instrumental content 'delivery'. It is, of course, easy to understand why such an approach has evolved as part of a high-stakes accountability culture in schools focussing on 'teaching to the test'. Leszek Iwaskow, former HMI for geography, clearly expressed his view of this approach (2013, p. 54):

> 'At key stage 4, teaching has become more functional: often the focus of a lesson is an exam question rather than the development of knowledge and understanding in the subject ... This increasing evidence for 'teaching to the test' reflects narrow and prescriptive teaching approaches; these may lead to good exam results but do not necessarily inspire students to love the subject. In order to improve the quality of geography, teaching needs to refocus on learning rather than training in exam technique. Currently, there is an imbalance in far too many schools.'

Where teachers equate curriculum directly with the exam specification they are likely to limit their planning to a consideration of the content, or the body of knowledge, that they wish to transmit, linked to use of past paper questions to determine the success of the transmission. What is often ditched is hard thinking about the educational purpose of teaching this content and how to create a strong 'interpretive narrative' in order to provide coherence.

Objectives-led outcomes model

Organising the curriculum around objectives is the basis for 'rational curriculum planning', and like the simple transmission delivery curriculum model is essentially linear. The intended learning is identified as tightly prescribed and measurable objectives, taught to students. Outcomes are assessed in order to make judgements about learning – and the effectiveness of teaching. This model or approach is a highly technical view of curriculum planning rooted in management economic principles of production – inputs, processes and outputs applied to education, and ultimately school effectiveness. Many schools have fully embraced this model in a hyper-socialised, data-hungry, assessment for management environment – an environment of accountability measured by student performance data, judged by Ofsted inspection and league tables.

The objectives approach has encouraged thinking about different types of learning outcomes that can be identified. Perhaps the most influential categorisation of outcomes was devised by Bloom (1956), in his taxonomy of educational objectives, a highly questionable hierarchy of thinking skills. Biddulph (2014) identifies a fundamental problem with an approach to curriculum planning that is overenthusiastic about objectives and outcomes:

> '... the casualty in this model is the subject as experienced by students. Broken down into ever smaller units, the tendency is to focus only on the parts and not the whole, and prioritise small detail over broader and more significant conceptual understanding. Such fragmentation means that the "big picture" of the discipline is lost for students and the idea of education is reduced to schooling' (p. 7)

Again, the issue here is about the loss of 'interpretative narrative' and a lack of coherence in the geography curriculum as experienced by the student.

Process-praxis model

The main challenge in curriculum thinking, if we take it seriously, is to imagine the curriculum in a manner that is not a linear, delivery model (the key issue with the transmission and objective-led models discussed above). In this sense curriculum is not a physical thing, but rather a series of interactions between teachers, students and the knowledge to be imparted. The curriculum is more a human, rather than a technical, process. In other words, curriculum is far messier and more dynamic than the clean, 'scientific' process implied by 'rational curriculum planning.' A key focus is on the classroom, and what teachers do to prepare lessons and to evaluate the students' responses. The curriculum as enacted is in turn responsive to evaluation. Thus, in the process-praxis model a number of elements are in constant interaction.

In this approach teachers are highly attentive not only to the sequence of lessons and learning activities they provide for students (and why), but also to what sense the students make of them. New ways to evaluate teaching and learning are developed, including action research. In this model teachers as active curriculum-makers think more deeply about the subject as a whole, considering its conceptual underpinning, and how to progress students' geographical understanding. The teacher makes pedagogical choices related to developing this understanding, engaging students in active enquiry learning to stimulate the capability to think geographically.

Roberts (1997) identifies a significant advantage of this process-praxis model in its focus on the quality of learning and recognising 'the role of pupils in shaping what they learn and in constructing geography for themselves ... the complexity of classroom interaction ... It values the learning that takes place, whether it is intended, unintended or unexpected' (p. 46).

The major weakness and, indeed, strength of the process-praxis model is that it relies on the quality of teachers and teaching. The approach is dependent on the teacher's balance and understanding of the interactions in the classroom, which is why the process model is usually linked to the notion of praxis – referring to the act of engaging, applying, exercising, realising or practising theoretical ideas.

Thus a teacher immersed in *praxis* would bring their theoretical thoughts to every decision as they make it. Furthermore, their theoretical perspectives would continually be shaped and re-formed by practical experience. As Roberts (1997) explains, 'Planning and developing a curriculum using the process model became not only a means of providing a curriculum for pupils, but also a means of continuous professional development' (p. 44). This approach situates the learning as a conversation between learner and teacher rather than as a teacher carrying out their plans.

A mixed economy approach

In practice it is a bit of a stretch to think that teachers somehow 'choose' their theoretical stance and follow its principles as if they were pure and mutually exclusive. Thus, Graves (1979) believed the difference between an objective-led and process model to be one of emphasis, and rarely cut and dried. He concluded that his 'natural inclination would be to combine them into an eclectic objectives and process model of curriculum planning' (p. 39).

This view is also supported by Wiliam (2013), stating that 'The curriculum should be child-centred and subject-centred (and society-centred too) ... The curriculum has to take into account the needs of individuals and society while at the same time being sensitive to local constraints and affordances ...' (p. 14) The curriculum problem (i.e. resolving the question of what to teach and how to sequence it) can never be satisfactorily addressed by a step-by-step technical template. The problem is just too complex to be solved with a recipe. Moreover, such a step-by-step model is unlikely to encourage the kind of creativity that is needed from teachers to produce effective, imaginative and engaging curricula.

Curriculum making – the GA's articulation of the process curriculum model

'Curriculum making', as described in the GA's manifesto for geography, *A Different View* (GA, 2009) and discussed by Lambert and Morgan (2010), is an articulation of the process model with the focus squarely on enactment in the classroom.

A Different View was published as part of a reaction to the NC revisions in 2007 (see Chapter 1, pp. 12–13). The manifesto saw teachers as part of the route to high-quality geography in schools: 'The GA believes that teachers should be accountable, but also that they are autonomous professionals driven by educational goals and purposes: that is, they are the curriculum makers and the subject leaders' (p. 27).

In *A Different View*, the GA defined curriculum making as the creative act of interpreting an NC or examination specification and turning it into a coherent, challenging and engaging sequence of teaching and learning: curriculum enactment in practice.

The model shows three main ingredients (described as sources of energy or resources) available to teachers enacting the curriculum in the classroom, by drawing from their knowledge of:

- the discipline of geography – its key ideas and purposes
- subject-specialist teaching – its techniques and general approaches
- their students – who they are and how they learn.

The well-known diagram in Figure 2.2 captures the essence of curriculum making. Teachers should usually aim for somewhere in the middle, where the competing priorities of teaching, students and the subject are held in some kind of balance. The diagram encourages teachers to engage with their subject, consider the needs of their students and think critically about both the purpose of what they are teaching and their approach to teaching it.

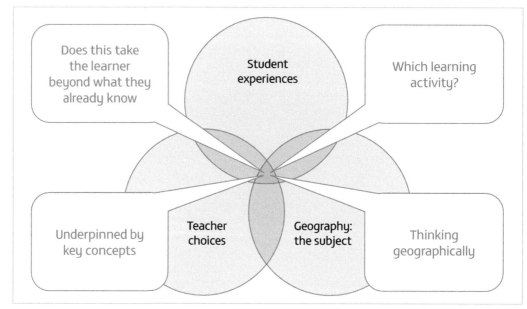

Figure 2.2: Curriculum making in geography. **Source:** Geographical Association at: www.geography. org.uk/Curriculum-making

As Lambert and Morgan (2010) explain: 'The three zones of influence in the figure may also be thought of as sources of energy that feed educational encounters in schools.' (p. 50) Mitchell (2017) adds that 'Curriculum making is located in an understanding of curriculum as process, rather than as predetermined or fixed content to be "delivered" ... It is a more fluid and immediate process than the longer-term curriculum planning and curriculum development. Curriculum making is not lesson planning, but is what Lambert and Morgan call the "in between work" (2010, p. 50) of translating curriculum planning into lesson sequences, or "medium-term planning"'. (pp. 99–100)

The curriculum-making model implies that each of the three elements plays an equally significant role in the process. Over-emphasising one over another may lead to an unproductive, unbalanced curriculum experience. In extremis – for example, in a situation where only the subject content matters, the student's needs are ignored and no attention is paid to teaching strategy – almost certainly a transmission model results. If, on the other hand, the curriculum is developed solely with the focus on the student's experience (it is entirely 'child-centred') it runs the risk of not taking them anywhere new in their learning; becoming unproductive. Finally, if the teacher is only really interested in the 'pedagogical adventure', the risk is that (s)he is only interested in their own performance: lessons might be technically outstanding in terms of structure and technique but empty of any geographical meaning!

The curriculum-making model is a reminder of the process-praxis curriculum model, and provides a useful way to think this through in practice.

ACTIVITY 2.1

Investigate the significance of curriculum making and PDK further in this online module of the GeoCapabilities project, which includes a video of David Lambert explaining the process.

https://www.geocapabilities.org/training-materials/module-2-curriculum-making-by-teachers/theory/

The GA manifesto identified three challenges teachers face as curriculum makers:

1. The subject matter of geography is constantly evolving.

2. The subject discipline is not always well understood. A synoptic understanding of the subject is not easy, particularly for non-specialist teachers of geography. It might even be difficult for some head teachers to see the importance of geography.

3. The subject content is potentially infinite, so we need a clear rationale for making selections from it.

A Different View publicly launched the argument for curriculum making, for teachers to reclaim their curriculum authority. Since then Lambert, and other geography educators, have continued to debate the issue (see Biddulph et al., 2015; Mitchell, 2016). These researchers have also refined their efforts to bring to light the question that is at the heart of curriculum making – in what does geographical knowledge contribute to educational processes in schools? Mitchell (2017) makes clear that 'The notion of "GeoCapabilities" (Bustin, 2019) can be read as such a refinement of (and an addition to) curriculum making, because it explains why geographical knowledge matters.' (p. 100)

How does geographical knowledge contribute?

A crucial aspect of the geography curriculum-making process is the teacher's ongoing relationship with the subject discipline. From this, teachers develop a vision of how the geography they teach contributes, bit by bit, to their students' capacity to think geographically (explained in more detail in Chapter 3 (pp. 36–43). It is for this reason that both teachers and researchers in geography education have been interested in exploring the idea of geography as powerful knowledge: the idea that geography can impart particular kinds of knowledge, understanding and skills that are empowering to the student. It is this hypothesis that has fired and continues to nourish the GeoCapabilities approach.

What is powerful disciplinary knowledge?

It is vital to grasp what is meant by 'powerful knowledge' – and what it doesn't mean – because it is the kind of term that can end up meaning whatever you want, which is profoundly unhelpful. The term 'powerful knowledge' (or 'powerful disciplinary knowledge', as the GeoCapabilities project prefers (see Bustin, 2019), has a history and a particular purpose.

The concept of 'powerful knowledge' was introduced into educational debate following a landmark book by Michael Young (2008) called *Bringing Knowledge Back In: From Social Constructivism to Social Realism in the Sociology of Education*. This book was considered at the time to be a volte face by Young, who had been a leading light in the so-called 'new sociology of education' signalled by his 1971 book, *Knowledge and Control: New Directions for the Sociology of Education*. This book revealed the exclusive and alienated nature of the school curriculum to many children. The argument was that the school curriculum was constructed by and for the ruling elite. Its role was to impart the 'knowledge of the powerful'. It is sobering to realise that geography, an academic subject born in the nineteenth century and which became the servant of empire and environmental determinism, was considered part of this. The GA has acknowledged this legacy through its statement on Black Lives Matter (GA, 2020). However, 35 years later, Young argued that in our haste to decolonise the curriculum and give students the skills they need in a more 'relevant' curriculum, organised around students' interests and experiences, we have thrown the baby out with the bath water. For while it is true that school subjects like geography can be transmissive of a profoundly exclusionary narrative, the fact remains that a geographical understanding – the ability to comprehend issues and problems geographically – leads to powerful insights and the capability to think about the way the world works in new ways. This is powerful knowledge.

The importance of subject knowledge in the school curriculum

Powerful knowledge provides a means to think progressively and imaginatively about the curriculum, in opposition to the focus on generic skills and learning outcomes favoured by those influential voices who would reform the curriculum away from 'traditional subjects'. Young (2009) argued that an emphasis on generic skills does not enable young people to gain the knowledge to understand and to think beyond the limits of their own experience – i.e. to develop a kind of knowledge that he describes as 'powerful'.

The National Curriculum Expert Panel Report (DfE, 2011) made reference to the views of Young's proposition of powerful knowledge:

'Subject knowledge can be seen as representing the accumulated experience of the past and the representation of this for the future. The concepts, facts, processes, language, narratives and conventions of each subject constitute socially refined forms of knowledge – knowledge that is regarded as "powerful"'. (p. 7)

Young makes the point that for any thinking about the curriculum, the most basic distinction is between the kinds of knowledge learned in school and the everyday knowledge and experiences that students bring to school. The former tends to be independent of context, socially produced of course, but validated by the subject community through the dynamic processes of argument, contestation and peer-review. It exists externally to the teacher and the student – unlike the knowledge based on experience that students bring to school, which is tied to the contexts and communities in which they live. The task of the teacher is to enable students to engage productively with the selected subject content and to move beyond their experience equipped with the new knowledge that they would not readily encounter at home and with ways to think about this – making generalisations, using abstract models or theories, etc. This knowledge is specialised knowledge that gives students the ability to think about and do things that otherwise they couldn't. Young calls this powerful knowledge, not because it exerts power *over* students, but because it gives power *to* students. Bustin (2019) identifies the educational potential of school geography '... to help young people discern fact from fiction; a potential to understand the nature of the changing world; and a potential to be able to think knowledgeably, live and work in the modern world' (p. 4).

Alaric Maude (2016), an Australian geography educator, attempted to develop a way of identifying powerful geographical knowledge derived from Young's concept. He aimed to help teachers recognise that some of what they already teach is powerful knowledge, as well as identify opportunities to develop their curriculum. He identified a typology of powerful knowledge in high-quality geography education:

1. Knowledge that provides students with 'new ways of thinking about the world'.

2. Knowledge that provides students with powerful ways to analyse, explain and understand the world.

3. Knowledge that gives students some power over their own knowledge.

4. Knowledge that enables young people to follow and participate in debates on significant local, national and global issues.

5. Knowledge of the world.

Maude concludes that by adopting a coherent approach to curriculum design, beyond a list of content to be taught, developing these powerful ways of thinking, whatever content is selected could 'help students to make more sense of the factual content of the curriculum, by learning how to synthesise information into generalisations or to use explanatory concepts, and to see coherence in what can often appear a somewhat disordered and sprawling discipline.' (p. 75)

Powerful knowledge and 'three Futures'

Michael Young and his collaborator Johan Muller (2010) have tried to sketch the significance of powerful knowledge in distinguishing different kinds of curriculum scenarios. They refer to these as 'three Futures': Future 1, Future 2 and Future 3. The numbering is slightly misleading, because they can also exist side by side; although one way to grasp Future 3 (which is the scenario based on powerful knowledge) is to imagine that it fuses or merges aspects of Future 1 and Future 2.

We can characterise the alternative curricular scenarios as:

1. Traditional: knowledge-led

2. Progressive: generic/skills-led

3. Progressive: knowledge-led (see Figure 2.3).

Young and Muller's naming of these three 'Futures' indicates that all three are realistic options for any future curriculum we might implement. But we should be clear: it is Future 3 that is based upon the potentially rich notion of powerful knowledge.

Young and Lambert (2014) expanded on the Future 3 school curriculum, and the GeoCapabilities approach is based upon achieving the educational potential (Bustin, 2019) of Future 3 curriculum thinking. We can also confirm that Future 3 is achievable through a curriculum making process aligned to a process-praxis model of curriculum.

Future 3 is a reaction to the inadequacies both of Future 1 and Future 2 (but particularly the latter). Lambert (2017) points out that:

'... Future 3 is a way of conceptualising the curriculum – not a recipe or set of techniques to adopt. It enables the process of 'curriculum making' by focusing first and foremost on why teaching geography (or any other specialist subject) is important and following that what (therefore) is worth teaching. The question of how to teach this is then appropriate, with a strong sense of fitness for purpose.' (p. 14)

Mark Enser (2020) summarises the significance of powerful knowledge and Futures 3 thinking in his TES article, 'The next "big thing" in teaching? It's all about you':

'In this Future 3 approach, the teacher once again takes centre stage as their role becomes one of selecting and re-contextualising academic ideas about their subject and introducing their students to them. They are also the ones best placed to model the disciplinary thinking of their subject and show their students how knowledge is debated and contested within this subject. My hope is that if teachers are able to regain control of their classrooms and of their curriculum we will see fewer of them being imposed on from outside and increasingly be left alone to just teach.'

GeoCapabilities

The idea of 'capability' derives from the conceptual framework developed by the economist Amartya Sen and US philosopher Martha Nussbaum (Nussbaum and Sen, 1993). David Lambert and others have discussed powerful knowledge in the context of 'capabilities' – where people are enabled to act and think differently as a result of their powerful, knowledge-rich education. A capabilities approach to geography education asks teachers to consider the role of geography in helping young people reach their full human potential.

Figure 2.3: Key characteristics of Futures 1, 2 and 3 curricular scenarios.

Future 1. Traditional: knowledge-led

Boundaries between subjects are rigid and curriculum content given and fixed. The curriculum is based upon a naturalised or 'under-socialised' concept of knowledge and the teaching governed by cultural transmission curriculum model.

Characteristics:

- originates in an elitist educational system in which cultural knowledge is passed on to a select group. The knowledge of the powerful – frequently exclusive and alienating to students.
- this is 'knowledge for knowledge's sake', with a lot of factual knowledge in an often static and conservative curriculum
- little or no student engagement. Teaching consists of literal 'delivery' by the teacher and is aimed at reproduction

The traditional curriculum is found in geography teaching from the 19th and most of the 20th centuries, which heavily emphasised a regional knowledge. It can be found today in some 'knowledge-led' schools and may even be characterised by 'scripted lessons'.

Future 2. Progressive: generic/skills-led

The boundaries between specialist subject knowledge are relaxed or even dissolved. The curriculum is based on an 'over-socialised' concept of knowledge – implying that knowledge has to be created *in situ*, only by the students themselves through experience.

Characteristics:

- knowledge no longer treated as a given, but very contingent, fluid and flexible
- attention shifts from teaching to learning – from knowledge acquisition to experience
- steady weakening of subject boundaries and the valorisation of cross-curricular skills, themes and dimensions
- integration of some school subjects
- curriculum attention paid to learning and thinking as educational aims in their own right, unconnected to the subject: emergence of 'learning to learn' 'building learning power'
- learning objectives are expressed in terms of general skills, such as cooperating with others or problem-solving, with measurable outcomes
- pedagogy supersedes curriculum – 'facilitating learning', e-learning and personalised learning
- pedagogic innovation at the expense of subject content renewal.

Future 3. Progressive: knowledge-led

Boundary maintenance between subjects but prior to encouraging boundary crossing. Based on subjects understood as powerful knowledge that is specialised, abstract, open to contest and challenge (and therefore) dynamic, systemic.

Characteristics:

- based on social realism (captured by Young's 'Bringing knowledge back in') a perspective that arose in response to the predominance of naïve social constructivism in educational studies, policy and practice. (All knowledge is socially constructed – but it is naïve then to think that everyone has to invent the wheel for themselves!)
- treats subjects as the most reliable tools we have to enable students to acquire knowledge and make sense of the world
- progressive and motivated by social justice –all students (not just the 'academic' or privileged few) need access to powerful knowledge that is outside their sphere of experience
- such knowledge is dynamic and related to discipline-based concepts and ways of thinking
- a curriculum of engagement with selected knowledge and special ways of thinking
- school subjects are not a given (as in Future 1), but neither are they arbitrary (as in Future 2)
- clear conceptual distinction between curriculum (its aims, aspirations and purpose) and teaching methods (the pedagogy) – though in practice these merge!

David Lambert presented his early thinking about a capability approach at his inaugural Professorial lecture at IoE in June 2009 (Lambert, 2009), observing that 'Geography is a moving, changing and sometimes restless idea ... and the geography curriculum needs to move with it.' He went on to comment that the GA manifesto created the brand 'Living Geography':

> '... living geography is ... not concerned with delivering slabs of content as an end in itself but with inducting young people into a geographical enquiry and how to think geographically ... Living geography is concerned with young people learning about themselves in the world through a geographical lens.' (p. 13)

The capabilities approach both steers and motivates geography teachers to focus on the agency that a high-quality 'living geography' imparts to students: geography lessons do not tell us how to live, but thinking geographically and developing our innate geographical imaginations can provide the intellectual means for visioning ourselves on planet Earth.

The GeoCapabilities Project (GeoCapabilities, 2016) is an internationally-funded project, with partners from the USA, Finland, Greece and the UK (including the GA) and a growing pool of 'associate partners' from all over the world. Its main output is a framework of practicable ideas, designed to develop curriculum leadership in geography teachers, that can be explored through four flexible online training modules. These can be undertaken by individual teachers, form part of in-school CPD training or be integrated into teacher training.

Since 2019, with the implementation of Ofsted's EIF focusing on curriculum, the evolution of thinking and research about the geography curriculum outlined in this chapter has the chance to flourish in schools. The following section introduces the research Ofsted conducted, to be clear about what they meant by curriculum and how to inspect schools, to determine the quality of their curriculum. Consideration of the findings of this Ofsted research clearly demonstrate the significance, and synergy with, the ideas about a geography curriculum, outlined in this chapter.

Ofsted curriculum research, 2017–2018

In January 2017 Her Majesty's Chief Inspector, Amanda Spielman, commissioned a major research study into the curriculum (Ofsted, 2017b). The purpose of this research was to ensure that Ofsted could assess in a valid and reliable way the 'quality of education' on offer in schools, with a welcome and radically new focus on the curriculum itself.

The curriculum research that informed the 2019 Education Inspection Framework (Ofsted, 2019) can be considered in the context of ideas and approaches to curriculum design and development in geography outlined in this chapter.

ACTIVITY 2.2

Listen to the video overview of Ofsted research.

Ofsted have published a series of video clips about the new EIF, including one by Professor Daniel Muijs, former Ofsted Head of Research, discussing the findings of three phases of their curriculum research. This provides a useful overview of findings of the three phases of research.

www.youtube.com/watch?v=08Iofb-KjI4

Phase 1: October 2017 (Ofsted, 2017a)

Spielman (Ofsted, 2017a) launched her commentary on phase 1 of Ofsted's curriculum research with a bold statement about the curriculum:

> 'At the very heart of education sits the vast accumulated wealth of human knowledge and what we choose to impart to the next generation: the curriculum ... Without a curriculum, a building full of teachers, leaders and students is not a school. Without receiving knowledge, students have learned nothing and no progress has been made – whatever the measures might indicate. This is why exams should exist in the service of the curriculum rather than the other way round.'

This research identified a lack of curriculum thinking in schools. In identifying next steps, Spielman acknowledged that Ofsted may have contributed to the state of curriculum thinking in schools through its former frameworks over-emphasising performance data:

'There is a serious risk of schools not fulfilling the promise and potential of the 2014 National Curriculum or of academies not using their freedoms to achieve the same. School leaders need to recognise how easy it is to focus on the performance of the school and lose sight of the pupil. I acknowledge that inspection may well have helped to tip this balance in the past.'

Phase 2: September 2018 (Ofsted, 2018a)

The purpose of phase 2 of the curriculum research was to identify positive influences on curriculum design, to provide inspectors with a rounded enough view of quality to be able to make accurate judgements on the curriculum.

Phase 3: December 2018 (Ofsted, 2018b)

The aim in phase 3 of Ofsted's curriculum research was to develop a series of indicators to evaluate curriculum quality. This model was then trialled in a range of schools by a small group of Her Majesty's Inspectors (HMI).

Ofsted discovered that effective curriculum 'planning' was not just about having a written plan of the content being taught. Words on the page were necessary but in themselves not sufficient to ensure high-quality curriculum thinking! It is important that curriculum leaders ensured that:

- content was **sequenced** to ensure that components of knowledge lead to conceptual understanding

- opportunities for students to practise what they knew – so they could deepen their understanding in a discipline – were built into the curriculum

- the layering of knowledge and concepts were secure so that students could make progress in the curriculum form their starting points.

HMI involved in the Phase 3 research were asked which of the indicators they felt were the most important to determine the intent of the curriculum. They identified that it should have a **coherent rationale**; that teacher's **knowledge of the concepts** to be imparted should be deep and fluent; and that the **curriculum should be ambitious** in its aims and purpose.

Furthermore, it is clear from this preparatory work that if curriculum lies at the heart of education,

and subjects lies at the heart of curriculum, then it follows that teachers need solid knowledge and understanding of the subject(s) they teach. As well as this, they need to know how to teach that subject and, more generally, how to teach. These three types of essential knowledge are known as content knowledge, pedagogical knowledge and pedagogical content knowledge. Content knowledge can be defined as teachers' knowledge of the subject they are teaching; pedagogical knowledge as teachers' knowledge of effective teaching methods; and pedagogical content knowledge as teachers' knowledge of how to teach the particular subject or topic. Developing these professional attributes takes time and can be assisted by high-quality, subject-focused professional development opportunities – within school departments, between schools (see Chapter 8) and of course within the wider association of subject specialists such as GA journals, events and conferences (see Chapter 9).

Ofsted's curriculum research (2019) used a working definition of the curriculum, which recognises that it passes through different states: how it is conceived, how it is taught and how students experience it. Thus:

'The curriculum is the substance of what is taught. It is a specific plan of what pupils need to know and should be able to do. The curriculum shapes and determines what pupils will get out of their educational experience. It is distinct from pedagogy, which is how the curriculum is taught. And, it is distinct from assessment, which is a means of setting out the desired outcomes we wish pupils to achieve and evaluating whether they have achieved those outcomes.' (p. 4)

This was the working definition of curriculum that emerged:

*'The curriculum is a framework for setting out the aims of a programme of education, including the knowledge and understanding to be gained at each stage (**intent**); for translating that framework over time into a structure and narrative, within an institutional context (**implementation**), and for evaluating what knowledge and understanding pupils have gained against expectations (**impact**/achievement).'* (p. 4)

Conclusion

In a special edition of the Ofsted School Inspection Update (Ofsted, 2019), to coincide with the launch of the formal consultation for the 2019 EIF, a stark and profound message was made clear:

> 'There is ample evidence of the extent to which an accountability system that does not look at what pupils are learning, and why they are learning it, diverts schools from the real substance of education. We have seen a 'school improvement' industry develop ... However, the results that young people achieve are only meaningful if the learning that underpins them is rich and deep. At present, what pupils learn too often comes second to the delivery of im-proved performance table data.' (p. 3)

This statement must be welcomed by any teacher who has the interests of their students at heart. It is an invitation for teachers to engage, both individually and in groups, with deeper, theoreti-cally robust curriculum thinking.

The focus on core knowledge in the NC, together with Ofsted's new focus on inspecting a curriculum, where they have identified the distinctive but interconnected and dynamic relationship between curriculum, pedagogy and assessment, is a breath of fresh air. These changes have the potential to change mindsets and behaviour patterns in the hyper-socialised school environment. This chapter has tried to provide a starting point for a new era of curriculum design to enable teachers to create their own coherent 11–16 geography curriculum. At the heart of this curriculum design process teachers need to develop a vision of what it means to make progress in geography. This is the focus of the next chapter.

References

All websites last accessed 27/07/2021.

Biddulph, M. (2014) 'What kind of curriculum do we want?', *Teaching Geography*, 39, 1, pp. 6–9.

Biddulph, M. (2017) 'What do we mean by curriculum?' in Jones, M. (ed) *The Handbook of Secondary Geography*. Sheffield: Geographical Association. pp. 30–39.

Biddulph, M., Lambert, D. and Balderstone, D. (2015) *Learning to Teach Geography in the Secondary School*. Abingdon: Routledge.

Bloom, B. S. (ed) (1956) *Taxonomy of Educational Objectives*. London: Longman.

Bruner, J. (1996) *The Culture of Education*. Cambridge, MA: Harvard University Press.

Bustin, R. (2019) *Geography Education's Potential and the Capability Approach*. Cham, Switzerland: Palgrave Macmillan.

DfE (2011) *The Framework for the National Curriculum: A report by the Expert Panel for the National Curriculum Review*. Available at https://assets.publishing.service.gov.uk/government/uploads/system/uploads/attachment_data/file/175439/NCR-Expert_Panel_Report.pdf

DfE (2013) *Geography: programmes of study: key stage 3*. Available at https://assets.publishing.service.gov.uk/government/uploads/system/uploads/attachment_data/file/239087/SECONDARY_national_curriculum_-_Geography.pdf

Enser, M. (2020) 'The next "big thing" in teaching?', TES, 12 January. Available at www.tes.com/news/next-big-thing-teaching-its-all-about-you

GA (2009) *A Different View: A Manifesto from the Geographical Association*. Sheffield: Geographical Association. Available at www.geography.org.uk/GA-Manifesto-for-geography

GA (2020) 'Black Lives Matter' – news statement 12 June 2020. Available at https://www.geography.org.uk/Announcements-and-updates/black-lives-matter/255912

GA (n.d.) 'Curriculum Making'. Available at www.geography.org.uk/Curriculum-making

GeoCapabilities (2016). Available at www.geocapabilities.org

Graves, N. (1979) *Curriculum Planning in Geography*. London: Heinemann Educational.

Hesslewood, A. (2017) 'Geography against learning?', *Teaching Geography*, 42, 1, pp. 23–5.

Iwaskow, L. (2013) 'Geography: a fragile environment?', *Teaching Geography*, 38, 2, pp. 53–5.

Lambert, D. (2009) 'Geography in education: Lost in the post?', IoE, University of London. Based on an inaugural Professorial lecture delivered at IoE 23 June 2009.

Lambert, D. (2017) 'Powerful Knowledge and Curriculum Futures' in Pyyry, N., Tainio, L., Juuti, K., Vasquez, R. and Paananen, M. (eds) *Changing Subjects, Changing Pedagogies: Diversities in School and Education*. Helsinki: Finnish Research Association for Subject Didactics.

Lambert, D. and Hopkin, J. (2014) 'A Possibilist Analysis of the Geography National Curriculum in England', *International Research in Geographical and Environmental Education*, 23, 1, pp. 64–78.

Lambert, D. and Morgan, J. (2010) *Teaching Geography 11–18: A conceptual approach*. Maidenhead: the Open University.

Maude, A. (2016) 'What might powerful geographical knowledge look like?', *Geography*, 101, 2, pp. 70-76.

Mitchell, D. (2016) 'Geography teachers and curriculum making in "changing times"', *International Research in Geographical and Environmental Education*, 25, 2, pp. 121–33.

Mitchell, D. (2017) '"Curriculum making", teacher and learner identities in changing times', *Geography*, 102, 2, pp. 99–103.

Chapter 2 | Emerging opportunities to plan a coherent geography curriculum?

31

Myatt, M. (2018) *The Curriculum: Gallimaufry to coherence*. Woodbridge: John Catt Educational Ltd.

Nussbaum, M. and Sen, M. (1993) *The Quality of Life*. Oxford Scholarship Online. Available at https://oxford.universitypressscholarship.com/view/10.1093/0198287976.001.0001/acprof-9780198287971

Oates, T. (2010) *Could do better: Using international comparisons to refine the National Curriculum in England*. Cambridge: University of Cambridge, Cambridge Assessment. Available at www.cambridgeassessment.org.uk/Images/112281-could-do-better-using-international-comparisons-to-refine-the-national-curriculum-in-england.pdf

Ofsted (2017a) *HMCI's commentary: recent primary and secondary curriculum research*. Phase 1: October 2017. Available at www.gov.uk/government/speeches/hmcis-commentary-october-2017

Ofsted (2017b) *Enriching the fabric of education*. Amanda Spielman's speech at the Festival of Education. Available at www.gov.uk/government/speeches/amanda-spielmans-speech-at-the-festival-of-education

Ofsted (2018a) *HMCI's commentary: curriculum and the new education inspection framework*. Phase 2: September 2018. Available at www.gov.uk/government/speeches/hmci-commentary-curriculum-and-the-new-education-inspection-framework

Ofsted (2018b) *Curriculum research: assessing intent, implementation and impact*. Phase 3. December 2018. Available at www.gov.uk/government/publications/curriculum-research-assessing-intent-implementation-and-impact

Ofsted (2019) *School inspection update: special edition*. Available at https://assets.publishing.service.gov.uk/government/uploads/system/uploads/attachment_data/file/772056/School_inspection_update_-_January_2019_Special_Edition_180119.pdf

Ofsted (2019) *Education inspection framework* (EIF) Available at https://assets.publishing.service.gov.uk/government/uploads/system/uploads/attachment_data/file/801429/Education_inspection_framework.pdf

Rawding, C. (2015) 'Constructing the geography curriculum 5', pp. 67–79 in Butt, G. (ed) *Master Class in Geography Education: Transforming Teaching and Learning*. London: Bloomsbury.

Roberts, M. (1997) 'Curriculum planning and course development: a matter of professional judgement', in Tilbury, D. and Williams, M. (eds) *Teaching and Learning Geography*. Abingdon: Routledge. pp. 35–48.

Wiliam, D. (2013) *Redesigning Schooling 3: Principled curriculum design*. London: SSAT. Available at https://webcontent.ssatuk.co.uk/wp-content/uploads/2013/09/Dylan-Wiliam-Principled-curriculum-design-chapter-1.pdf

Young, M. (2008) *Bringing Knowledge Back In: From social constructivism to social realism in the sociology of education*. Abingdon: Routledge.

Young, M., Lambert, D., Roberts, C., Roberts, M. (2014) *Knowledge and the Future School*. Bloomsbury: London.

Young, M. and Muller, J. (2010) 'Three educational scenarios for the future: lessons from the sociology of knowledge', *European Journal of Education*, 45, 1. pp. 11–27.

Progression and its significance in designing a Future 3 curriculum

'If we did not hope that our students would, in some sense, progress we would have no foundation on which to construct a curriculum or embark on the act of teaching ... It is ... a daunting prospect to look across the whole of the period of formal geography teaching in schools and colleges and to ask what concept of progression, implicit or explicit, is informing the design of the curriculum.'
(Daugherty, 1996, p. 195)

Daugherty's words capture the essence of curriculum planning. Over a period of time, we intend that students learn, and thus make progress. However, progression in geography is not a linear process. It is not always predictable. There can be sudden bursts of progress, sometimes followed by periods of consolidation – or even periods when students appear to go backwards! What is daunting for the teacher is the realisation that students' progress is often determined by the type of activity, or nature of a unit of work, that they provide. Compared with subjects that have the appearance of being linear or hierarchical, such as science or maths, progress in geography is more difficult to conceive of and plan for. What we mean by geography, how we think students get better at it, and how we know what students have achieved in it, have all proved difficult to be definitive about.

There are many reasons for this, but perhaps the key is to recognise that geography as a discipline is very 'horizontal' in structure, in contrast to more vertical (hierarchical) subjects such as maths (Vernon, 2016). Geographical knowledge develops partly by ideas becoming more abstract and/or difficult (vertically), but also by accretion – new ideas (and information) are constantly being added to the way we make sense of the world (horizontally). This mix makes it devilishly difficult to say with ease how students make progress in geography. And yet we have to try, because it is central to teacher's work.

This chapter explores the nature of progression in geography, as well as its fundamental significance

in the curriculum design process with reference to the importance of geographical concepts to progression, to a framework for progression, and thence to designing a coherent curriculum.

Definitions of progression in geography

In the main considerations of progression – the idea of what getting better at geography looks like – tend to focus on broad assertions about the character of such progression. Long ago, HMI (1978) stated that:

'It has been shown that while some geographical ideas vary in the degree of difficulty they present to pupils, many ideas can be approached at different levels of understanding. Although what can be achieved at a particular stage will depend largely upon pupils' experience and their intellectual capabilities, important ideas need to be returned to time and time again, with a gradual extension and deepening of understanding. The notion of a "spiral curriculum", in which key ideas and skills are progressively developed in a carefully structured manner, has obvious attractions.'
(DES, 1978, p. 11)

Building on this Trevor Bennetts, former chief HMI for geography (1995), defined progression as:

'... how pupils' learning advances. It can be applied both to the design of a curriculum, in particular how the structure of the content and sequence of learning activities are intended to facilitate advances in learning, and to the gradual gains in knowledge, understanding and skills and competencies which pupils actually achieve. Progression has to be planned for and monitored, and the only effective way of doing the latter is by the use of assessment' (p. 75).

The importance of planning is abundantly clear. Bennetts goes on to point out that:

'Planning for progression should, therefore, take account of the past, present and future:

what pupils have already experienced and achieved; what they can reasonably be expected to do at the time; and what will best serve their future needs' (p. 75).

Eleanor Rawling (2007) further developed this view, considering three aspects of progression that implicitly relate to the three 'sources of energy' in the classroom identified in the process of curriculum making (see Chapter 2, p. 24):

- ■ **Progression in relation to students' understanding and performance** – identifying the key features of performance we expect to see in a student's work as they progress – the outcomes of teaching and learning.

- ■ **Progression in relation to the curriculum experiences planned by the teacher** – the kinds of learning experiences provided as opportunities for students to make progress.

- ■ **Progression in relation to the inherent structure of the subject** – creating a sequence of content, concepts and skills in curriculum intent to guide the establishment of the curriculum journey and the implementation of the curriculum.

Why is understanding progress in geography important?

Key stage 3 is crucial in supporting the development of future 'geographers' in our society and for educating geographically-literate citizens. This may be the only time in their lives that students study the subject in a systematic manner. A geography teacher needs a clear idea about how curriculum, assessment, teaching and learning interact. To help students acquire and develop their geographical capability, teachers need to clarify their understanding of progression in geography. Ofsted identified in their curriculum research that teachers' subject knowledge is important in terms of designing a curriculum (Chapter 2, p. 30) The significance of subject knowledge linked to student progression is very clearly articulated by the GA in its online guidance (GA, n.d.1) for people considering a career as a geography teacher:

'You may be thinking here about a list of themes (e.g. coasts, volcanoes, cities) or issues (e.g. migration, development) or places (e.g. Japan, Russia). What you know about these

topics is described by teachers as *content knowledge. This is not merely geographical facts. It is also an understanding of underlying physical and human processes, systems and interrelationships, as well as geographical terminology, and skills, such as fieldwork, mapping, data handling and research.*

Through your training you will develop your subject knowledge for teaching. *A geography teacher needs to know about students' experience of geography, how they learn the subject and their misconceptions; they need to know how to plan a curriculum and teach geography so that students make progress. Your challenge, as you become a geography teacher, will be to take your geographical content knowledge and present it to students so they learn to think geographically.'*

The clear emphasis here, then, is planning a curriculum, designed with student progress in mind. But what does this progress in geography look like? Figures 3.1 and 3.2 provide two useful tools to help consider this question. The GA has identified five broad dimensions of progress (Figure 3.1) which are essential when thinking about both curriculum planning for progression and assessment.

1. Demonstrating greater fluency with world knowledge by drawing on increasing breadth and depth of content and contexts.

2. Extending from the familiar and concrete to the unfamiliar and abstract.

3. Making greater sense of the world by organising and connecting information and ideas about people, places, processes and environments.

4. Working with more complex information about the world, including the relevance of people's attitudes, values and beliefs.

5. Increasing the range and accuracy of investigative skills, and advancing their ability to select and apply these with increasing independence to geographical enquiry.

Figure 3.1: Five dimensions of progress in geography. **Source:** GA (2020, p. 2)

The GA website support for trainees and NQTs provides the following useful table (Figure 3.2) identifying aspects of progression in geography, which is an adaptation of the QCA *Geography scheme of work for key stage 3 Teacher's guide* (2000, p. 21). You can use this to keep thoughts about progression to the forefront of your mind when planning units of work across the curriculum.

So far, this chapter has focussed on defining progression in geography. A Future 3 curriculum, designed to empower students to think geographically, requires teachers to develop an ongoing and deep relationship with the subject discipline. At its heart this means considering the conceptual understanding required by students to think geographically. It is now important to think about powerful knowledge, GeoCapabilities and thinking geographically (introduced in Chapter 2, p. 26), to explore the concepts that underpin the subject and consider their significance in planning a coherent curriculum with progression in mind.

Aspect of geography	From year 7	To year 9	Comment
Vocabulary	Using a limited vocabulary	Precise use of a wider range of vocabulary	Students develop accurate and precise use of geographical vocabulary
Knowledge of place	Geographical knowledge of some places	Understanding of a wider range of places and links between them	Students broaden their scale and contexts of study and explain the links between places
Human/physical patterns and processes	Describing patterns and processes	Explaining patterns and processes	Students begin to cope with increasingly complex patterns and processes
Geographical thinking	Participating in practical activities involving geographical thinking	Building increasingly abstract models of real situations	Students understand increasingly complex abstract ideas and are capable of operating within abstract ideas
Geographical explanation	Explaining events and geographical phenomena in terms of their own ideas	Explaining these in terms of accepting ideas or models and using generalisations	Explanations become more accurate and precise. Students increasingly recognise links, interrelationships and complexity
Geographical enquiry	Following teacher guidance for investigations	Forming relevant geographical questions and investigating them systematically	Students increasingly understand the meaning of geographical enquiry and the steps they need to follow to carry it out and present findings
Map skills	Using simple drawings and maps	Using a wide range of maps and diagrams, and selecting the most appropriate way to use them to represent information	Students make increasing use of cognitive skills for interpretation, analysis and communication
Fieldwork	Guided practical activities	Working independently outside the classroom	Students, with increasing independence, use geographical skills in more complex and precise ways

Figure 3.2: Aspects of progression in geography. **Source:** GA (2017). ⤓

Thinking geographically: the significance of geographical concepts for progression

The review of the National Curriculum launched by the government in 2010 provided an opportunity for the GA to expand and develop the thinking of its Manifesto, published in 2009 (GA, 2009). Given the government intended to re-write the curriculum based on what seemed like the limited notion of 'core knowledge', the GA developed its own typology of geographical knowledge (Figure 3.3) drawing on, amongst other things, Michael Young's idea of 'powerful knowledge' (2008). The GA was attempting to expand government thinking that appeared to limit the curriculum to teaching the basic facts (heavily influenced by the notion of 'cultural literacy' – see Hirsch, 1987; 2007). 'We have nothing against facts', the GA was to say, 'but geographical knowledge includes more than facts alone'. The GA Manifesto compared geography to a language that provides a way of thinking about the world – 'Languages have vocabulary. You need vocabulary to speak the language, but it is not enough. Languages also have grammar, rules, concepts and procedures which allow you to construct meanings. The grammar of geography is its big ideas, which help us organise and attach significance to the vocabulary (geographical information or knowledge)'. The typology (Figure 3.3) expands on this idea.

Kn1, Kn2 and Kn3 provide a platform on which we can build a definition of what it means to study geography. Or to put this another way, to learn how to think geographically. In 2012, the GA developed its own curriculum proposals for the GNC that expanded on this thinking. Part of the approach was to consider the distinctive conceptual underpinning of geography. The GA published this as 'Thinking Geographically', explaining its purpose as: 'looking for a form of conceptual knowledge development which links facts together through geographic thought' (GA, 2012, p. 1), within an overarching framework of place, space, environment and geographical enquiry. Although the final version of the 2014 GNC did not fully embrace these ideas, thinking geographically is one of the four aims for GCSE, and underpins A level geography. All five of the case study schools in Chapter 8 clearly identify thinking geographically in their curriculum intent.

Core knowledge [Kn1]: the vocabulary of geography. This refers to the subject as it resides in the popular imagination: if geography is the 'world subject' its core knowledge is gleaned and created from the information communicated in globes and atlases. Much of this amounts to geographical *context*, and in this sense can be distinguished from the main *content* of the curriculum. It is not low-level or trivial material but it can become so if taught badly, e.g. as an end in itself. It may be thought of as *extensive* world knowledge, in itself fairly superficial yet enabling.

Content knowledge [Kn2]: the grammar of geography. Sometimes referred to as concepts or generalisations, and the key to developing understanding. This may be seen as the main content of the geography curriculum. Key concepts and generalisations in geography show how geography contributes to students' acquisition and development of 'powerful knowledge'. It may also be thought of as more *intensive* world knowledge, taking in the realm of processes, different perspectives and values.

Procedural knowledge [Kn3]: Thinking geographically is a distinctive procedure – it is not the same as thinking historically, or scientifically, or mathematically (etc.) The teacher can model this by example, but it is also learned through exposure to, and direct experience of, high-quality geographical enquiry which might include decision making or problem-solving scenarios. Learning geography requires students to engage mentally with questions about people, society, environment and the planet. This means they identify, assimilate, analyse and communicate data of various kinds, and learn the skills to do so productively. This will often entail using information technology – manipulating maps, diagrams, graphs and images (sometimes referred to collectively as 'graphicacy') – structured talk and debate and writing for a variety of audiences.

Figure 3.3: The GA's knowledge framework: three mutually inter- dependent types of geographical knowledge.
Source: GA (2011), pp. 2–3.

The thinking developed at this time by the GA is of great value to the process of curriculum design. David Lambert (2017) revisited these ideas in his excellent review of thinking geographically, Chapter 2 in the GA's *Handbook of Secondary Geography*. Here, Lambert proposes a three-part framework for schools to contribute to the growth of young people's capabilities to think geographically:

■ the acquisition and development of deep descriptive and explanatory 'world knowledge'; we can think of this as geography's core knowledge, its 'vocabulary'

■ the development of the relational thinking that underpins geographical thought; we can think of this as geography's conceptual subject identity, its 'grammar'

■ a propensity to ask questions, explore and apply analysis to alternative social, economic and environmental futures in particular place contexts; we can think of this as 'geographical enquiry' (p. 25).

As curriculum developers, therefore, we need to plan for progression that sequentially links units of work to:

■ what we want students to know (statements of essential knowledge)

with

■ what we want students to understand (conceptual understanding)

with

■ what we want students to be able to do (geographical skills and enquiry).

This provides a clear view of what thinking geographically involves, and how to plan a curriculum to achieve student progress towards it. This framework builds on the GA's typology of geographical knowledge (Figure 3.3). This 'relational thinking that underpins geographical thought' requires careful consideration.

What are concepts?

Concepts are fundamental to making progress towards thinking geographically. It is, therefore, important to understand what concepts are in order to design a curriculum with this idea of progression in mind.

ACTIVITY 3.1

A good place to start thinking about the role of concepts in your curriculum is provided, with excellent online CPD, at 'Getting Started with Key Concepts' by Cambridge Assessment International Education, led by Dr Liz Taylor.

https://cambridge-community.org.uk/professional-development/gswkey/index.html

Concepts are a way of categorising or labelling things to create a shared framework for understanding, communication and action. So, for example, if someone refers to a 'farm' we have a basic idea what they're talking about, even if our idea 'farm' might be a bit different from theirs. Concepts are classifiers that help us make sense of a very complex world. Each school subject incorporates a large number of concepts; geography has many, and the world of geography education has described them in different ways. Concepts range from simple, substantive or **concrete things**, for example, river or city (similar to Kn1 in Figure 3.3), to those that refer to **abstract or complex things** or even **processes**, for example, environment or urbanisation (similar to Kn2 in Figure 3.3). Some concepts include a sub-set of 'smaller' concepts for example, biome includes rainforest and desert.

Bennetts (2008) explains that 'concepts enable us to cope mentally with the complexities of our environment, our experiences and the information available to us. The labels that we attach to individual concepts represent underlying ideas, which can vary greatly in the challenges that they pose for learners' (p. 56).

Clare Brooks (2018) classifies concepts into three categories: hierarchical, organisational and developmental:

■ hierarchical – concepts as a content container, focussing on the subject

■ organisational – concepts helping to link ideas, experiences and processes, focussing on pedagogy

■ developmental – concepts reflecting the process of deepening understanding, focussing on the learner (pp. 104–5).

Hierarchical concepts or big ideas

The hierarchical concepts, or big ideas, a person or group chooses as 'key' in a subject vary according to your view of the subject and the purpose in selecting the set of key concepts. (See 'Concepts used in curriculum design in case study schools', Chapter 8.) There is no one definitive list of key geographical concepts and no correct categorisation of concepts. The subject of geography, just like the world, is constantly growing and changing, so it is unlikely there could ever be just one agreed set of key concepts for all learning situations. Furthermore, if we favour Future 3 curriculum scenarios (see Chapter 2, p. 27), underpinned by a notion of 'powerful knowledge', then we expect the knowledge component in our teaching to be dynamic, contingent and developing (rather than predefined, stable and 'given'). Taylor (2008) summarised a number of sets of geographical key concepts, identified by various authors in geography education, as well as in the National Curriculum (Figure 3.4).

The 2007 GNC identified seven concepts, shown in Figure 3.4, which represented an 'official' view of the big ideas in geography. While most geographers would probably agree place, space and scale, and environmental interaction as being key to geography, the other three were more contested (partly because they were more 'cross-curricular' and listed in other NC subjects). The Action Plan for Geography (DfES/GA/RGS-IBG, 2006) lists five key concepts or big ideas that perform this role: place, connectedness, scale, process and skills. Peter Jackson (2006) captured the *relational thinking* that characterises distinctively geographical perspectives, again emphasising what it means to think geographically. His device was to identify a short series of deliberately paired concepts:

- space and place
- scale and connection
- proximity and distance.

Jackson concludes, 'Thinking geographically ... provides a set of concepts and ideas that can help us see the connections between places and scales that others frequently miss ...That is the power of thinking geographically.' (p. 203)

There is general agreement that the main hierarchical concepts of geography are place, space and environment. Beneath this level of big ideas there is a wide range of substantive concepts, such as river basin, city, development, sustainability. As students are introduced to and progress their understanding of such substantive

Schools Council Project *History, Geography and Social Science* (1976) in Marsden (1995)	Leat (1998)		Geography Advisers and Inspectors Network (2002)		
Communication	Cause and effect	Planning	Bias	Futures	Perception
Power	Classification	Systems	Causation	Inequality	Region
Beliefs and values	Decision-making		Change	Interdependence	Environment
Conflict/consensus	Development		Conflict	Landscape	Uncertainty
Similarity/difference	Inequality		Development	Scale	
Causes and consequences	Location		Distribution	Location	
Holloway *et al* (2003)	**Jackson (2006)**		**English 2008 key stage 3 Curriculum (QCA, 2007)**		
Space	Space and place		Place	Physical and human processes	
Time	Scale and connection		Space	Environmental interaction and sustainable development	
Place	Proximity and distance		Scale		
Scale	Relational thinking		Interdependence	Cultural understanding and diversity	
Social formations					
Physical systems					
Landscape and environment					

Figure 3.4: Some suggested sets of important concepts in geography. **Source:** Taylor (2008), p. 51.

concepts, they begin to grasp the more abstract ideas and generalisations of place, space and environment. The difficulty of planning a curriculum with these hierarchical concepts in mind, is that there is no clear meaning in the words themselves: they represent a complex array of smaller ideas. The GA attempted to unpack these ideas in the paper 'Thinking geographically' (2012) reproduced here as Figure 3.5, and also further explained in David Lambert's chapter in the GA's *Handbook of Secondary Geography* (Lambert, 2017).

Place (places, territories, regions)	Space (patterns and links)	Environment (physical and human interaction)
A place is a specific part of Earth's surface that has been named and given meaning by people, although these meanings may differ. Places range in size from the home and locality to a major world region. Doreen Massey suggests we view the planet as a place. They are interconnected with other places, often in complex ways. Places are unique, but do not have to be studied as if they were singular, for in seeking understanding and explanation geographers study general processes and look for similarities as well as differences.	Space in geography is the three-dimensional surface of the Earth. While historians study change over time, geographical study emphasises differences across space. This is of particular interest in understanding the rich diversity of environments, peoples, cultures and economies that exist together on the surface of the Earth.	The term environment means our living and non-living surroundings. The features of the environment can be classified as natural, managed, or constructed. However, we also recognise that these boundaries can be contested and are 'fuzzy': there is much interaction and cross-over. The concept of environment provides a powerful way of understanding, explaining and thinking about the world.
In studying place in school we can:	**In geography we develop a deeper understanding of space (the 'spatial') by:**	**In geography we do this by:**
■ progress from describing the characteristics of places to explaining them. Characteristics include climate, economy, population, landforms, built environment, soils and vegetation, communities, water resources, cultures, minerals, landscape, and recreational and scenic quality. Some are tangible, such as rivers and buildings, while others are less so, such as wilderness and socioeconomic status.	■ investigating the spatial distribution of phenomena and explaining them, often by looking for a spatial association between several distributions.	■ recognising the environment as an ecosystem – with environmental benefits, such as genetic diversity, pollination or nutrient cycling.
■ explore people's aesthetic, emotional, cultural and spiritual connections with places; the role of places in their own feelings of identity, sense of place and belonging; and the ways they experience and use places.	■ learning how to evaluate the economic, social, environmental and political consequences of particular spatial distributions.	■ investigating the structure and functioning of environments as systems: of weather, climate, hydrology, geomorphology, biogeography and soils.
■ recognise that places may be altered and remade by people, and that changes promoted by one group may be contested by others. The values and beliefs people and groups hold are variables which contribute to our understanding of why change in places is often controversial.	■ studying the influence of absolute and relative location on the characteristics of places and on people's lives.	■ examining the ways that people use, alter and manage environments (intentionally and unintentionally).
■ use the uniqueness of places to explain why the outcomes of universal environmental and human processes may vary, and why similar problems may require different strategies in different places.	■ recognising that improvements in transport and communication systems have greatly reduced the time taken to send goods, capital and information between places, which has increased the speed at which economic and cultural impacts spread around the world.	■ exploring different world views about the relationship between humans and the environment, and applying ideas such as sustainability and stewardship in studies of the environment.
	■ investigating the ways that space is structured, organised and managed by people for different purposes.	■ recognising that studies of environmental change have an ethical dimension, succinctly captured by the question: who gets what, why and where (and why care)?
	■ recognising that people perceive and use space differently, and may feel accepted and safe in some and unwelcome or unsafe in others.	■ investigating the effects of the environment on people and places through the opportunities and constraints it presents for economic development and human settlement.
	■ understanding the role of values and beliefs in influencing decision-making about how space may be used in the future.	■ reflecting on the extent to which the environment contributes to human beings' sense of identity.
	■ exploring the ways space is represented, e.g. in maps, art, literature, films, songs, stories and dance, and the influences of these representations on people's perceptions.	

Figure 3.5: Geography – the three organisational concepts, explained. **Source:** GA (2012) 'Thinking geographically' GNC discussion paper. ⬇

Threshold concepts

'A threshold concept can be considered as akin to a portal, opening up a new and previously inaccessible way of thinking about something. It represents a transformed way of understanding, or interpreting, or viewing something without which the learner cannot progress. As a consequence of comprehending a threshold concept there may thus be a transformed internal view of subject matter, subject landscape, or even world view.' (Meyer and Land, 2006, p. 412).

The idea of threshold concepts emerged from a UK national research project into the possible characteristics of strong teaching and learning environments in the disciplines for undergraduate education. The idea has been applied to a wide range of higher education disciplines (Cousin, 2006).

Slinger (2011) summarises the characteristics of a threshold concept, identified by Meyer and Land. It is likely to be:

■ *Transformative:* causing students to perceive the subject differently. It can also involve a 'transformation of personal identity, a reconstruction of subjectivity'. This can also include an affective component such as a shift in values, feelings or attitude.

■ *Probably irreversible:* once crossed it is unlikely to be forgotten or unlearned.

■ *Integrative:* in that it 'exposes the previously hidden interrelatedness of something'.

■ *Possibly bounded:* the conceptual space occupied by the threshold concept has a boundary; often one that defines where the disciplinary boundary itself might lie.

■ *Potentially troublesome:* there are barriers to understanding that can take a variety of forms and that have the effect of delaying, frustrating, limiting or possibly preventing understanding. Troublesomeness results in students not 'getting it'.

Thus, threshold concepts are big ideas or concepts that link with other concepts; understanding them can enable students to integrate their thinking across the subject, and see the bigger picture. Once this is achieved, sometimes through a 'wow' moment, the student's understanding is transformed to another level. As Margaret Roberts explains: 'Threshold concepts are not like building blocks which add to other concepts; instead they lead to a change in conceptual understanding ... before ... they [students] tend to understand a subject in more fragmented ways which can create a barrier to their progress.' (2013, p. 87)

A geographer who has a deep interest in the conceptual basis of the subject, Alaric Maude identified a fourth key concept beyond place, space and environment, namely **interconnection** (Maude, 2020). All four have the potential to be threshold concepts, but in relation to interconnections Maude explains, 'The concept of interconnection is about recognising that nothing studied in geography exists in isolation, because everything is influenced by its relationships with other phenomena, both within and between places.' He sees this concept at the top of a hierarchy of some pretty important ideas that include interdependence, interaction, processes and systems. A powerful and potentially transformational aspect of fully grasped interconnections is that this helps students understand 'that the places in which they live are connected to places around the world, and that their climate, population, economy and culture are influenced by these interconnections at all scales from the local to the global' (p. 237). This promotes high levels of relational and holistic thinking, and once achieved, a deeper geographical understanding: it literally enables in the learner 'a different view' (GA, 2009).

Slinger's research into threshold concepts identified a number of implications for curriculum and pedagogy, including:

■ **Progression within the curriculum.** This can be conceived of in terms of the development of geographical thinking rather than accumulation of content. In 11–16 school geography, there can be a tendency to pack the curriculum with content and focus on a narrow view of knowledge. As Slinger states, 'A focus on threshold concepts enables teachers to make refined decisions about what is fundamental to a grasp of the subject they are teaching, a 'less is more' approach to curriculum design' (2011, p. 4). This gives over more control to the teacher in making professional judgements about where next to take the learning journey. Cousin (2006) sees the potential of threshold concepts to constitute the 'jewels in the curriculum' providing powerful transformative points in the student's learning experience.

- **New forms of assessment** that are formative in a way that assess both the qualities of learners but also the nature of the understanding, the modes of reasoning or explanation and the ability to construct discipline-specific narratives and argument.

Organisational concepts – that help focus on pedagogy

Brooks (2018) identifies a second category: an organisational approach to concepts, focussed on pedagogy. She provides the example of Taylor (2008) where concepts are used as a way of linking everyday experiences with higher-level, big geographical ideas. Taylor considers organisational concepts that she feels are central to asking geographical concepts. Figure 3.6 shows her four organisational concepts, and the sorts of geographical questions which each organising concept enables us to ask. Brooks explains that 'organisational concepts are different to hierarchical concepts, as they are not the goal of learning geography but a facilitating tool to get to those

goals, and hence they emphasise linked processes and ideas rather than outcomes'. (p. 109). These concepts tend to be more generic.

Developmental concepts – developing understanding

As we have seen above, the third category of concept identified by Brooks (2018) was developmental. This focuses on the learner and involves the student's own conceptualisation of school geography. The significance of this made clear by Brooks: '... while teachers may organise their curriculums around hierarchical or organisational concepts, the way that students make sense of their lessons may be determined by their own conceptual frameworks.' (p. 109) It seems important, therefore, that teachers consider the processes by which students learn, as they devise and implement their curriculum intent.

Trevor Bennetts is one of very few people who have researched the development of understanding in geography (Bennetts, 2005a). In Figure 3.7, he models the process of learning to develop understanding. It shows how experience and geographical ideas need to be developed by various mental processes in order to lead to understanding. Understanding is the way in which students connect their prior experiences and knowledge to a concept at that moment in time.

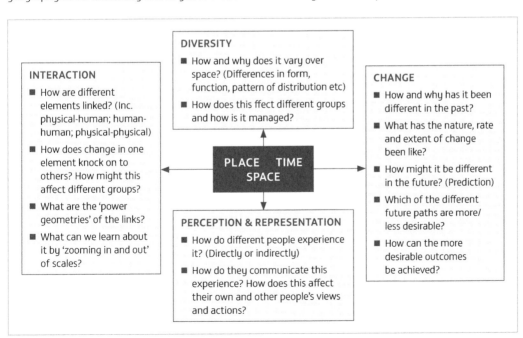

Figure 3.6: Four organisational concepts (Taylor, 2008).

DIVERSITY
- How and why does it vary over space? (Differences in form, function, pattern of distribution etc)
- How does this ffect different groups and how is it managed?

INTERACTION
- How are different elements linked? (Inc. physical-human; human-human; physical-physical)
- How does change in one element knock on to others? How might this affect different groups?
- What are the 'power geometries' of the links?
- What can we learn about it by 'zooming in and out' of scales?

PLACE TIME SPACE

CHANGE
- How and why has it been different in the past?
- What has the nature, rate and extent of change been like?
- How might it be different in the future? (Prediction)
- Which of the different future paths are more/less desirable?
- How can the more desirable outcomes be achieved?

PERCEPTION & REPRESENTATION
- How do different people experience it? (Directly or indirectly)
- How do they communicate this experience? How does this affect their own and other people's views and actions?

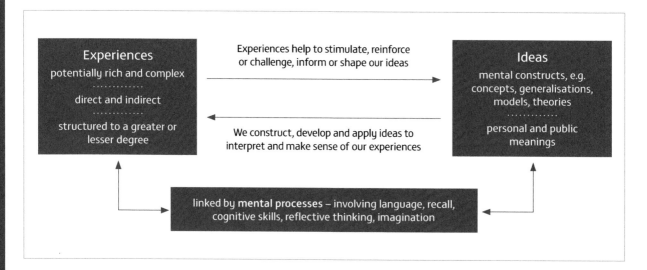

Figure 3.7:
The roots of understanding.
Source: Bennetts (2005b), p. 154.

As Bennetts (2005b) explains, the model:

'... draws attention to the strong interrelationships between experiences and ideas, with our experiences helping to stimulate and shape our ideas; and our ideas influencing how we perceive reality, and how we interpret and make sense of our experiences. We construct the links between our experiences and our ideas by mental processes, sometimes consciously, as when we engage in analytical and reflective thinking, but also subconsciously ... development of understanding is in some respects an imaginative and creative activity, which cannot be explained solely in terms of the logical relationships between ideas.' (pp. 155–6)

Bennetts has made a significant contribution to consideration of the pedagogy required to support students towards understanding, with activities stimulating mental processes. He identified activities that require them to reflect on:

■ the meaning of relevant ideas

■ the relationships between related ideas

■ the relationships between these ideas and their experience

■ the information or geographical data that is presented to them.

The activities that stimulate mental processes relate to the process of geographical enquiry (see Roberts, 2013). Enquiry can enable learners to link information, concepts and activities so as to reveal and progress the essential and distinctive thinking that our discipline contributes to a student's perspective on the world (Kn3, GA typology of knowledge) (see Chapter 6, p. 102).

The role of concepts in your curriculum intent

Concepts are important in curriculum enactment. As Bennetts (2008) writes, '... teachers of geography would benefit from a view of conceptual structures within their subject which goes beyond that of a limited number of highly generalised "key concepts"' (p. 60). As we have seen above, concepts come in many different sizes and shapes – from the tiniest substantive 'thing' such as a particle of clay to the largest, rambling complex big idea such as 'sustainable development'. But when advocating a conceptual approach to the curriculum most writers, including Bennetts, are trying to distinguish the curriculum as a vehicle for the delivery of facts (sometimes confusingly referred to as 'knowledge') from a process curriculum focussed on developing understanding.

Thus Clare Brooks (2018) asserts that 'Concepts are at the centre of geography education' (p. 103). She goes on to explain: 'A programme of study articulated without concepts runs the risk of focusing entirely on knowledge or skill acquisition, and not on how to develop the building blocks of geographical understanding. Not only will this affect progression in geographical learning, but it will also affect how we distinguish what is distinctively different about learning geography from other school subject areas' (p. 106).

Eleanor Rawling (2007) encourages us to think of the big concepts '... as a framework or skeleton of geography on which to hang the more detailed curriculum flesh ... It is intended that students will gradually move towards understanding them better as they study the particular geographical topics you have chosen.' (pp. 17–18)

Rawling added that 'the concepts and ideas of the subject represent economies of thought which are useful if geography is not just to be a mass of memorised facts.' (p. 23). These principles about the significance of concepts are reinforced by the GA:

> 'An effective teacher builds students' understanding of concepts so that geography becomes accessible to them and they can progress. They make concepts transparent to students, to help them to think geographically and to develop transferable geographical understanding. This will take students beyond learning a set of dislocated facts and move them into the realms of informed geographical thinking. All this relies, of course, on teachers having a good grasp of the key geographical concepts themselves'. (GA, n.d.2)

GA – A progression framework for geography

The GA produced the original version of *A progression framework for geography* (fully revised in 2020) for the 2014 National Curriculum (GA, 2014). It connects GA guidance on aspects of achievement, dimensions of progress and benchmarks in geography. It is based on a clear vision of what it means to make progress in geography, anchored by age-specific national expectations for students aged 7–16 years. This guidance aims to support teachers in planning a geography curriculum that is ambitious, coherently planned and sequenced, and which anticipates high standards for their students. In other words, it supports teachers, to show how they connect the intent, implementation and impact of their geography curriculum. The progression framework underpins the practical guidance provided in Chapters 4–8 of this book.

The framework for progression has used the aims of the geography National Curriculum as three

aspects of achievement, which can act as 'progression strands' around which you can design your own curriculum. These aims/aspects of achievement/progression strands are:

- contextual world knowledge of locations, places and geographical features
- conceptual understanding of the conditions, processes and interactions that explain features, distribution patterns, and changes in places over time and space
- competence in geographical enquiry, and the application of skills in observing, collecting, analysing, evaluating and communicating geographical ideas and information.

These 'strands' are deeply embedded in the epistemology of the discipline. They can be applied flexibly to curricula based on systematic or thematic geography, geographical issues or even regional geography. Systematic geography appears as a series of sub-disciplines, identified in the GNC as aspects of physical and human geography. Regional or place-based geography is organised by analysing the interaction of such systematic themes, in the particular context of one place or region. Issues-based geography curricula are guided by problems, dilemmas or issues (such as development, or the impact of climate change) and investigates these geographical ideas and perspectives.

The strands underpin achievement and progress, and help bring a sense of coherence to learning geography. They naturally progress and interconnect with the aims and AOs for geography at GCSE, thus forming the basis for planning a coherent 11–16 geography curriculum.

Benchmark expectations

By combining the progress strands, teachers can gain an overview of what they expect students to achieve. The GA has developed age-related benchmark statements for 7, 9, 11, 14 and 16 years. These statements are based explicitly on the three progression strands, providing us with a 'map' of the 'expected' geographical achievement up to and including GCSE (Figure 3.8). They are by necessity quite generalised – and always open to some debate and refinement. But they are a good starting point for teachers to use in their planning.

Contextual world knowledge of locations, places and geographical features.

- demonstrating greater fluency with world knowledge by drawing on increasing breadth and depth of content and contexts.

Expectations by age 7	by age 9	by age 11	by age 14	by age 16
Have simple locational knowledge about individual places and environments, especially in the local area, but also in the UK and wider world.	Have begun to develop a framework of world locational knowledge, including knowledge of places in the local area, UK and wider world, and some globally significant physical and human features.	Have a more detailed and extensive framework of knowledge of the world, including globally significant physical and human features and places in the news.	Have extensive knowledge relating to a wide range of places, environments and features at a variety of appropriate spatial scales, extending from local to global.	Have a broader and deeper understanding of locational contexts, including greater awareness of the importance of scale and the concept of global.

Understanding of the conditions, processes and interactions that explain features, distribution patterns, and changes over time and space.

- extending from the familiar and concrete to the unfamiliar and abstract
- making greater sense of the world by organising and connecting information and ideas about people, places, processes and environments
- working with more complex information about the world, including the relevance of people's attitudes, values and beliefs.

Expectations by age 7	by age 9	by age 11	by age 14	by age 16
Show understanding by describing the places and features they study using simple geographical vocabulary, identifying some similarities and differences and simple patterns in the environment.	Demonstrate their knowledge and understanding of the wider world by investigating places beyond their immediate surroundings, including human and physical features and patterns, how places change and some links between people and environments. They become more adept at comparing places, and understand some reasons for similarities and differences.	Understand in some detail what a number of places are like, how and why they are similar and different, and how and why they are changing. They know about some spatial patterns in physical and human geography, the conditions that influence those patterns, and the processes that lead to change. They show some understanding of the links between places, people and environments.	Understand the physical and human conditions and processes that lead to the development of, and change in, a variety of geographical features, systems and places. They can explain various ways in which places are linked and the impact such links have on people and environments. They can make connections between different geographical phenomena they have studied.	Gain a deeper understanding of the processes that lead to geographical changes and the multivariate nature of human-physical relationships and interactions, with a stronger focus on forming valid general isations and abstractions, together with a growing awareness of the importance of theoretical perspectives and conceptual frameworks in geography.

Competence in **geographical enquiry**, and the application of skills in observing, collecting, analysing, evaluating and communicating geographical information.

- increasing the range and accuracy of pupils' investigative skills, and advancing their ability to select and apply these with increasing independence to geographical enquiry.

Expectations by age 7	by age 9	by age 11	by age 14	by age 16
Be able to investigate places and environments by asking and answering questions, making observations and using sources such as simple maps, atlases, globes, images and aerial photos.	Be able to investigate places and environments by asking and responding to geographical questions, making observations and using sources such as maps, atlases, globes, images and aerial photos. They can express their opinions and recognise that others may think differently.	Be able to carry out investigations using a range of geographical questions, skills and sources of information including a variety of maps, graphs and images. They can express and explain their opinions, and recognise why others may have different points of view.	Be able, with increasing independence, to choose and use a wide range of data to help investigate, interpret, make judgements and draw conclusions about geographical questions, issues and problems, and express and engage with different points of view about these.	Be able to plan and undertake independent enquiry in which skills, knowledge and understanding are applied to investigate geographical questions, and show competence in a range of intellectual and communication skills, including the formulation of arguments, that include elements of synthesis and evaluation of material.

Figure 3.8: The GA's progression framework. **Source**: GA (2020).

The benchmark statements can also be used to inform and set expectations for students' achievement and develop assessment criteria in individual teaching units. The latter won't use the same general or abstract language as the benchmark statements, but will contextualise the expectations into a mark scheme or assessment criteria that will make sense not only to students, but teachers too: i.e. they will provide 'pitch'. This provides the basis for planning assessment opportunities into lesson sequences – enabling benchmark expectations to be developed in practice.

Thus, the purpose of these benchmark statements is to:

- support your thinking about progress in geography as part of your curriculum design process

- to be used or modified to underpin long- and medium-term judgements of students' attainment and shared with students and parents

- provide a shared language to help set expectations and standards in your school, and so form the backdrop to planning for progress

- indirectly support both discussions with students about their progress as well as teachers' practice in planning and differentiation

- support your periodic judgements about students' attainment (particularly at the end of key stages) by providing a national framework of standards

- provide a starting point for you to customise the statements linked to your geography curriculum and developed to suit the needs of your students, e.g. by adding specific places, themes and skills, personalised and differentiated to show expectations for different year groups, e.g. 'an expert geographer in year 7 knows ...'

- offer the flexibility to develop your own stepping stones in learning; learning that is at the heart of your key stage plan and linked, clearly, to the topics/places you plan to investigate

- support curriculum review. For example:

'Did we have sufficient curriculum time to teach 'X' in sufficient depth?''In key stage 3, did we provide sufficient opportunities for students to develop independence in enquiry?'.

Designing a curriculum using progression strands and benchmark statements

It is possible to use the progression strands and benchmark statements to create a coherent key stage 3 geography curriculum. As a starting point, compare the benchmark statements for each aspect of achievement/progression strand for an 11–14 year old. This will help you to consider the nature of the progression you will be planning for. You can use them to plan a curriculum journey to take your students from the benchmark statement for an 11-year old to those of a 14-year old, following a journey along the GA's dimensions of progression.

A key stage 3 plan should consist of more than a list of topics to be taught over the two or three years. How these topics are sequenced can appear quite random! However, using the progression strands can influence the sequencing to support student progress: how a geographical concept or skill can be introduced or progressed across topics, or how they build on and progress key stage 2 geography.

Figure 3.9 shows how the topics that make up a key stage 3 curriculum can be interconnected in a coherent way by the three progression strands. This represents an approach to curriculum design that puts progression at the very heart. Once initiated, this approach makes the need transparent for sequencing units (topics 1–6) in each year group shown in Figure 3.9, to create logical stepping stones in teaching and learning. Each unit can be assigned 'responsibilities' to introduce or progress an aspect of achievement to work towards the long term vision of the key stage course. Planning in this way has the potential to naturally align geographical concepts, core knowledge and skills. This approach will be developed and explained further in Chapter 5.

Built-in progression in DfE curriculum documents

The Department for Education (and Ofqual) have approached curriculum reform in a manner that is more mindful of progression at a policy level. For example, the DfE (2014) subject content for GCSE geography set out the vision:

How do you plan for progression?

Plan for student progress across each topic

| Topic 1 | Topic 2 | Topic 3 | Topic 4 | Topic 5 | Topic 6 |

Year 7

Contextual world knowledge – how do you plan for opportunities for students to demonstrate greater fluency with world knowledge by drawing on an increasing breadth and depth of content and contexts?

Geographical understanding – how do you plan for opportunities for students to demonstrate that they can make greater sense of the world, organising and connecting more complex information about people, places, processes and environments?

Competence in geographical enquiry and skills – how do you plan for opportunities for students to demonstrate increasing range and accuracy of investigative skills, with advancing ability to select and apply these with increasing independence to geographical enquiry?

Year 8

Contextual world knowledge – how do you plan for opportunities for students to demonstrate greater fluency with world knowledge by drawing on an increasing breadth and depth of content and contexts?

Geographical understanding – how do you plan for opportunities for students to demonstrate that they can make greater sense of the world, organising and connecting more complex information about people, places, processes and environments?

Competence in geographical enquiry and skills – how do you plan for opportunities for students to demonstrate increasing range and accuracy of investigative skills, with advancing ability to select and apply these with increasing independence to geographical enquiry?

Year 9

Contextual world knowledge – how do you plan for opportunities for students to demonstrate greater fluency with world knowledge by drawing on an increasing breadth and depth of content and contexts?

Geographical understanding – how do you plan for opportunities for students to demonstrate that they can make greater sense of the world, organising and connecting more complex information about people, places, processes and environments?

Competence in geographical enquiry and skills – how do you plan for opportunities for students to demonstrate increasing range and accuracy of investigative skills, with advancing ability to select and apply these with increasing independence to geographical enquiry?

Plan for progression across topics in each year group

Contextual world knowledge

Geographical understanding

Competence in geographical enquiry and skills

Figure 3.9: Interconnecting unit topics using the progression strands. **Source:** Author's own.

'The GCSE subject content sets out the knowledge, understanding and skills common to all GCSE specifications in a given subject. Together with the AOs it provides the framework within which awarding organisations create the detail of their specifications, so ensuring progression from key stage 3 national curriculum requirements and the possibilities for development into A level.' (p. 3)

Eleanor Rawling (2016) highlighted what the new content framework means for secondary teachers of geography, and attempted to trace the opportunities for progression in teaching and learning across the whole 5–19 age range. She helpfully summarised the subject content frameworks that

now exist across GNC, GCSE and A level, shown in Figure 3.10. She provides lists for locational knowledge, place, physical and human geography across the National Frameworks 5–19, with more detailed tables available to download on the GA website in the additional resources section for this specific edition of *Teaching Geography*. These tables provide an excellent overview of the opportunities for progression 5–19.

Rawling explains how each DfE national document for each key stage (including A level) was developed with progression in mind:

'One of the main areas of discussion among the subject professionals involved in the national curriculum, GCSE and AS/A-level development

National Curriculum 11–14 years	GCSE 14–16 years	AS/A level 16–19 years
Knowledge-led, emphasis on locational knowledge, a regional study in Africa and one in Asia, coverage of traditional physical and human topics, including rocks, weathering, weather/climate, population, urban development, economic activity, resources. Brief key stage paragraphs identify some aspects of progression. Not all aspects of geography present (e.g. people-environment). No mention of enquiry.	Detailed subject knowledge via headings: locational knowledge; place; human geography; people-environment; physical geography; maps, fieldwork, geographical skills (including enquiry). 'Place' includes 'Geography of UK' in overview and in some depth. Fieldwork strengthened – in two contrasting environments. Full statement about progression from key stage 3. Terminal examinations only.	Subject knowledge framed within clear rationale and structure (from A level Content Advisory Board [ALCAB] report). Core (60%) content includes two human and two physical themes for A level (1 each for AS). Updated content especially in human geography – place meaning, identity, representation; and in physical geography – water/carbon cycles. Progression from GCSE stated. Independent learning and research stressed (student investigation 20%).

Figure 3.10: National Frameworks for geography 11–19. **Source:** *Teaching Geography*, 41, 1, p. 6.

exercises was how to set out the subject content required at each key stage in a way that clarified the conceptual structure and coherence of the subject, rather than just outlining a random list of topics. Accordingly, the statements of aims and purposes for each key stage highlight the big organising ideas of geography – place, space, environment, process and scale … the message from the aims and purpose statements is that the specific and detailed knowledge of locations, places, processes and environments listed at all scales from local to global is not just "stuff" to be learned: it is a basis for developing greater understanding of these big ideas of geography which students will build up throughout the key stages.' (p. 6)

As a result, there is a clear advantage for teachers in using the aims and purposes – in conjunction with the GA's benchmark statements and progression strands – **before** delving into the detailed knowledge outlined in the GCSE specification. A progression statement, making it clear how GCSE is designed to progress learning from key stage 3 geography, is also included in the GCSE subject content document for geography (Figure 3.11).

It is interesting that this statement seems to be targeted at the awarding bodies, designing specifications from this subject content. But it is certainly also of great use for the teacher, using the specification to enact the curriculum. This progression statement provides an invaluable starting point for planning your coherent 11–16 geography curriculum.

When designing specifications, awarding organisations should note the following ways in which curriculum emphases should progress from key stage 3 and ensure that specifications facilitate this:

■ broadening and deepening understanding of locational contexts, including greater awareness of the importance of scale and the concept of global

■ a greater emphasis given to process studies that lead to an understanding of change

■ a greater stress on the multivariate nature of 'human-physical' relationships and interactions

■ a stronger focus on forming generalisations and/or abstractions, including some awareness of theoretical perspectives and of the subject's conceptual frameworks

■ an increased involvement of students in planning and undertaking independent enquiry in which skills and knowledge are applied to investigate geographical questions

■ enhancing competence in a range of intellectual and communication skills, including the formulation of arguments, that include elements of synthesis and evaluation of material.

There is a clear link between this GCSE progression statement and the GA's dimensions of progression with which we began this chapter (Figure 3.1). The aims, AOs and the prescribed content provided by the DfE have been developed with progression from key stage 3 and to A level in mind. Figure 3.12 shows the aims/progression strands for GNC, as well as the aims and AOs for GCSE and A level geography.

Figure 3.11: GCSE Subject content for geography progression statement. **Source:** DfE (2014), p. 4.

NC Key Stage 3	Contextual world knowledge of locations, places and geographical features.	Understanding conditions, processes and interactions that explain geographical features, distribution patterns and changes over time and space.	Competence in geographical enquiry and the application of skills in observing, collecting, analysing, evaluating and communicating geographical information.
GCSE Aims	Know geographical material	Think like a geographer	Study like a geographer Applying geography
AOs	**AO1** Demonstrate knowledge of locations, places, processes, environments and different scales. 15%	**AO2** Demonstrate geographical understanding of concepts and how they are used in relation to places, environments and processes, and the interrelationships between places, environments and processes. 25%	**AO3** Apply knowledge and understanding to interpret, analyse and evaluate geographical information and issues. 35% **AO4** Select, adapt and use a variety of skills and techniques to investigate questions and issues and communicate findings and to make judgements. 25%
A level AOs	**AO1** Demonstrate knowledge and understanding of places, environments, concepts, processes, interactions and change, at a variety of scales. 30–40%		**AO2** Apply knowledge and understanding in different contexts to interpret, analyse and evaluate geographical information and issues. 30–40% **AO3** Use a variety of relevant quantitative, qualitative and fieldwork skills to: ■ investigate geographical questions and issues ■ interpret, analyse and evaluate data and evidence ■ construct arguments and draw conclusions. 20–30%

Figure 3.12: Progression in aims and AOs for 11–19. **Source:** Adapted from Gardner, 2018.

The alignment between these is clear, demonstrating the potential to plan for progression in geography 5–19. This is the first time it has been possible quite so explicitly to build in this progression across the NC, GCSEs and A level.

'The post-14 scene is currently a good news story, not least the opportunities the reforms have created for coherent planning for genuine progression and continuity 11–19' (Gardner, 2018, p. 43). And addressing teachers directly Rawling (2016), concludes that the DfE curriculum documents for geography '... are guidelines for professional development and expansion. They require, firstly, recognition and application of the broad principles of progression in geography subject knowledge ... and secondly, creative development by awarding bodies (for GCSE and AS/A) and ultimately by teachers. The opportunities are all yours.' (p. 9)

The curriculum as the progression model and the importance of sequencing learning

So far, this chapter has focussed on defining progression in geography and what it looks like. We have done this with reference to the GA (represented by the geography education community), and the 'built in' progression framework provided in the official documents for geography 5–19. We should finish this chapter with reference to Ofsted's inspection requirements. It is of no surprise that in its own curriculum research (2018) Ofsted identified progression as central to curriculum quality. The evidence gathered demonstrated that effective curriculum 'planning' was not just about having a written plan of the content being taught. In the better schools planning focused more on, for instance, how curriculum leaders ensured that:

- content is **sequenced** to ensure that components of knowledge lead to **conceptual understanding**

- opportunities for pupils to practise what they knew – so they could **deepen their understanding** in a discipline – were built into the curriculum

- the **layering** of knowledge and concepts were secure so that pupils could **make progress** in the curriculum from their various starting points.

The highlighted words all imply consideration of progression. In terms of curriculum implementation, Ofsted generally advocate that **subject leadership knowledge** is essential. The focus on the **progression model** was mentioned by all the HMI involved in the research in schools, as being helpful in building an effective curriculum, and in deepening their concept of curriculum progression.

ACTIVITY 3.2

Heather Fearn, Inspector Curriculum and Development Lead, captures in a video clip Ofsted's view of the significance of progression in terms of the curriculum.

https://www.youtube.com/watch?v=tRkdJegSTWs

Curriculum sequencing

Ofsted's curriculum research (Ofsted, 2019a) has led to an interconnected focus on curriculum coherence and sequencing, as important indicators of a quality curriculum, in the inspection framework, as shown below.

Intent

- the provider's curriculum is **coherently** planned and **sequenced** towards **cumulatively** sufficient knowledge and skills for future learning and employment

Implementation

- teachers create an environment that allows the learner to focus on learning. The resources and materials that teachers select – in a way that does not create unnecessary workload for staff – reflect the provider's ambitious intentions for the course of study and clearly support

the intent of a coherently planned curriculum, sequenced towards cumulatively sufficient knowledge and skills for future learning and employment (pp 9-10)

This focus on sequencing the introduction and development of content, concepts and skills in a co-ordinated, logical order is vitally important. If students are to progress towards cumulative knowledge and skills, in an efficient and effective manner, they need a carefully planned curriculum with clear stepping stones for intended progress.

Wiliam (2013) explains:

'In other less linear subjects [such as geography], there is even greater freedom for us to teach things in the sequence that makes most sense. I do not mean to suggest that "anything goes". Rather teachers have both considerable freedom, and considerable responsibility, to sequence the curriculum. However, this must be done in a way that is accountable both to their students and their needs, and to the discipline or subject ... As with so much else to do with curriculum design, curricular sequencing is a creative process, and cannot be reduced to a set of procedures.' (pp. 30–31)

Bennetts (2005a) helpfully distinguishes between sequencing and progression:

'Sequence, in the context of the curriculum, is essentially about the order in which content and activities are introduced and organised. While a sequence of some sort is inevitable within any curriculum, progression in learning is not an inevitable outcome. Progression focuses attention on the quality of students' learning, and how that can be developed over periods of their education. Although it can be applied to different time scales, the idea becomes especially pertinent when applied to long periods, during which students' cognitive abilities, depth of understanding, and development of value systems are affected by maturation processes, as well as by experience.' (p. 113)

As Bennett points out, all key stage plans or curricula have a sequence, but not necessarily an interconnected sequence developed with progression in mind, as suggested in Figure 3.9. A better appreciation of the student qualities as outlined by Bennetts would help fully inform some of the detailed decisions which have to be made when designing a curriculum to support progression in learning.

Healy (2020) further emphasises the significance of sequencing:

> 'Curriculum sequencing matters. This is ulti-mately about how and why a certain section of the curriculum prepares students for future content, such that it has a proximal function to make the next stage possible and an ultimate function to do an enduring job ... In terms of curriculum thinking, this means we need to think about the incidence, blend and interplay of different types of geographical content to serve as part of students' wider geography cur-riculum journey. This is also why it is necessary to think about the key geographical concepts that students encounter repeatedly and how we could use this as an opportunity to ensure students develop more nuanced understand-ings of these concepts over time.' (p. 31)

How does thinking geographically relate to Ofsted's view of learning in the new EIF?

Ofsted (2019b) published a paper presenting the research evidence underpinning the Education Inspection Framework (EIF). Their research on memory and learning led them to conclude:

> 'Learning is at least in part defined as a change in long-term memory. As Sweller et al. (2011) have pointed out, 'if nothing in the long-term memory has been altered, nothing has been learned'; although there are, of course, other aspects to learning. It is, therefore, important that we use approaches that help students to integrate new knowledge into the long-term memory and make enduring connections that foster understanding.'

> 'Cognitive load theory (CLT). CLT is concerned with the architecture of memory and the brain, and in particular the capacity of the short-term memory to process information. The long-term memory consists of a range of schemata, which are complex structures that link knowl-edge and create meaning and which are built up over time. Experts possess far more detailed and complex schemata than novice learners. Learning is essentially about changing those schemata, through acquiring knowledge and making connections with different schemata. However, before entering long-term memory and developing schemata, information must first be processed by the short-term or working memory. As this has limited capacity, retention of knowledge and development of schema-ta will not happen if the working memory is overloaded. In educational terms, this suggests teaching in small chunks and not organising activities that require too much memory capacity, until learners acquire the knowledge that allows them to spend less time processing content.' (pp.15–17)

This focus by Ofsted on cognitive science, relating the dynamic of short-term and long-term memory to learning, has stimulated a wide range of training for approaches to teaching and learning in schools. New 'buzz words' include dual coding, active schema building, retrieval. It is really important that these ideas are not implemented in a vacuum, separate from the subject discipline.

Bennetts (2005a) identifies the significance of a 'spiral curriculum' proposed by Bruner (1960), in planning for progression in the long term. He explains: 'In this model, progression is linked to carefully selected recurrent elements, such as themes, ideas and skills, which are conceived as forming threads that weave through a programme, linking various units of study to provide the means, for example, to reinforce, extend and refine under-standing.' (pp 120–21)

Such an approach is underpinned by the assump-tion that students are capable of transferring what they have learnt in one context to different con-texts, providing the opportunity to deepen their understanding, by enhancing the interconnections between experiences, ideas and mental process outlined in Figure 3.8. Planning a curriculum that develops conceptual understanding, as outlined in this chapter, is a pivotal aspect of this planning.

As Bennetts points out: 'An effective strategy for transfer of learning over a fairly long period will depend, to some extent, on students developing their long-term memories; and that in itself may depend on how often particular ideas are encoun-tered and used in a geography course.' (p. 121)

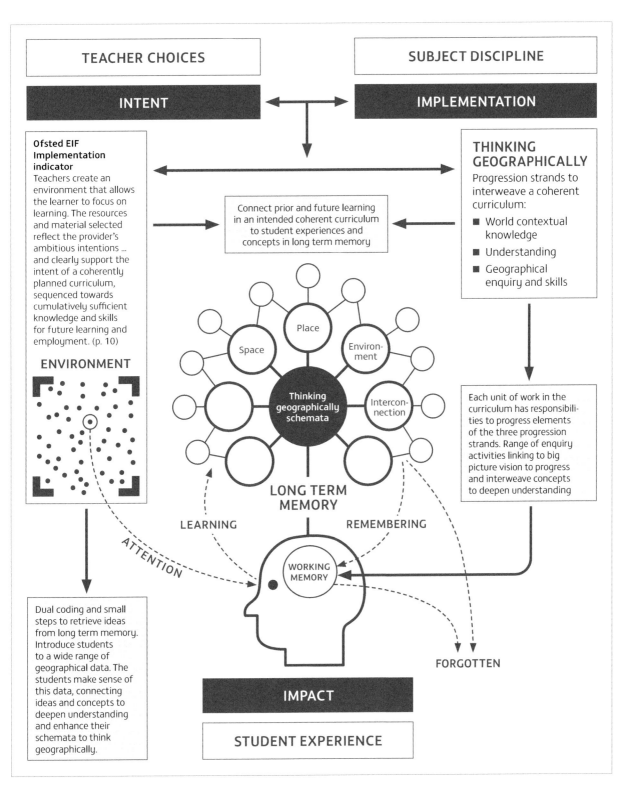

Figure 3.13: Curriculum making in action – the learning process. **Source:** Adapted from Sherrington, T. (2020).

This transfer of learning, then, does not take place as a matter of course. As Bennetts explains: 'Teachers need to identify which ideas are suitable for transfer; develop strategies which help their students acquire a satisfactory initial grasp of meanings; and provide opportunities for them to explore application to other content and contexts.' (p. 121)

This overview of curriculum in geography clearly links to the cognitive science that underpins Ofsted curriculum thinking in the new EIF. When a geographical concept is explored in a different context, it will be initially retrieved from the long-term memory, applied in a different context, with the potential to deepen understanding, further linking knowledge in the schema of the long-term memory. This is what Ofsted (2019a) means by 'the provider's curriculum is **coherently** planned and **sequenced** towards **cumulatively** sufficient knowledge' (pp. 9–21). Figure 3.13 attempts to demonstrate the synergy between the Ofsted research on learning and the research and ideas of the geography subject discipline.

Conclusion

What model of progression do we have? A legitimate question, which may feel difficult to answer in a simple, straightforward way. But Fordham (2017) maintains that the curriculum *is* the progression model. He believes that if a student has learnt the curriculum, they have made progress. This sounds helpful.

Grace Healy (2020) reinforces this point: 'As geography teachers, we ought to be driven by what we can define as the gold standard of geography education. This should be planned for and visible in the enacted curriculum. The assessment strategy follows, and should be designed to serve in relation to the curriculum rather than assessment structures determining what is taught.' (p. 30)

This chapter has attempted to explore what progression in geography looks like, together with its intimate relationship with the curriculum and its design. The ideas and tools introduced form the basis of Chapters 4–7, which provide guidance on the curriculum design process utilising the Ofsted research, EIF, and the GA progression framework.

The GA progression framework, combining aspects of achievement or progression strands, and benchmarks for geography, provides a tool to design a coherent and interconnected curriculum with progression and assessment at its heart. It will support your thinking about the three interconnected phases of the curriculum design process, expressed in the 2019 Ofsted framework as intent, implementation and impact:

- **Intent:** how ambitious, coherently planned and sequenced is the curriculum, in order for all students to learn successfully in geography?

- **Implementation:** based on the intent, how do we teach and assess learning to ensure students make progress in geography?

- **Impact:** as a result of teaching the curriculum, to what extent have students developed geographical knowledge, understanding and skills ready for the next stage of their education?

This chapter has highlighted that geography benefits from a spiral approach to the curriculum: revisiting places, concepts and skills to build up students' depth of knowledge, understanding and competence, so enabling them to make progress. However, although some progression may happen automatically and of its own accord – sometimes even despite the teacher – the professional view is that it can be supported and enhanced by good planning and preparation.

Perhaps we should let the words 'so that', highlighted in Mark Enser's TES article (2020) 'Why the words "so that" are so important for teachers', provide the concluding remarks:

"So that" are two words I often hear from experienced teachers in a classroom, but hear a lot less from trainees and those who are more recently qualified. Experienced teachers will make very clear how what a class is learning today links to what they will be learning about tomorrow. "We are going to learn about Russia's climate so that you can understand the country's reaction to the threat of climate change ..." From the teacher's point of view, it is obvious why they have asked the class to create a climate graph ... It turns out, this is often a lot less clear to those doing the work. "We are drawing a climate graph so that you can see the relationship between temperature and rainfall" helps the pupil to see how the task fits into the bigger picture of the lesson, and hopefully then into the bigger picture of the subject.'

A curriculum built with progression at its heart probably guarantees 'so that' words are fully integrated into lessons. The in-depth thinking about a curriculum designed for student progression means that teachers naturally make links between stepping stones of learning along the curriculum journey.

References

All websites last accessed 27/07/2021.

Bennetts, T.H. (1995) 'Continuity and progression', *Teaching Geography*, 20, 2, pp. 75–9.

Bennetts, T.H. (2005a) 'Progression in Geographical Understanding', *International Research in Geographical and Environmental Education*, 14, 2, pp. 112–32.

Bennetts, T.H. (2005b) 'The links between understanding, progression and assessment in the secondary geography curriculum', *Geography*, 90, 2, pp. 152–70

Bennetts, T.H. (2008) 'Improving geographical understanding at KS3', *Teaching Geography*, 33, 2, pp. 55–60.

Brooks, C. (2018) 'Understanding conceptual development in school geography' in Jones, M. and Lambert, D. (eds) *Debates in Geography (2nd edition)*. Abingdon: Routledge. pp. 103–14.

Bruner, J.S. (1960) *The Process of Education*. New York:Vintage.

Cousin, G. (2006) 'An introduction to threshold concepts', *Planet*, 17, pp. 4–5.

Daugherty, R. (1996) 'Defining and Measuring Progression in Geography' in Daugherty, R. and Rawling, E. (eds) *Geography into the Twenty-First Century*. Oxford: Wiley-Blackwell.

DeS (1978) *The Teaching of ideas in Geography*, HMI Series Matters for Discussion No.5. London: HMSO. Available at www.educationengland.org.uk/documents/hmi-discussion/geography.html

DfE (2014) *GCSE subject content for geography*. Available at www.gov.uk/government/publications/gcse-geography

Enser, M. (2020) 'Why the words "so that" are so important for teachers'. TES, 22 March. Available at www.tes.com/news/why-words-so-are-so-important-teachers

Fordham, M. (2017) *The Curriculum as progression model*. Available at https://clioetcetera.com/2017/03/04/the-curriculum-as-progression-model/

Gardner, D. (2018) 'Geography in the examination system', in Jones, M. and Lambert, D. (eds) *Debates in Geography (3rd edition)*. Abingdon: Routledge. pp. 33–45.

Geographical Association

(2009) *A Different View: A Manifesto from the Geographical Association*. Sheffield: Geographical Association. Available at www.geography.org.uk/GA-Manifesto-for-geography

(2011) 'The geography national curriculum: GA curriculum proposals and rationale'. Available at https://www.geography.org.uk/write/MediaUploads/download/GA_GIGCCCurriculumProposals.pdf

(2012) 'Thinking Geographically' Available at https://www.geography.org.uk/write/mediauploads/download/ga_ginconsultation%20thinkinggeographically%20nc%202012.pdf

(2014) 'An assessment and progression framework for geography'. Sheffield: Geographical Association.

(2020) 'A progression framework for geography'. Sheffield: Geographical Association

(2017) *Support for trainees and NQTs: Aspects of progression in geography*. Available at www.geography.org.uk/write/MediaUploads/teaching%20resources/GA_ITE_TTIS_Aspects_of_progression.pdf

(n.d.1) *What geography subject knowledge do I need?* Available at www.geography.org.uk/What-geography-subject-knowledge-do-I-need

(n.d.2) *Concepts in geography*. Available at www.geography.org.uk/Concepts-in-geography

Healy, G. (2020) 'Placing the geography curriculum at the heart of assessment practice', *Teaching Geography*, 45, 1, pp. 30–33.

Hirsch, E.D. (1987) *Cultural Literacy: What every American needs to know*. Boston, MA: Houghton Mifflin.

Jackson, P. (2006) 'Thinking geographically', *Geography*, 91, 3, pp. 199–204

Lambert, D. (2010) Progression Think Piece *Issues in Geography Education: Session 8*. Available at https://www.geography.org.uk/download/ga_prmghprogressionthinkpiece.pdf

Lambert, D. (2017) 'Thinking geographically' in Jones, M. (ed) *The Handbook of Secondary Geography*. Sheffield: Geographical Association (pp. 20–29).

Meyer, J. and Land, R. (2006) 'Threshold concepts and troublesome knowledge: an introduction' in Meyer, J. and Land, R. (eds) *Overcoming barriers to student understanding: threshold concepts and troublesome knowledge*. Abingdon: Routledge. pp. 3–18.

Maude, A. (2020) 'The role of geography's concepts and powerful knowledge in a Future 3 curriculum', *International Research in Geographical and Environmental Education*, 29, 3, pp. 232–43.

Ofsted

(2018) *Curriculum research: assessing intent, implementation and impact*. Phase 3, December 2018. Available at www.gov.uk/government/publications/curriculum-research-assessing-intent-implementation-and-impact

(2019a) Education Inspection Framework. Available at https://www.gov.uk/government/publications/education-inspection-framework/education-inspection-framework

(2019b) Education Inspection Framework. *Overview of research*. Available at https://assets.publishing.service.gov.uk/government/uploads/system/uploads/attachment_data/file/813228/Research_for_EIF_framework_100619__16_.pdf

QCA (2000) *Geography: A scheme of work for key stage 3 Teacher's guide*. Available at https://webarchive.nationalarchives.gov.uk/20100512143620/http://www.standards.dfes.gov.uk/schemes2/secondary_geography/teaching?view=get

Rawling, E. (2007) *Planning your Key Stage 3 geography curriculum*. Sheffield: Geographical Association.

Rawling, E. (2016) 'The geography curriculum 5–19: what does it all mean?' *Teaching Geography*, 41, 1, pp. 6–9.

Roberts, M. (2013) *Geography Through Enquiry: Approaches to teaching and learning in the secondary school*. Sheffield: Geographical Association.

Sherrington, T. (2020) 'A model for the learning process. And why it helps to have one', *Teacherhead*. Available at https://teacherhead.com/2020/03/10/a-model-for-the-learning-process-and-why-it-helps-to-have-one

Slinger, J. (2011) *Threshold Concepts in Secondary Geography Education*. Research report presented at GA Annual Conference 2011. Available at www.geography.org.uk/download/ga_conf11slinger.pdf

Sweller, J., Ayres, P. and Kalyuga, S. (2011) *Cognitive load theory (Vol 1)*. Berlin: Springer Science & Business Media.

Taylor, L. (2008) 'Key concepts and medium term planning', *Teaching Geography*, 33, 2, p. 51.

Vernon, E. (2016) 'The structure of knowledge: does theory matter?' *Geography*, 101, 2, pp. 100–104.

Young, M. (2008) *Bringing Knowledge Back In: From social constructivism to social realism in the sociology of education*. Abingdon: Routledge.

Wiliam, D. (2013) 'Principled curriculum design', SSAT *Redesigning Schooling 3, The Campaign for a schools-led vision of education*. Available at https://webcontent.ssatuk.co.uk/wp-content/uploads/2013/09/Dylan-Wiliam-Principled-curriculum-design-chapter-1.pdf

Curriculum guidance

Intent, implementation and impact – connected steps in curriculum design

The guidance section of this book considers the whole curriculum design process. Chapters 4–7 provide more detailed guidance to support each stage of this interconnected process.

What is the purpose of key stage 3 geography?

Before a geography department embarks on the process of 11–16 curriculum design, it is important to consider the existing curriculum and the whole-school view of the purpose of curricula at different key stages. In particular, in secondary schools, there is a need to be clear about the purpose of key stage 3, where it has not always been seen as a priority. Ofsted's survey (2015) *Key Stage 3: the wasted years?* identified weaknesses in teaching and student progress, due to priority being given staffing key stages 4 and 5 over key stage 3 – classes were often split between more than one teacher, or taught by non-specialists. Ofsted also identified an issue with transition from primary schools: too many secondary schools did not understand students' prior learning, to ensure that they built on this during key stage 3. Phase 1 of Ofsted's curriculum research (2017) expressed concern about reducing the key stage 3 curriculum to two years, often to provide more time to cover the content of GCSEs.

Key stage 3's purpose is to progress student understanding and the capability of the subject to enhance their ability to think geographically so all students are ready for their next stage of learning, regardless of whether they go on to study the subject at GCSE. It is important to acknowledge the statutory contribution of key stage 3 geography to a broad and balanced curriculum for all students. Figure 1 demonstrates the continuum of school geography 5–19 and the built-in progression explained in Chapter 3. It shows the broad view of curriculum progression in geography through all key stages, outlining the character and intent

of each key stage, as well as the statutory nature of key stages 1–3, and the option of continuing progression in geography at key stages 4 and 5.

Within the continuum, key stage 3 has a pivotal and multi-functional role. It can be perceived as the 'engine room' of geography education 5–19. It provides a transition from the primary to secondary phases of education and consolidates the foundations of geographical learning provided in key stages 1 and 2. For many students, key stage 3 is their first experience of being taught by specialist geography teachers. Key stage 3 can consolidate a student's capability to understand the interconnected world they will live and work in throughout their lives. The elements of progression provided at a policy level, shown in Figure 1, provide the opportunity to plan a curriculum 5–19 that is coherent, yet at the same time distinctive, at each key stage. The function of key stage 3 geography is, therefore, much more complex than just preparing for GCSE. An appreciation of the functions of key stage 3 is fundamental to designing a coherent 11–16 geography curriculum.

Introduction to a curriculum design process

Ofsted (2019b) provided a much clearer and more helpful view of their perception of curriculum in the revised inspection methodology to support the EIF, than the working definition provided in Chapter 2 (p. 30):

'At the heart of the EIF is the new "quality of education" judgement, the purpose of which is to put a single conversation about education at the centre of inspection. This conversation draws together curriculum, teaching, assessment and standards. In doing this, we draw heavily on the working definition of the curriculum that Ofsted has used over the last couple of years. This definition uses the concepts of "intent", "implementation" and "impact" to

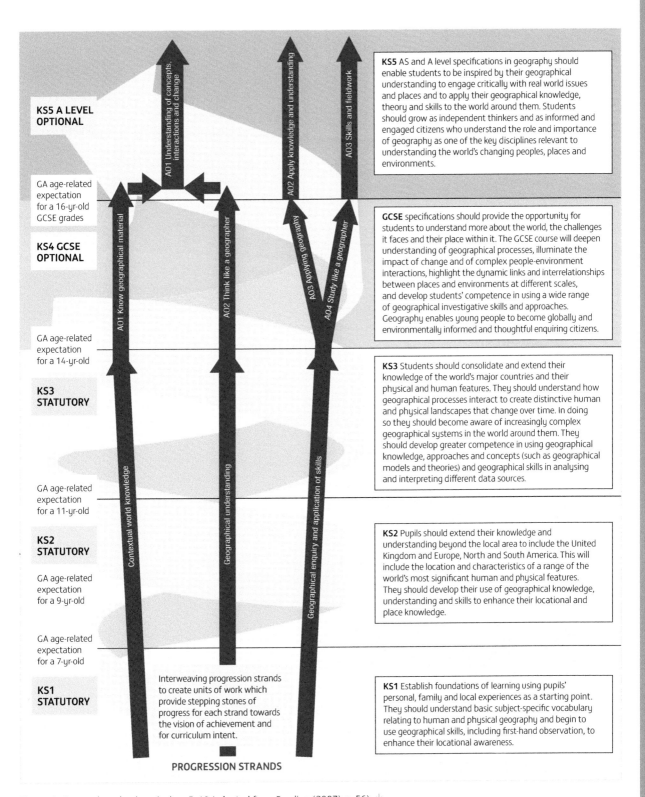

KS5 A LEVEL OPTIONAL

GA age-related expectation for a 16-yr-old GCSE grades

KS4 GCSE OPTIONAL

GA age-related expectation for a 14-yr-old

KS3 STATUTORY

GA age-related expectation for an 11-yr-old

KS2 STATUTORY

GA age-related expectation for a 9-yr-old

GA age-related expectation for a 7-yr-old

KS1 STATUTORY

AO1 Understanding of concepts, interactions and change

AO2 Apply knowledge and understanding

AO3 Skills and fieldwork

AO1 Know geographical material

AO2 Think like a geographer

AO3 Applying geography

AO4 Study like a geographer

Contextual world knowledge

Geographical understanding

Geographical enquiry and application of skills

Interweaving progression strands to create units of work which provide stepping stones of progress for each strand towards the vision of achievement and for curriculum intent.

PROGRESSION STRANDS

KS5 AS and A level specifications in geography should enable students to be inspired by their geographical understanding to engage critically with real world issues and places and to apply their geographical knowledge, theory and skills to the world around them. Students should grow as independent thinkers and as informed and engaged citizens who understand the role and importance of geography as one of the key disciplines relevant to understanding the world's changing peoples, places and environments.

GCSE specifications should provide the opportunity for students to understand more about the world, the challenges it faces and their place within it. The GCSE course will deepen understanding of geographical processes, illuminate the impact of change and of complex people-environment interactions, highlight the dynamic links and interrelationships between places and environments at different scales, and develop students' competence in using a wide range of geographical investigative skills and approaches. Geography enables young people to become globally and environmentally informed and thoughtful enquiring citizens.

KS3 Students should consolidate and extend their knowledge of the world's major countries and their physical and human features. They should understand how geographical processes interact to create distinctive human and physical landscapes that change over time. In doing so they should become aware of increasingly complex geographical systems in the world around them. They should develop greater competence in using geographical knowledge, approaches and concepts (such as geographical models and theories) and geographical skills in analysing and interpreting different data sources.

KS2 Pupils should extend their knowledge and understanding beyond the local area to include the United Kingdom and Europe, North and South America. This will include the location and characteristics of a range of the world's most significant human and physical features. They should develop their use of geographical knowledge, understanding and skills to enhance their locational and place knowledge.

KS1 Establish foundations of learning using pupils' personal, family and local experiences as a starting point. They should understand basic subject-specific vocabulary relating to human and physical geography and begin to use geographical skills, including first-hand observation, to enhance their locational awareness.

Figure 1: Geography school curriculum 5–19 (adapted from Rawling (2007), p. 56). ⬇

recognise that the curriculum passes through different states: it is conceived, taught and experienced. Leaders and teachers design, structure and sequence a curriculum, which is then implemented through classroom teaching. The end result of a good, well-taught curriculum is that pupils know more and are able to do more. The positive results of students' learning can then be seen in the standards they achieve. The EIF starts from the understanding that all of these steps are connected.' (p. 3)

The most significant and helpful part of this statement is the last sentence. This interconnection, or coherence, has been a central theme to emerge in the first three chapters of this book, and will form the central tenet of the guidance (Chapters 4–7).

An initial knee-jerk reaction by some school leadership teams to the new EIF led to an Ofsted blog 'Busting the "intent" myth' (2019). Heather Fearn, Inspector Curriculum and Professional Development lead for Ofsted, explained: 'We have even heard of courses for schools to write an "intent

statement" in half a day, so it's time to bust the first myth that has arisen around "intent". She reinforces the point that intent is far more than a statement and is a key aspect of a series of interconnected steps.

Alan Kinder and Paula Owens were both members of an Ofsted geography reference group that worked throughout the summer term of 2019. The aim of the group was to help devise training guidance for Ofsted inspectors, so that they would be better equipped to apply the new framework to inspect the quality of geography education in schools. Kinder and Owen have used this experience to write an invaluable article (2019), published in both *Teaching Geography* and *Primary Geography*, to provide an overview of the interconnected steps involved in the curriculum:

'Subject leaders should note that, overall, the EIF is built around the idea of the connectedness of curriculum, teaching, assessment and standards. In that sense, it echoes the GA's take on curriculum making, which suggests that

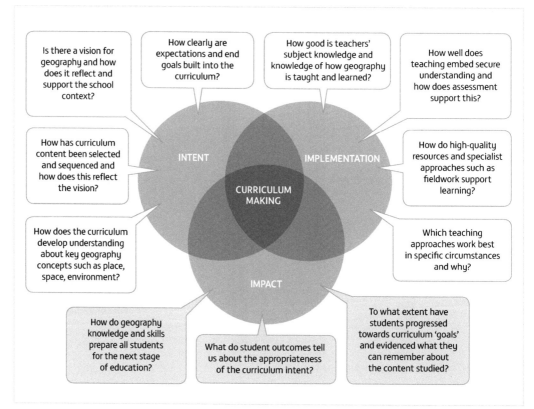

Figure 2:
Key questions link intent, implementation and impact around the notion of curriculum making. Adapted from Kinder and Owens (2019).

effective teaching draws on the rich resources offered by the subject discipline, specialist pedagogies and students' own experiences' (p. 99).

The article includes an excellent overview diagram, reproduced here as Figure 2, to illustrate this thinking by showing how curriculum intent, implementation and impact – the 'three Is' – interconnect around the process of curriculum making. Curriculum development, design or making is an ongoing process driven by questions. A number of important questions relating to each of the three I's is helpfully included in Figure 2. These questions are an invaluable aid, and will be revisited and explored through chapters 4–7.

Guidance introduction

Ofsted (2021a) acknowledge that the curriculum is built around subjects and as a consequence the inspection processes are largely based on subject 'deep dives'. An overview of deep dives is provided in Chapter 7 pp. 127–29. In 2019, Ofsted appointed HMI subject leads, in part to train fellow HMIs, and contracted Ofsted inspectors from the same subject background to create a network of subject expertise, as well as train non-specialists.

ACTIVITY

The HMI subject lead for geography appointed in 2019, was Iain Freeland. Listen to Iain Freeland talking to John Lyon, about his career path as well as some of things Ofsted are looking for in terms of 'good geography in the GA's GeogPod, Series 5, episode 31 at: https://www.geography.org.uk/GeogPod-The-GAs-Podcast

From April 2021 Ofsted began publishing a series of documents, coordinated and led by the HMI subject leads including:

- research reviews: which collate available research evidence about a high-quality education in each subject
- subject reports: designed to inform the education community, what inspection evidence, particularly deep dives.

Ofsted (2021a) envisage that these reviews will provide a shared understanding of high-quality education for each subject, what they call the 'conception of subject quality'. Ofsted believe the reviews outline subject-specific principles that can be used by inspectors to conduct deep dives in schools.

The research reviews, therefore, provide an idea of what Ofsted are looking for in terms of a high-quality subject curriculum, making them a significant starting point for designing a coherent 11–16 geography curriculum.

The Ofsted Research Review for geography (2021b) includes the following in its conclusion, which provides a helpful snapshot of the subject-specific principles for geography:

'Through teachers' careful identification of each component of geographical knowledge and thoughtful sequencing, pupils learn and remember more and more. Curriculum plans reflect the importance of each interrelated form of substantive knowledge (locational knowledge; place knowledge; environmental, human and physical processes; geographical skills and fieldwork). They consider each in a proportionate manner and reveal the connections between them. Through teachers' curriculum planning and pedagogical approaches, pupils gain an insight into the discipline. Research shows that this is most effective when pupils build on their existing knowledge'.

Figure 3 provides a more detailed overview of principles for geography identified in the Ofsted review for geography, and how they are integrated into the various sections and chapters of this book.

The publication of this research review for geography, received mixed responses from the geography community, with some clear warnings regarding the narrow view of curriculum presented. The GA (2021) was pleased:

'that a wide range of research and insights from the geography education community itself proved of such great help in its production … The report begins to explore the importance not only of learning well-sequenced geographical content, but of learning geography as a discipline. Much more work is needed here to create clear messages and understandings. From a GA perspective, disciplinary knowledge

Ofsted research review subject specific principles	Explanation of principles in this book
Organising concepts – a means of categorising geographical knowledge of natural and human phenomena.	Chapter 3, pp. 37–43
Forms of geographical knowledge: ■ locational knowledge ■ place knowledge and understanding ■ knowledge of environmental, physical and human geography processes ■ geographical skills.	Chapter 5, pp. 82–96
The case for fieldwork	Chapter 6, pp. 111–13
Map skills	Chapter 5, pp. 87–9
Spatial thinking – a curriculum to think like a geographer	Chapter 3, pp. 36–43
Disciplinary knowledge – powerful knowledge	Chapter 2, pp, 25–28
Curriculum structure, sequencing and how knowledge is remembered	Chapters 3 and 5
Pedagogy – enquiry	Chapter 6, pp. 99–107
Assessment	Chapter 6, pp. 113–19
Professional development	Chapter 6, pp. 99–101 Chapter 9
Resources	Chapter 6, pp. 107–111

Figure 3: Ofsted research review – overview of principles for geography.

means learning about the purposes of geography, how geographers think, about the methods geographers use to create valuable insights about the world and the range of ideas and perspectives that make geography a truly global subject.'

Steve Brace, Head of Education and Outdoor Learning at the RGS (with IBG), said: 'This is an important report which will help geographers reflect on and review their own practice and also offer important lessons for school leaders in how geography can be better supported in primary and secondary schools.'

John Morgan, (2021), whilst acknowledging there is much to learn from the review, comments on the review's 'impoverished understanding of "curriculum"'. He believes 'The review is the latest manifestation of the tendency to ensure school geography not only remains insulated from the wider discipline but also from social, economic, political and environmental contexts in which it operates.' As the GA commented, Morgan believes the nature of disciplinary knowledge is not explored in detail. He is surprised that the review ignores the voices

of geographers themselves who explore the question of why geography matters, and how to make sense of a world in the making. Morgan makes the point that in the absence of this ongoing debate the review presents the latest version of the National Curriculum as 'the done deal' He also maintains that the review ignores the current state of flux the world finds itself in as a result of economic crashes, social divisions and the rise of Black Lives Matters. He concludes, 'Importantly, the warrant for teaching about "actually existing geographies" rather than "Ofsted's geography" comes from the discipline of geography itself, which, at its best and at times of social change, has provided us with maps of meaning with which to make sense of a changing world.'

Nayeri and Rushton (2021) believe the review does what it tells teachers not to do, in presenting a single story of what makes a high-quality geography curriculum. In particular, they highlight the silence regarding race, at a time when geography academics identify its significance.

It is important, however, not to lose sight of the significance of subjects and the curriculum, presented by Ofsted in this work. This represents a significant step forward from the misaligned educational system; the hypersocialised school environment and Future 1 and Future 2 scenarios outlined in Chapters 1 and 2. The abolition of levels the built-in progression of the DfE geography curriculum documents shown in Figure 1, the curriculum focus of the Ofsted EIF, as well as the introduction of the ITT Core Content Framework and the Early Career Framework, all recognise and depend on subject-specific expertise. This all suggests an important alignment of the 13 control factors on the education system, identified by Tim Oates (Chapter 2 pp. 19–20), moving towards coherence and opportunities for geography teachers to become curriculum makers, placing their students' progress at the heart of the design process. The Ofsted review is a useful tool that summarises and references principles of the subject. It is not a curriculum model; it is merely a starting point for teachers to build from, much like the first three chapters of this book. The guidance section of this book, provides a range of tools to help you consider these principles to create your own learning journey for your students, interconnecting your curriculum intent, implementation and impact with pupil progress at its heart, linked to the questions shown in Figure 2.

Where to start?

Rawling (2007) presented a very useful diagram 'Where to start?' (p. 12), to highlight the key considerations to focus on when embarking on a process of curriculum design. Figure 4 has adapted this diagram to suit the needs of creating a coherent 11–16 geography curriculum with the post-2014 GNC and GCSEs in mind. It also references where you can read about different aspects of these considerations in this book.

Figure 4: 'Where to start?' Adapted from Rawling (2007), p. 12. ⬇

WHERE TO START?

Current geography curriculum
- Existing KS3 curriculum and resources
- Developments and plans for GCSE and AS/A2
- Links with primary schools over KS1/2

Wider school issues (chapter 4)
- The students, their background and experiences brought to learning
- School curriculum decisions already made, e.g. integrated year 7; two-year KS3; move back to three-year KS3
- Existing school priorities, e.g. funding for ICT, academy status

National requirements
- Revised KS3 requirements including geography
- Other initiatives and strategies, e.g. importance of subjects, prescribed, knowledge at each key stage
- Ofsted foci for quality of education (Chapters 4–7)

THE IMPORTANT QUESTIONS (Chapter 4)

What is the rationale for geography in our school? How do we make a case for it? What are the aims and purposes of geography at KS3? What do we hope students will gain as a result of studying it? How might geography change their lives for the better?

What are the special characteristics of our students and their experiences? What is distinctive about the school and its locality/community that will affect the geography we teach? What are the opportunities? What are the issues to face? What specific resources do we have as a school that offer potential? What can we learn from past experience?

What are the opportunities implicit in the new national curriculum requirements and what particular contributions can geography make to developing them, as opposed to other subjects? What potential lies in new trends in geography and how can they be developed?

Past curriculum experience
- What went well or badly at KS3 in the past?
- Performance of geography at KS3, GCSE, A level over past five years
- Which resources or approaches are tired or dated?

Local area and community
- Existing links and contacts in the local area, e.g. planning contact, museum link
- Special geographical features in the area, e.g. coastal scenery, new motorway link
- Opportunities for geographical study/activity, e.g. students' work experience

Geography as a subject
- New trends or developments in the subject, e.g. cultural and global perspectives in human geography
- Possibilities afforded by new technology and GIS
- Link made with geography departments of local HE institutions (Chapter 6)

Towards a curriculum design process

QCA (2008) developed guidance for a process of 'disciplined curriculum innovation' built around the three curriculum questions identified in Chapter 1 (p. 12–13). This process has been adapted for the curriculum guidance for this book. The three I's of the Ofsted definition of curriculum form the arrows on the outside of the circular process to demonstrate their interconnected nature. Figure 5 introduces the seven-stage process used in this curriculum guidance.

This seven-stage process is designed to help develop an ambitious and coherently planned curriculum that clearly supports the intent, sequenced towards cumulatively sufficient knowledge and skills for future learning and employment.

A seven stage curriculum process

Intent

1. **Create a vision**. Identify your priorities to create a long-term vision of what you want your students to be like by the end of the key stage. There are a number of key documents to support this process, explained in the next chapter.

2. **Record your starting point**. You will only know what impact you've made if you know where you started. Before you initiate changes to your curriculum, you need to establish a baseline. Consider your current curriculum and what your students are like. Consider your new long-term vision, to describe what you hope to see in your students. The best way to do this is to develop

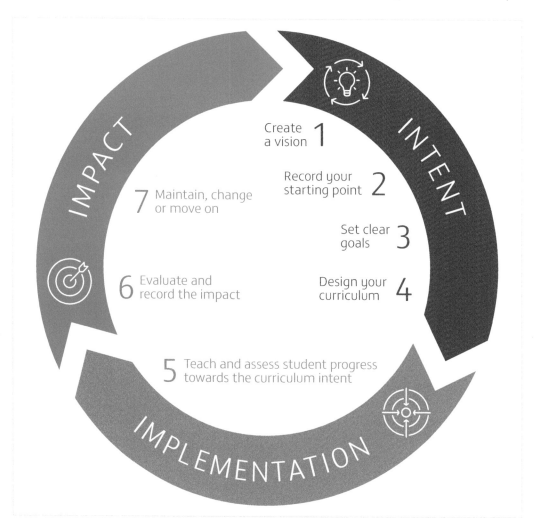

Figure 5: The curriculum design process.

an overview of your students at the moment and define how you would like this to change.

3. **Set clear goals.** To bring your long-term vision to life, use the GA benchmark statements, and dimensions of progression, to consider the progress you will plan for in your curriculum. Identify key elements of your curriculum – geographical concepts, linked to knowledge content, and skills. Chapter 4 provides tools and activities to support you in these initial stages.

4. **Design your curriculum.** Only when you are clear about your priorities and goals can you make decisions about how to build a coherently planned curriculum, sequenced towards cumulatively sufficient knowledge, understanding and skills that will best help you realise your vision. Chapter 5 will introduce a number of tools to support this stage.

Implementation

5. **Teach and assess student progress towards the curriculum intent.** Think carefully about the three energies in your classroom before you embark on curriculum making. Incorporate the most appropriate pedagogies, resources and approaches to assessment to support the implementation of your vision. Consider how these will help your students to remember, in the long term, knowledge they have been taught, and to integrate new knowledge into larger concepts. Chapter 6 will introduce ideas and approaches to support you in considering implementation of your curriculum.

Impact

6. **Evaluate and record the impact.** This can be done periodically to identify and report the differences between your students' starting point and the current situation. Are they on course to achieving your long-term vision for the curriculum? Tools to support this stage are provided in Chapter 7.

7. **Maintain, change or move on.** Reflect on how successful your new curriculum is in supporting students to develop detailed knowledge and skills across the curriculum, and as a result achieve well. Activities and ideas are provided in Chapter 7 to support this stage of the process.

References

All websites last accessed 28/07/2021.

Fearn, H. (2019) 'Busting the 'intent' myth'. Ofsted blog. Available at https://educationinspection.blog.gov.uk/2019/07/01/busting-the-intent-myth

Geographical Association (2021) GA response to the Ofsted research report on geography (June 2021). Available at https://www.geography.org.uk/Announcements-and-updates/ga-response-to-the-ofsted-research-report-on-geography-june-2021/273086

Kinder, A. and Owens, P. (2019) 'The new Education Inspection Framework – through a geographical lens', *Teaching Geography*, 44, 3, pp. 97–100.

Morgan, J. (2021) One Review to rule them all? Ofsted's Review of Research in Geography, Impolite Geography, GEReCO, https://impolitegeography.wordpress.com

Nayeri, C. and Rushton, E. (2012) Response to Ofsted's curriculum research review for geography, Routes. Available at https://routesjournal.org/2021/06/20/ofstedreviewgeog/

Ofsted (2017) HMCI's commentary: recent primary and secondary curriculum research. Available at https://www.gov.uk/government/speeches/hmcis-commentary-october-2017

Ofsted (2019a) *The education inspection framework*. Available at www.gov.uk/government/publications/education-inspection-framework

Ofsted (2019b) *Inspecting the curriculum: revising inspection methodology to support the education inspection framework*. Available at https://assets.publishing.service.gov.uk/government/uploads/system/uploads/attachment_data/file/814685/Inspecting_the_curriculum.pdf

Ofsted (2021a) *Research and analysis: Principles behind Ofsted's research reviews and subject reports*, https://www.gov.uk/government/publications/principles-behind-ofsteds-research-reviews-and-subject-reports/principles-behind-ofsteds-research-reviews-and-subject-reports

Ofsted (2021b) *Research and analysis: Research review series: geography* https://www.gov.uk/government/publications/research-review-series-geography/research-review-series-geography

QCA (2008) *Disciplined curriculum innovation: Making a difference to learners* London: QCA. Available at http://archive.teachfind.com/qcda/www.qcda.gov.uk/resources/publicationdf21.html

Royal Geographical Society (with IBG) (2021) Response to Ofsted's review of research in geography. Available at https://www.rgs.org/geography/news/ofsted-research-review-on-geography/

4 Curriculum design guidance – Intent

 INTENT **1** Create a vision **2** Record your starting point **3** Set clear goals **4** Design your curriculum

As we saw in Chapters 2 and 3, the geography curriculum is driven by the big ideas of the subject. It is important, therefore, that geography departments spend time thinking strategically about what they are trying to achieve with their curriculum – which big ideas or concepts are important to introduce, develop and progress in a key stage 3 curriculum to help form the building blocks of geographical knowledge, understanding and skills, to prepare students for their next stage of learning. The same thinking is required at GCSE level, although the aims of GCSE do provide, together with the detailed thinking and planning you do at key stage 3, a base from which to design your coherent 11–16 curriculum.

It is really important that this strategic thinking involves all the teachers of geography in the department. This needs to be a shared vision of curriculum intent, utilising each teacher's geography subject knowledge and expertise. Once this vision is established, the department can begin to create a key stage plan that provides the building blocks, or steps in learning, which will support student progress en route to achieving the shared vision.

Curriculum design – intent

Initially, a clear idea of what is meant by intent is required. Heather Fearn, an author of the Ofsted blog (2019) reiterates its meaning and purpose for curriculum design:

'Intent is about what leaders intend pupils to learn. It's as simple as that. Intent is everything up to the point at which teaching happens ... all the curriculum planning ...what do you want pupils to know? ... Does it contain the right knowledge in the right order? Is the curriculum providing pupils with the building blocks of what they need to know and be able to do to succeed in each subject?'

Fearn maintains, that '... intent is nothing new ... Intent is not the next big thing'.

But, for many geography departments that have not always thought strategically about what they are trying to achieve in the curriculum, writing an intent or vision statement will be new, and very necessary, as a starting point to creating a vision: very much 'the next big thing' – but not necessarily in the way school leadership teams may have initially thought.

Gleen (2020) makes the point that considering intent, is 'not just to tick the box for Ofsted'. She goes on to share her initial experiences of this process, reflecting that 'I really hope that this direction from Ofsted achieves what it set out to do: encourage departments to discuss their intent, jointly plan the shape of their curriculum and agree their priorities for ensuring all students make good progress.' (p. 110)

This chapter has been designed to provide guidance, resources, and tools to support curriculum design through the intent phase; in this case, the first three stages of the curriculum design process shown in the introduction to this section in Figure 5 (p. 62):

1. Create a vision.

2. Record your starting point.

3. Set clear goals.

Stage 1 – Create a vision

This strategic thinking needs careful planning, as it ultimately involves considering the end point you want your students to get to by the end of each key stage. This vision will form the driving force of your curriculum design.

Chapters 2 and 3 of this book provide an introduction to a 'Future 3' geography curriculum: powerful disciplinary knowledge, as well as the role of teachers as curriculum makers, to support students to think geographically. It is important, therefore, that a geography department has a clear idea of what it means to think geographically.

Thinking geographically – the significance of critical thinking

Chapter 3, page 36, provides a useful starting point to consider how to progress your students' capabilities to think geographically. The GA has further expanded on these ideas with a focus on critical thinking in the classroom: its website guidance begins 'Being a good geographer means thinking critically about the world'. The GA believes that critical thinking 'combines capability, the tools to think deeper and the curriculum context to do so – centred on geographical thought.' It identifies three key ingredients of critical thinking, summarised in Figure 4.1.

Margaret Roberts (2015) helpfully relates critical thinking, and critical pedagogy, to global learning. She believes critical thinking incorporates rigour, rationality and reasoning and provides a useful summary of the characteristics of critical thinking that she suggests could be used as a checklist (Figure 4.2). She distinguishes between critical thinking and pedagogy: 'Whereas critical thinking encourages an approach to education underpinned by a commitment to reasoned rationality, critical pedagogy is concerned with the potential emancipatory power of reasoned thinking and is underpinned by a commitment to equality and social justice.' (p. 56) Roberts goes on to identify a similar list of characteristics for critical pedagogy, relevant to global learning in geography (Figure 4.3).

Figures 4.1 to 4.3 are invaluable tools to consider when creating a vision for your curriculum, to help clarify what it means to think geographically. Incorporating these ideas into your vision and curriculum intent will have significant implications for its implementation, as geographical enquiry is the fundamental process which underpins the identified ingredients and characteristics of critical thinking, as explained and exemplified by Margaret Roberts. The GA website guidance on critical thinking in the classroom also provides a range of strategies that you could implement, leading to student progress towards this vision. This will be explored in greater detail in Chapter 6.

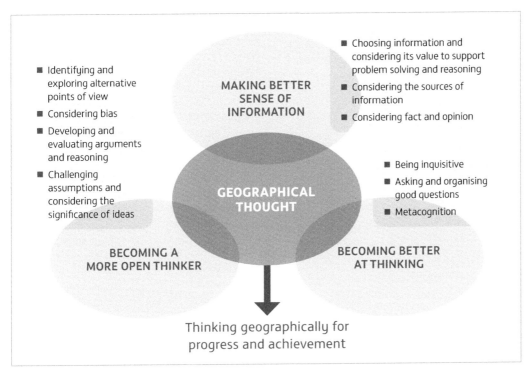

Figure 4.1:
The ingredients of critical thinking in geography
Source: Geographical Association (2019).

- Being inquisitive and asking good questions
- Judging the appropriateness and value of sources of geographical information
- Evaluating geographical data as evidence
- Distinguishing between fact and opinion
- Evaluating arguments and reasoning in what is presented
- Developing reasoned arguments based on evidence
- Probing assumptions
- Identifying the point of view or perspective
- Assessing the importance and significance of the ideas presented
- Evaluating conclusions and generalisations
- Justifying conclusions using evidence and reasoned arguments

Figure 4.2: Characteristics of critical thinking. **Source:** Roberts (2015) p. 56.

- Recognising the political nature of issues
- Asking questions that challenge the status quo
- Exposing hidden meanings of data, by examining the language used and what is included and excluded
- Examining power relations involved in an issue: who has the power to influence a decision about an issue and why?
- Considering ethical issues involved in situations and decisions. Are some situations or actions morally good or bad? Are some better or worse? Why? Who gains and who loses from decisions? What would be a socially just decision?
- Understanding different perspectives on issues including those related to class, race and gender
- Becoming aware of possibilities for changing things

Figure 4.3: Characteristics of critical pedagogy. **Source:** Roberts (2015) p. 56.

Social justice and inequality – the role of thinking geographically

The shocking and tragic death of George Floyd in the USA in 2020 has rightly led to renewed calls, nationally and internationally, for the ongoing injustices of racism and inequality to be addressed. Black Lives Matter – the GA has published a statement about this on the website, making it clear that school geography has a distinct role to play in addressing these issues. Since 2020, a growing number of GA journal articles and Annual Conference sessions have explored the nature of this injustice, and the role school geography can play.

Critical thinking and pedagogy, as part of thinking like a geographer, clearly have great relevance in responding to the injustice of racism and inequality. Issues of race and racism are of central concern to geography teachers' work as curriculum makers. A significant characteristic of critical pedagogy identified by Roberts (Figure 4.3), for example, is understanding different perspectives on issues including those related to class, race and gender.

Puttick and Murrey (2020), however, point out that race is not mentioned in either the GNC, GCSE or A level geography subject content. They regard this omission as racist. They maintain that 'School geography requires an explicitly anti-racist curriculum that seeks to actively dismantle racist ideas, practices and institutions as well as holistically engage with the range of human experiences and knowledges of place, space and lived environments.' (p. 128) They go on to explain how cultural literacy and powerful knowledge 'offer support for the development of anti-racist and race-conscious school geography.' (p. 129) They provide examples of a critical approach to the interpretation of geographical data, such as news articles, and the way the continent of Africa and other parts of the colonial world are often portrayed as a 'single story' in need of aid and support. An example of this occurred in 2020 when Vanessa Nakate, a Ugandan environmental activist, was cropped out of a photo that then just showed white activists (Evelyn, 2020). Puttick and Murrey conclude with a call for a more holistic and sustained anti-racist geography curriculum, with attention given to Black, indigenous and decolonial thought. This, they maintain, 'will help to ensure that young people have the skills and critical thinking necessary to understand complex and shifting politics of space, place and knowledge at a global scale. And, based upon such knowledge, our students might be better situated to contribute to meaningful anti-racist futures.' (p. 132)

Milner (2020) has also identified a number of issues in school geography, in particular the careless representation of other countries, often presented to students in a one-dimensional way. The students' experiences of other countries were not always in line with the content taught in geography lessons, leading to student questions, for example 'Why do we look at ... blood diamonds in Angola but we don't focus on the rich resources that we have?' (p. 106). The Nigerian author Chimamanda Ngozi Adichie (2009) refers to this as 'the danger of the single story': 'The single story creates stereotypes, and the problem with stereotypes is not that they are untrue, but that they are incomplete. They make one story become the only story.' Milner outlines different strategies to 'enable geography teachers to tackle the subject's whiteness through approaching geographical knowledge critically; diversifying knowledge production processes at the classroom level; changing the way other countries are represented; and examining colonialism and racialisation'. (p. 107)

The report from the Commission on Race and Ethnic Disparities (CRED) (2021), recommends the development of high-quality teaching resources about the making of modern Britain. The Commission sees this as an opportunity 'to link the story of different ethnic groups to a unifying sense of Britishness.' (p. 89) Alan Lester, Professor of Historical Geography at the University of Sussex, has raised a number of concerns about this report in his blog (2021). In particular, he is concerned that 'the Report's refusal to acknowledge that the British Empire was not only founded on, but also governed according to ... racial division fuels further division today rather than healing it.'

The Decolonising Geography Educators Group was formed in response to the killing of George Floyd in the USA in 2020. This group explores ways to decolonise the curriculum, challenging 'the reproduction of colonial practices of knowledge in our classrooms.' The group has developed an excellent website (https://decolonisegeography. com), sharing pedagogical techniques and teaching resources. It is designed to empower students to co-create knowledge and build critical geographies and help geography teachers to *reflect on* and *question* the content they currently teach.

ACTIVITY 4.1: WHAT DOES IT MEAN TO THINK GEOGRAPHICALLY? ⬇

Designing a curriculum provides an opportunity to consider and refresh your department's idea of thinking geographically, as well as its role in addressing issues of social injustice and inequality in the world.

One of the aims of GCSE geography shown in Figure 4.7 is 'think like a geographer', providing a basic definition of what this means. In designing a coherent 11–16 geography curriculum you need to consider how you will develop and progress your student's geographical thinking capabilities across both key stages. Developing a shared understanding across a geography department of what thinking geographically means, in theory and practice, is vitally important to this endeavour.

This chapter, along with Chapters 2 and 3, provide a starting point to achieve this, and if required you can dig deeper using the references provided.

Useful videos

The following video clips and podcasts produced by the GA are also very useful starting points in this process:

- In the pilot episode of GeogPod Rebecca Kitchen provides an overview of the Critical Thinking for Achievement programme.
- GeogPod, episode 13. Hina Robinson, a secondary geography teacher, and Tariq Jazeel, Professor of Geography at UCL, talk about defining and decolonising geography: www.geography. org.uk/GeogPod-The-GAs-Podcast
- In 'Geographical Connections', Professor Peter Jackson explains how geographic thinking can be used to find connections in the world which are not immediately apparent: www. geography.org.uk/teaching-resources/videos/connections
- In 'The Power of Geographical Thinking', Professor Peter Jackson explains how a painting can be reinterpreted using multiple strands of geographical thinking: www.geography. org.uk/teaching-resources/videos/thinking

This group are also critical of CRED, pointing out that one of the case studies of lesson resources, highlighted and recommended in the report, fails to properly present a clear picture of the relationship between urban change in Liverpool, and processes associated with race and racism. In particular, they claim it understates the great wealth generated in the city from its pivotal role in the slave trade, and the global slave-cotton industry, as well as ignoring racially motivated rioting in the city in 1919. The group believes the lessons to be politically biased rather than impartial.

Clearly these responses to the CRED Report demonstrate critical thinking in action, the sort of thinking you may wish to develop in your students. The significance of such thinking in supporting students to become open thinkers, able to understand different perspectives on social issues, is clear. Mary Biddulph (2017), considering inclusive geographies, argues that all students have the right to access powerful knowledge, believing that 'there is an imperative for all young people to develop the knowledge, skills and understanding necessary to interrogate what they read, see and hear ... [enabling] them to question the ideas and issues they encounter in their everyday lives, now and in the future.' (p. 48)

ACTIVITY 4.2: CREATING A VISION FOR GEOGRAPHY ⬇

TALKING POINT: How would you describe a well-educated geographer?

In a department meeting, take a look at your existing mission statement or aims for geography.

- How well do you think it describes a well-educated geographer, able to think geographically?

- How well does it integrate your considerations in Activity 4.1?

- What knowledge, understanding and skills do they need?

- Are there things that it would be helpful to add?

- Compare your department aims with the whole-school aims. What distinctive contribution to the whole-school aims can geography make?

PRACTICAL ACTION: Picturing the ideal

- Draw a cartoon student in the middle of a large sheet of paper.

- Introduce this activity in the meeting. Ask everyone to write words around the drawing to create a description of a well-educated geographer, using the ideas from your earlier discussion, and phrases from your whole-school aims identifying the distinctive contribution of geography together with your thinking from Activity 4.1.

- You could bring the student to life by incorporating knowledge, understanding and skills into the cartoon student.

- Make a start on this activity, and then leave it pinned up in the department office for a few days, so members of the department can reflect, and then add their further thoughts to the cartoon.

You could develop two of these cartoon visualisations of intent for key stage 3 and GCSE (Figure 4.11).

PRACTICAL ACTION: Clarify and share your vision

Once all geography teachers have added to the cartoon, compare the vision with the following:

- the purpose of study of the key stage 3 geography curriculum (Figure 4.4)

- the aims of the geography National Curriculum (Figure 4.5)

- the introduction to the National Curriculum subject content for key stage 3 (Figure 4.6)

- the GCSE subject aims (Figure 4.7) and assessment objectives (Figure 4.8)

- *A Different View: A Manifesto from the GA* is also useful here (Figure 4.9)

- Ofsted (2013) subject-specific guidance for geography (Figure 4.10).

Use these documents to clarify your vision for geography at key stage 3 and GCSE. Create a final cartoon or poster to show the vision, and display it in each geography classroom. It will be particularly important to share this vision with students, on a regular basis, once you begin implementing your curriculum. It provides a clear purpose for the learning, for the teacher to make clear how each unit of work is a stepping stone on the learning journey towards achieving this vision (Figures 4.11–4.13).

A high-quality geography education should inspire in pupils a curiosity and fascination about the world and its people that will remain with them for the rest of their lives. Teaching should equip pupils with knowledge about diverse places, people, resources and natural and human environments, together with a deep understanding of the Earth's key physical and human processes. As pupils progress, their growing knowledge about the world should help them to deepen their understanding of the interaction between physical and human processes, and of the formation and use of landscapes and environments. Geographical knowledge, understanding and skills provide the frameworks and approaches that explain how the Earth's features at different scales are shaped, interconnected and change over time.

Figure 4.4: Key stage 3 geography National Curriculum: the purpose of study. **Source:** DfE (2013).

The national curriculum for geography aims to ensure that all pupils:

- develop contextual knowledge of the location of globally significant places – both terrestrial and marine – including their defining physical and human characteristics and how these provide a geographical context for understanding the actions of processes

- understand the processes that give rise to key physical and human geographical features of the world, how these are interdependent and how they bring about spatial variation and change over time

- are competent in the geographical skills needed to:

  - collect, analyse and communicate with a range of data gathered through experiences of fieldwork that deepen their understanding of geographical processes

  - interpret a range of sources of geographical information, including maps, diagrams, globes, aerial photographs and Geographical Information Systems (GIS)

  - communicate geographical information in a variety of ways, including through maps, numerical and quantitative skills and writing at length.

Figure 4.5: Aims of the geography National Curriculum. **Source:** DfE (2013).

Pupils should consolidate and extend their knowledge of the world's major countries and their physical and human features. They should understand how geographical processes interact to create distinctive human and physical landscapes that change over time. In doing so, they should become aware of increasingly complex geographical systems in the world around them. They should develop greater competence in using geographical knowledge, approaches and concepts [such as models and theories] and geographical skills in analysing and interpreting different data sources. In this way pupils will continue to enrich their locational knowledge and spatial and environmental understanding.

Figure 4.6: Geography National Curriculum – introduction to the key stage 3 subject content. **Source:** DfE (2013).

GCSE specifications for the discipline of geography should provide the opportunity for students to understand more about the world, the challenges it faces and their place within it. The GCSE course will deepen understanding of geographical processes, illuminate the impact of change and of complex people-environment interactions, highlight the dynamic links and interrelationships between places and environments at different scales, and develop students' competence in using a wide range of geographical investigative skills and approaches. Geography enables young people to become globally and environmentally informed and thoughtful, enquiring citizens. >>>

Figure 4.7: GCSE geography aims. **Source:** DfE (2014).

GCSE specifications in geography should enable students to build on their key stage 3 knowledge and skills to:

- develop and extend their knowledge of locations, places, environments and processes, and of different scales including global; and of social, political and cultural contexts (**know geographical material**)

- gain understanding of the interactions between people and environments, change in places and processes over space and time, and the interrelationship between geographical phenomena at different scales and in different contexts (**think like a geographer**)

- develop and extend their competence in a range of skills including those used in fieldwork, in using maps and Geographical Information Systems (GIS) and in researching secondary evidence, including digital sources; and develop their competence in applying sound enquiry and investigative approaches to questions and hypotheses (**study like a geographer**)

- apply geographical knowledge, understanding, skills and approaches appropriately and creatively to real world contexts, including fieldwork, and to contemporary situations and issues; and develop well-evidenced arguments drawing on their geographical knowledge and understanding (**applying geography**).

Figure 4.7 (continued): GCSE geography aims. **Source:** DfE (2014).

The exams will measure how students have achieved the following assessment objectives.

- AO1: Demonstrate knowledge of locations, places, processes, environments and different scales (15%).

- AO2: Demonstrate geographical understanding of: concepts and how they are used in relation to places, environments and processes; the interrelationships between places, environments and processes (25%).

- AO3: Apply knowledge and understanding to interpret, analyse and evaluate geographical information and issues to make judgements (35%, including 10% applied to fieldwork context(s)).

- AO4: Select, adapt and use a variety of skills and techniques to investigate questions and issues and communicate findings (25%, including 5% used to respond to fieldwork data and context(s)).

Figure 4.8: GCSE geography Assessment Objectives. **Source:** DfE (2014).

The GA's charitable mission is to 'further geographical knowledge and understanding through education' and one of our underpinning beliefs is that geographical education enriches the lives of all young people.

The GA's vision for geography is developed from the following principles:

- geography underpins a lifelong 'conversation' about Earth as the home of humankind, and therefore contributes to a balanced education for all young people in schools, colleges and other settings

- an essential outcome of learning geography is to be able to apply knowledge and conceptual understanding to new settings: that is, to 'think geographically' about the changing world

- geography in schools, colleges and other educational settings is concerned with perceptive and deep description of the real world. It seeks explanations about how the world works and helps us think about alternative futures

- young people, working with their teachers and drawing from their own experiences and curiosity, should be encouraged to help shape the geography curriculum

- students must be active participants and investigators in geographical enquiry, not just the passive recipients of knowledge

- fieldwork – learning directly in the untidy real world outside the classroom – is an essential component of geography education

- teachers should be accountable, but are also autonomous professionals driven by educational goals and purposes: they are curriculum makers and subject leaders.

Figure 4.9: Extracts from *A different view: A Manifesto from the Geographical Association*. **Source:** GA (2009).

Outstanding student achievement descriptors

- Pupils have excellent knowledge of where places are and what they are like. They have excellent understanding of the ways in which places are interdependent and interconnected and how human and physical environments are interrelated.

- Pupils have an extensive base of core geographical knowledge and vocabulary.

- Pupils are able to carry out increasingly complex geographical enquiry, apply questioning skills and use effective analytical and presentational techniques in a wide range of environments, scales and contexts. They reach clear conclusions and are able to develop reasoned argument to explain their findings.

- Pupils show exceptional independence; they are able to think for themselves and take the initiative in, for example, asking questions, carrying out their own

investigations and working constructively with others. They show significant levels of originality, imagination or creativity in their understanding and skills within the subject.

- Fieldwork and other geographical skills, including numerical and quantitative skills, and techniques are highly developed and frequently utilised.

- Pupils develop passion and commitment to the subject and exhibit a real sense of curiosity in finding out about the world around them and the people who live there.

- Pupils are able to express well-balanced opinions, rooted in very good knowledge and understanding about current and contemporary issues in society and the environment.

Figure 4.10: Ofsted subject-specific guidance for geography. **Source:** Ofsted (2013)

This is a vitally important activity which is fundamental to establishing a coherent curriculum designed to support pupil progress. It is an activity successfully used in training with

teachers all over the world. Figure 4.11 (Gardner, 2016, p. 54) shows two examples of 'vision visualisation' posters produced on a GA CPD day for curriculum design.

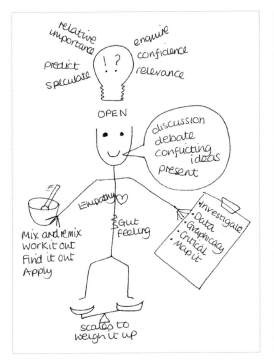

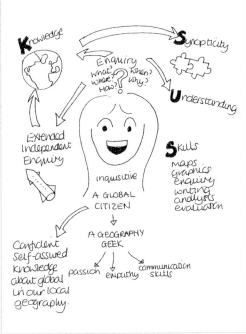

Figure 4.11: Two examples of vision visualisation posters. **Source:** Gardner (2016), p. 54.

Holistic geographies

At the outset of this curriculum design process in geography, a key challenge is to hold together what is an enormously broad subject – which can often appear to be an incoherent, endless list of 'stuff' to the learner. It is helpful, therefore, to consider a holistic approach to planning a coherent geography curriculum with progression in mind. Supporting students to think geographically should be the focus of a holistic vision, an approach which is clearly evident in the aims for GCSE. Rawding (2014) provides a helpful overview of 'holistic geographies', and concludes:

> 'Developing an understanding of the Earth in its entirety is an essential component in becoming a geographer. Without such an understanding, it is all too easy to see geography as a loosely connected list of topics, many of which could be taught under alternative subject headings.' (p. 13)

All the case study schools in Chapter 8 have spent a significant amount of time establishing a strategic vision for their curriculum. Spalding Grammar School embeds critical thinking across its curriculum. Harris MAT consider the significance of decolonisation in their curriculum. Kay (2021) explains her department has developed a vision for the curriculum with sustainability at its core: 'Our aim is that students think geographically about the changing world, becoming critical learners and knowledgeable, skilful and responsible citizens who care about the future of our planet.' (p. 11). Fortismere School introduces this vision, focussed on becoming a geographer, with an introductory unit of study to key stage 3 – 'What it means to be a geographer' This allows teachers to make clear right at the outset the purpose of key stage 3 geography. Also, this approach lends itself to finding out what the new year 7 students already know about being a geographer from their studies of the subject in key stages 1 and 2. This first unit then can be used to get to know new students, and where they are in their learning, as a transitional assessment unit.

Sharing the vision

The strategic vision is the fulcrum of a curriculum designed with student progress in mind. It is a statement of the intent of what the curriculum is trying to achieve for students. It represents a vision of how students will have developed by the end of the stage of learning. It provides the purpose, or the 'why', of learning for every stepping stone of the journey leading to its achievement by students. It is really important, therefore, that this vision is shared by teachers, who are collectively responsible for the quality of geography lessons experienced by students.

It is important that the vision is shared with the students, so they develop a sense of what geography is for and its value and what it means to think geographically, and see the world in an interconnected way. In this way, students can begin to see the importance of geography not just for their life now, but for their future. Fortismere School describes how their vision for intent is displayed in each geography classroom, and used in lessons to make connections to the vision. Jo Coles adopted a similar approach in her school for GCSE. She saw the importance of the aims for GCSE (Figure 4.7) and turned them into posters displayed in classroom (Figures 4.12 and 4.13). These were then used regularly in lessons to demonstrate what success looks like at GCSE.

Presenting a clear vision in this way is also invaluable within school, to make clear geography's distinctive contribution to the whole-school curriculum. This vision should be shared with school leadership teams; in fact, the new Education Inspection Framework means Ofsted inspectors will insist on this. The vision forms an invaluable starting point for cross-curricular approaches with other subject departments. The vision also demonstrates to parents what the subject is trying to achieve for their child's learning, and would be very helpful to share with them at parents' evenings.

Stage 2 – Record your starting point

You will only know what impact you've made if you know where you started. Before you initiate changes to your curriculum you need to establish a baseline. Consider your current curriculum and what your students are like. Reflect on your existing key stage 3 and 4 curricula; consider their strengths and weaknesses, and what resources you have to support them. Consider how the aims and structure of these curricula have embedded geographical concepts, and support students' abilities

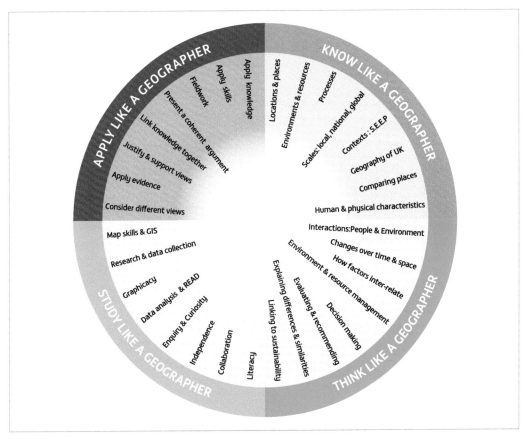

Figure 4.12: GCSE aims poster: What it means to think geographically. **Source:** Jo Coles.

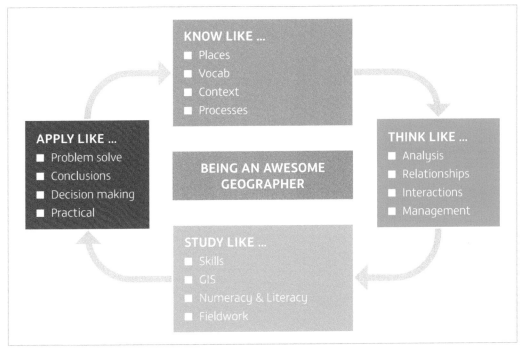

Figure 4.13: Student-friendly GCSE aims. **Source:** Jo Coles.

to think geographically. Think carefully about how far your current key stage 3 curriculum prepares your students for their next stage of learning. How can you design your key stage 3 curriculum to develop the building blocks of knowledge, understanding and skills as part of a broad and balanced curriculum, and also to provide a foundation from which to progress at GCSE?

Consider your new long-term vision to describe what you hope to see in your students. The best way to do this is to develop an overview of your students at the moment and define how you would like this to change. Which aspects of your vision developed in Stage 1 are currently a strength in your existing curriculum? Which aspects will you need to develop?

ACTIVITY 4.3: RECORD YOUR STARTING POINT ⤓

Taking a baseline is difficult. You can relate this analysis to the aims and objectives shown in Figure 4.5: for example, the aims GNC identifies communicate geographical information in a variety of ways, including through maps, numerical and quantitative skills and writing at length. How well developed are your students' communication skills currently, particularly in terms of the identified aspects of maps, numerical and quantitative skills? How effective are your students at extended writing in geography?

You might find it helpful to record this information in a table, so you have a clear benchmark against which to draw comparisons later on in your curriculum development work. An example of this is provided in Figure 4.14.

Vision	Set clear goals	How well are we achieving our aims?
What are our learners like now?	*What are the strengths of our current curriculum?*	*How will we evaluate the impact of our new curriculum?*
What do we want our learners to be like?	*What features do we need to have in our new curriculum?*	*What do we need to do to bring about change to our curriculum?*

Figure 4.14: Curriculum design process – intent. ⤓

Stage 3 – Set clear goals

So far you have visualised what successful student achievement could look like at key stage 3 and GCSE. The challenge now is to begin to consider how to bring this strategic vision to life.

A central goal of curriculum intent should be to develop the abilities of your students to make connections, to develop an holistic view. The aims of GNC provide a helpful starting point here: world contextual knowledge, understanding of physical and human processes, and competence in geographical skills. The GA utilised these aims to develop a progression framework explained in Chapter 3 (page 43). These aims are progressed at GCSE through the aims and Assessment Objectives – know geographical material, think like a geographer, study like a geographer, applying geography (Figures 4.7 and 4.8). Thinking geographically, using geographical skills independently as a matter of routine, and developing a locational matrix of

the world are central to thinking geographically. To achieve this you need to be clear about the big ideas or concepts of geography to be introduced and progressed, across your curriculum at key stage 3 and GCSE. Each school case study in Chapter 8 has identified concepts to be introduced and progressed in their key stage 3 geography curriculum. Activity 4.4 has been designed to help you set clear goals.

The next chapter provides guidance on Step 4 of this curriculum design process – designing a curriculum to bring your vision to life. This will involve creating a strategic plan to develop the relationships and interconnections between your intent vision, and the big ideas, skills and locations identified in your table. The guidance chapter will help you design a curriculum that sequences units of work across the plan in a coherent manner, introducing and progressing concepts, locational knowledge and skills, making student progress towards the vision transparent and achievable.

ACTIVITY 4.4: STAGE 3 – SET CLEAR GOALS ⬇

Practical action research

Match your strategic vision and department discussion to the following:

- ideas about concepts and thinking geographically, provided in Chapter 3 (page 36–43).
- GNC document
- GCSE subject content and specification
- *A different view: A manifesto from the Geographical Association*
- the curriculum design process explained in the case study schools (Chapter 8, pp. 37–43)

Talking point

Discuss with the department which concepts, locational knowledge, and skills, identified in the research will be central to bringing your vision to life in your key stage 3 and GCSE geography curricula.

Identify the concepts, or big ideas, that you think are central to bringing your vision to life.

Record your decisions in a table

Aspect of your vision	Big ideas/concepts	Skills	Locations

Reflections

Consider your findings about your existing curriculum in Step 2.

References

All websites last accessed 27/07/2021.

Adichie, C.N. (2009) *The danger of a single story*, Technology, Entertainment and Design Conference, Palm Springs, USA. Available at www.ted.com/talks/chimamanda_ngozi_adichie_the_danger_of_a_single_story/transcript?language=en

Biddulph, M. (2017) 'Inclusive geographies: the illusion of inclusion', *Teaching Geography*, 42, 2, pp. 46–8.

CRED (2021) *Commission on Race and Ethnic Disparities: The Report*. Available at https://assets.publishing.service.gov.uk/government/uploads/system/uploads/attachment_data/file/974507/20210331_-_CRED_Report_-_FINAL_-_Web_Accessible.pdf

Decolonising geography website available at https://decolonisegeography.com/

DfE (2013) National curriculum in England: geography programmes of study. Available at www.gov.uk/government/publications/national-curriculum-in-england-geography-programmes-of-study

DfE (2014) GCSE subject content for geography. Available at www.gov.uk/government/publications/gcse-geography

Evelyn, K. (2020) *'Like I wasn't there': climate activist Vanessa Nakate on being erased from a movement*. Available at https://www.theguardian.com/world/2020/jan/29/vanessa-nakate-interview-climate-activism-cropped-photo-davos

Fearn, H. (2019) 'Busting the "intent" myth'. Ofsted blog. Available at https://educationinspection.blog.gov.uk/2019/07/01/busting-the-intent-myth

Gardner, D. (2016) 'Planning for Progress in Geography', *Teaching Geography*, 41, 2, pp. 54–5.

Geographical Association (2020) *Critical thinking – a model for achievement*. Available at https://www.geography.org.uk/Critical-thinking-in-the-classroom

Geographical Association (2009) *A Different View: A Manifesto from the Geographical Association*. Sheffield: Geographical Association. Available at www.geography.org.uk/GA-Manifesto-for-geography

Geographical Association (2020) *Black Lives Matter statement*. Available at www.geography.org.uk/Announcements-and-Updates/black-lives-matter/255912

Geographical Association (2020-21) GeogPod – the GA's podcast, Series 1–6. Available at https://www.geography.org.uk/GeogPod-The-GAs-Podcast

Gleen, J. (2020) 'Geography's intent: developing your curriculum', *Teaching Geography*, 45, 3, pp. 108–10.

Kay, R. (2021) 'The deep dive geography experience: intent, implementation and impact', *Teaching Geography*, 46, 1, pp. 11–13.

Lister, A. (2021) *Comments on the Report of the Commission on Race and Ethnic Disparities, Snapshots of Empire Blog*. Available at https://blogs.sussex.ac.uk/snapshotsofempire/2021/04/01/comments-on-the-report-of-the-commission-on-race-and-ethnic-disparities

Milner, C. (2020) 'Classroom strategies for tackling the whiteness of geography', *Teaching Geography*, 45, 3, pp. 105–7.

Ofsted (2013) *Subject-specific guidance for geography*. Available at www.geography.org.uk/download/ga_ofsted%20subject-specific%20guidance%20for%20geography%20(dec%202013).pdf

Puttick, S. and Murrey, A. (2020) 'Confronting the deafening silence on race in geography education in England: learning from anti-racist, decolonial and Black geographies', *Geography*, 105, 3, pp.126–34.

Rawding, C. (2014) 'The importance of teaching "holistic" geographies', *Teaching Geography*, 39, 1, pp. 10–13.

Roberts, M. (2015) 'Critical thinking and global learning', *Teaching Geography*, 40, 2, pp. 55–9.

Curriculum Intent – turning the vision into a plan

 INTENT   **1** Create a vision   **2** Record your starting point   **3** Set clear goals   **4** Design your curriculum

Stage 4 – Design your curriculum

This stage involves planning how to organise the learning to achieve your vision. We discovered in Chapters 2 and 3 that good curriculum design incorporates coherence and sequencing, building students' knowledge and understanding cumulatively. The current EIF makes this an explicit requirement. The key indicator of curriculum intent in Ofsted's Education Inspection Framework (Ofsted, 2019a) is:

> 'the provider's curriculum is coherently planned and sequenced towards cumulatively sufficient knowledge and skills for future learning and employment' (p. 9)

This Ofsted key indicator of curriculum intent requires unpicking to determine what it ultimately means in practice. The Ofsted geography research and analysis review (2021), is a helpful starting point. It makes the following point in the conclusion:

> 'The curriculum organises and repeats substantive and disciplinary knowledge in ways that show pupils how each component fits together and how each composite idea fits with others. Through this, pupils gain a secure grasp of well-connected pieces of knowledge and consequently know more, remember more and are able to do more, thus making good progress in the subject ... Curriculums help pupils build an effective schema when they further embed previously learned knowledge in memory through recall and review, build on what pupils know and increase both the quantity and complexity of content and disciplinary appreciation.'

This chapter provides guidance on how to plan a coherent and sequenced geography curriculum 11–16.

Towards coherence

Long ago, the now defunct QCA (2000) explained the significance of a long-term or key stage plan:

> 'It draws parts of the programme of study together into coherent, manageable teaching units. It shows how these teaching units are distributed across the three years of the key stage in a sequence that promotes curriculum continuity and progression in students' learning.' (p. 5)

Curriculum coherence (Chapter 2, pages 19–21) requires deep thought about connectivity, bringing together what Lambert refers to as the grammar – the big ideas of the subject – with the vocabulary of the subject – the geographical content knowledge (Chapter 3, pages 36–7). The construction of a coherent curriculum can be seen as the creation of a world narrative, with internal elements (grammar and vocabulary) working together, towards an end goal – the vision you created in Stage 1. In developing your unfolding curriculum story, you will plan to progress your students towards the end goal, the visualisation of what you want your students to achieve.

Chapter 4 provides guidance and tools to support Stages 1–3 in designing the curriculum and encouraging the establishment of an agreed clear vision of the geography you are trying to achieve over the key stage. To do this, we take into account the nature of the subject – geography; the needs and context of your students; and the expertise we have available, embodied in the geography teaching team.

Stage 4 of the design process is all about thinking through the implications of these first three stages to create a coherent long-term plan for the key stage, made up of units of work. Stages 1–3 are about how to realise the vision. This requires an approach to thinking about curriculum that focusses on student progress. Thus units of work and lessons need to be carefully sequenced to progress student understanding of geographical concepts, world contextual knowledge and skills, towards the vision of what you want students to achieve – ultimately, how to think geographically. This approach to planning has the potential to align curriculum, progression and assessment in the manner outlined by Oates (Chapter 2, pages 19–20). As with the last chapter, you can see this guidance applied in practice in the five case study schools, presented in Chapter 8.

Gleen (2000) also outlines how her department worked together to establish a curriculum intent, concluding that these discussion are 'important for determining your department's curriculum rather than just because Ofsted said so' to ensure 'all students make good progress' (p. 110).

Key questions to consider in the design phase

The process of designing your curriculum is driven by a series of questions:

■ How will the selected curriculum content be sequenced to reflect and support student progress towards our vision?

■ How will our curriculum develop students' understanding of geography concepts?

■ How can we build our end goals and vision clearly into our curriculum?

■ How can we plan for student progress across the whole key stage, each unit, and lessons?

■ Should we maintain, modify or reject units of work we have previously used?

■ What should be the focus of the units: themes, places, issues, skills, particular experiences (e.g. individual investigations), fieldwork, or a mixture of all?

■ What opportunities are there for liaising, or cross-curricular working, with other subjects?

The following activity has been designed to help you begin to consider the implications of your vision for the design of your curriculum.

ACTIVITY 5.1: CONSIDER THE IMPLICATIONS OF YOUR VISION FOR YOUR CURRICULUM DESIGN ⬇

TALKING POINT: What are the key aspects of our curriculum intent?

In a department meeting, deconstruct the key elements of your vision statement for the key stage. Discuss each element and write them out as a list.

PRACTICAL ACTION: Visualise the implications for your curriculum design.

Use the 'if/then' template to consider the way your curriculum will bring the vision to life.

If ...
We want students who can become better geographers

Then ...
identify how the department plans for this

We need to design a curriculum that ...

PRACTICAL ACTION: Visualise the implications for your curriculum design, using an example case study.

You can use this 'if/then' device to stimulate discussion about other key elements of your vision statement.

Identifying the 'big ideas' to bring your vision to life

In the design of a coherent, sequenced and inter-connected geography curriculum with progression at its heart, it is important to consider the role of geographical concepts (see Chapter 3, pages 36–43). The Ofsted research review (2021) highlights the significance of concepts to designing a coherent geography curriculum:

'Concepts are important in geography as they draw out the links between processes and ideas. To develop their understanding of each of these concepts, pupils need to learn the range of relevant knowledge and skills. It is from this knowledge and development of these skills that pupils gain a more abstract appreciation of the subject. Therefore, it is critical that the content of the curriculum is broken down into component parts (or chunks) that pupils can first comprehend in their own right, before combining different components to gain a fuller conceptual appreciation.'

As you discovered in Chapter 3 (Figure 3.4, p. 38), there is no one definitive list of key geographical concepts and no correct categorisation of concepts. The concepts that underpin the curriculum intent of the five case study schools in Chapter 8, shown in Figure 5.1, while displaying some common ground, are also varied, dependent on the nature of the geography department's vision. This variety of ideas is related to what Lambert and Morgan (2010) refer to as a geography teacher's 'philosophy of geography'. They define this as 'an understanding of the geography that serves, or at least complements, their educational philosophy' (p. 164). This philosophy they maintain is important because it provides the basis for the autonomous professional activity of curriculum making.

In terms of GCSE geography subject content, DfE makes the following helpful statements about the nature of concepts at key stage 4:

Progression statement

4. designing specifications, awarding organisations should note the following ways in which curriculum emphases should progress from KS3 and ensure that specifications facilitate this:

- broadening and deepening understanding of locational contexts, including greater awareness of the importance of scale and the concept of global

- a greater emphasis given to process studies that lead to an understanding of change

- a greater stress on the multivariate nature of 'human-physical' relationships and interactions

- a stronger focus on forming generalisations and/or abstractions, including some awareness of theoretical perspectives and of the subject's conceptual frameworks

DfE (2014) p. 4

Schools	Organising concepts identified by schools (the 'grammar') to be embedded in the content to be studied (the 'vocabulary')							
Graveney School	Risk and resilience	Natural resources and consumption	Inequality	Physical processes and landscapes	Mitigation and adaptation	Geopolitics and globalisation	Conflict and resolution	Sustainability
Fortismere School	Place	Physical systems	Human systems	Interdependence	Spatial variation	Change over time		
Trinity Academy Grammar	Place	Space	Scale	Global geography	Interdependence	Sustainable development	Human and physical interactions	
The Harris Federation	Climate	Geomorphology	Development	Sustainability	Human/physical interactions			
Spalding Grammar School	Space	Place	Interdependence/interconnectedness	Physical processes and human actions	Context	Sustainability		

Figure 5.1: Concepts identified by the case study schools in Chapter 8.

A research project in Sweden carried out by Jankell et al. (2021) with a group of 18 geography teachers, designed a model based on geographical organising concepts that could be used as guiding principles for teacher's curriculum choices. Although developed for the Swedish geography curriculum, the approach and evolving model shown in Figure 5.2 offers a very useful tool for any geography department considering the role of concepts in designing a curriculum. The first step in the modelling activity is to define organising concepts that capture and mediate the very core of geographical knowing. This core can be used as a lens through which the student can learn to see, interpret and explore the world in a geographical way. As shown in the model diagram, the Swedish teachers identified Place, Space and Scale as the 'big ideas' of the subject. The second circle in the model represents organising concepts that capture what geographers study. The Swedish teachers identified Processes, Change, Connections and relationships between humans and nature. The third circle of the model relates to the geographical knowledge outcomes for students, and how they can learn to present what they have been studying in a geographical manner – what the aims for GCSE geography call 'study like a geographer' and 'applying geography'. Discussion led the teachers to identify spatial patterns; interrelated systems; and perspectives and values, believing that the third outcome was important to help students become aware of different ways to interpret and value an issue. Teachers then trialled the use of the prototype model with their department and students, finding it useful to scaffold discussions about geographical issues with students.

Figure 5.2:
The curriculum concepts model, and key questions to capture geographical understanding.
Source: Dessen Jankell *et al.* (2021), p. 73.

How can we use SCALE to interpret and compare phenomena and events in the world? Experience how to interpret phenomena at certain scales and to interlink different scales in relation to each other in the studied issue.

How can we use PROCESSES to explain driving forces of phenomena, events or situations? Experience how to observe factors and explain actions that drive and build up processes; be able to explain the process in steps.

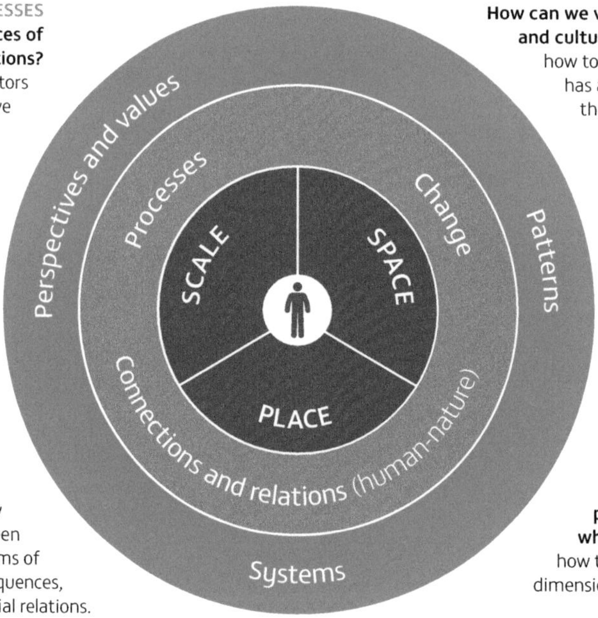

How can we use different PERSPECTIVES to interpret and VALUE phenomena? Experience how to value, argue and discuss from different perspectives.

How can we explain different CONNECTIONS and RELATIONS in the world? Experience how to interpret connections between human and nature in terms of causalities, cause and consequences, structure-agency or spatial relations.

How can we visualise CHANGES in natural and cultural landscapes? Experience how to describe and interpret what has and has not changed, and what that means in a certain place.

How can we make natural and cultural PATTERNS become visible? Experience how to interpret patterns of cultural and natural processes, events and phenomena.

How can we use PLACE to understand where natural phenomena or events occur and what it means? Becoming aware of how to use place contexts and spatial dimensions to interpret the world.

What do natural and cultural SYSTEMS look like, how do they function and what factors drive them? Experience different factors interconnected to larger systems and how they function and affect each other and the system as a whole.

Perspectives and values · Processes · Change · Patterns · Connections and relations (human-nature) · Systems · SCALE · SPACE · PLACE

Crucially, Jankell et al concluded:

'… since students and teachers used the same language (in terms of organising concepts), it became easier to give feedback on how to qualify students' knowing, e.g. how to use these concepts as a way to interpret and analyse an issue. In turn, this feedback was not limited to the specific task or topic, but was something that the students could take with them to the next module.' (p. 73)

This approach, therefore, demonstrates a potential for embedding concepts in curriculum design in order, as Ofsted states, to 'gain a more abstract appreciation of the subject', evolving the necessary holistic understanding to think like a geographer.

Activity 5.2 is designed to support thinking about the role of concepts in terms of planning a coherent, sequenced and interconnected geography curriculum with progression towards your intent vision at its heart.

ACTIVITY 5.2: WHAT ARE THE BIG IDEAS THAT UNDERPIN YOUR CURRICULUM VISION FOR THE KEY STAGE? ⬇

TALKING POINT

It is important that your department agrees the 'big ideas' or concepts of your vision for the key stage. Initially each member of the department will need to be clear on the role of concepts in designing a curriculum.

KEY READING

- Chapter 3, in particular the section about concepts (pp. 36–43).

- Chaper 8 and case study downloads to see how each of the case study schools considered concepts.

- Jankell *et al.* (2021).

Discuss the following questions:

- Why do we need to establish geographical concepts for the key stage?

- What concepts do we think emerge from our curriculum intent vision?

PRACTICAL ACTION: Create your own organising concepts model

Download a copy of the curriculum concept model adapted from Jankell *et al.* and discuss each question, recording your ideas on a copy of the model.

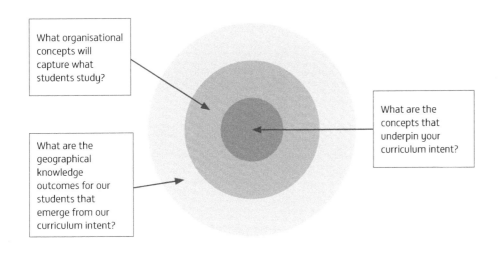

What organisational concepts will capture what students study?

What are the geographical knowledge outcomes for our students that emerge from our curriculum intent?

What are the concepts that underpin your curriculum intent?

Figure 5.3: Organising concepts model.

ACTIVITY 5.3: INITIAL THINKING TO CREATE YOUR LONG-TERM PLAN ⬇

Considering how topics are sequenced in a long-term plan is an important, but also fun and creative, part of the curriculum design process. Here the department team have an opportunity to really apply their depth of subject knowledge, to design a coherently sequenced key stage plan that helps students to progress. The work done on visioning end goals in Stages 1–3 of the curriculum intent is of considerable help here as it underpins the reasoning required in sequencing the topics. It is a very useful professional task to explore precisely how these 'topics' connect to a vision and goals for geography.

Stage 1
Use Fig 5.4 as a dummy run ...

Initially your department could use Figure 5.4 as a sort of 'dummy run', to establish the skills and understanding required to create a long-term plan, with topics sequenced in a logical order and student progression towards the vision in mind.

Stage 2
Consider your vision statement for key stage 3 ...

Consider the vision for key stage 3 geography you have established in Stage 1 of the curriculum design process:

- Identify how the topics shown in Figure 5.4 connect with your vision.

- Consider how far the sequence of topics shown would support student progress towards the vision.

- Are there any issues with the sequencing? For example, why might a school study of climate change before introducing the key features of weather and climate?

Stage 3
Consider your your existing plan

Consider your existing key stage 3 plan, to identify which topics support the vision, and how each can be sequenced to support cumulative knowledge and skills. Does your existing plan have sequencing issues?

Stage 4
Consider other long-term plans

All five case study schools in Chapter 8 provide glimpses of the reasoning applied, as does Gleen (2020), to create their coherent curriculum plans. There will be ideas and approaches here that you can apply to the sequencing of topics in your curriculum.

Year group	Autumn term		Spring term		Summer term	
7	What is a geographer? (skills)	Climate change	Africa	Glaciation	Development	Local fieldwork
8	Rivers and flooding	Geography of crime	India and China	Globalisation	Geography of fashion	Tourism
9	Weather and climate	Natural resources	Coasts	Natural hazards	Middle East	What future for the planet?

Figure 5.4: A composite key stage 3 geography plan.

ACTIVITY 5.4: SELECTING AND SEQUENCING THE KNOWLEDGE AND SKILLS FOR YOUR KEY STAGE 3 CURRICULUM ⬇

TALKING POINT: What knowledge and skills will form your curriculum?

In a department meeting, identify the core knowledge and skills of the GNC, together with other knowledge developed in Activity 5.3 that link to achieving your vision, and link clearly to the concepts you have identified in Activity 5.2.

PRACTICAL ACTIVITY: Begin to think about how to sequence the knowledge and skills.

The following list provides an overview of the content of GNC at key stage 3. You can create a series of cards for this content, together with additional knowledge and skills you have identified to support students to achieve your vision.

PRACTICAL ACTIVITY: Sequencing card sort

You could begin by watching HMI Paul Joyce explain planning and sequencing a curriculum, and consider how this can work for geography. This video is available at: www.youtube.com/watch?v=yQfYzZbOLYA

Read Gleen (2020) – this describes how the department followed a similar process.

In a department meeting, lay out the cards you have created on a sheet of paper. Spend time discussing:

- a logical sequence for this content; move the cards to create the sequence

- how the content and the key concepts you have identified will be brought together to form units of work

- how many units of work will make up your key stage plan

- how these units will be sequenced

- what should be the focus of the units of work this content will form: themes, skills, places, issues, particular experiences (e.g. individual investigations) fieldwork or a mixture of all

- how skills and fieldwork opportunities can be integrated across units to ensure students make progress in the skills.

Lay out the cards, sorted into a final agreed sequence, and take a photo of it: this will be important to begin to create a key stage plan in the next stage.

NC key stage 3 skills and content
The building blocks for progression 11–16

Collect, analyse, conclusions from geographical data	Russia	Rocks, weathering and soils

| Interpret OS maps | Interpret aerial and satellite photos | Middle East | GIS |

| Regions in Africa compared with India | Geological timescales and plate tectonics |

| Population and urbanisation | Economic activity | Use of natural resources |

| International development | Asia including China and India | Hydrology |

| Weather and climate, including climate change | Coasts | Glaciation | Fieldwork |

Planning a coherent curriculum – aligning curriculum, assessment and progression

Most schools have an overview plan that provides a list of topics, usually between five and six a year; roughly two units of work each term, often concluded with an end-of-unit test. Plans have often evolved with each successive National Curriculum review, with new topics added, and an understandable reluctance to change old, favourite topics. Some schools attempt to engage students by including enticing unit titles, for example: 'Will the slumbering giant awaken?' (volcanoes); others provide enquiry questions as unit titles. Figure 5.4 is a composite version of many different plans seen over the years. In recent years, many schools have reduced key stage 3 to two years, which has created problems for geography departments, who have attempted to reduce or amalgamate units of work from a plan such as that shown.

This whole creative process requires decisions that are matters for your professional judgement. There is no single correct way to sequence a key stage plan: it is how you justify and then implement any decision about sequencing topics that is important, together with evidence that your sequence demonstrates a positive impact on your students' progress towards your vision. Activities 5.2, 5.3 and 5.4 have been designed to support this process.

It is much easier to design the curriculum when you can plan with progress in mind, as highlighted in the Ofsted review (see earlier in this chapter). You can design your curriculum as the progression framework. Figure 5.5 shows the basis for such a framework for key stage 3 that integrates the thinking involved in Stages 1–3 of the curriculum design process, with the GA's dimensions of progression, aspects of achievement/progression strands, and benchmark statements explained in Chapter 3, pages 43–6.

At the stage when you have agreed a sequence of units for the key stage that the department feels will support students to make progress towards the vision, you can start planning and map out the nature of this progress. This is clearly a matter of professional judgement, made by the team, which depends on a range of factors. There is no approved GA or Ofsted model for how the long-term plan is sequenced. Indeed, if you compare the plans for the case study schools (Chapter 8), you will see a range of approaches, thinking and sequences. It is how your department team have justified your sequence that is important; and of course, the implementation stage of the curriculum design process might lead to changes in the sequence of topics, as the team realise through experience that X before Y doesn't work.

The three scales of curriculum planning

Curriculum planning operates at three interconnected scales – key stage; medium term; and lesson plan. As you zoom between the scales working through the process you will need to consider the role of each in planning for student progress.

Key stage plan

The key stage long-term plan provides the big picture, and is the scale of curriculum planning introduced so far in this chapter. This long-term plan is made up of a series of interconnected and sequenced medium-term plans or units of work.

The medium-term plan

The medium-term plan, or what many teachers know as a scheme of work or curriculum unit, is in effect a coherent sequence of lessons. These need to be ordered just as carefully as the long-term plan to create the coherence, and logical narrative, to ensure student progress. Each unit should have a clear purpose in the overall plan or vision. A medium-term plan can be assigned responsibilities for 'chunks' of the vision, which can be identified for the students as key objectives for each unit – stepping stones to progress. A year 7 unit, Natural Resources, for example, could introduce the concept of sustainability, in a local or UK context. A year 8 development unit could progress understanding of sustainability at a global scale, by introducing the UN Sustainable Development Goals. In the implementation of this unit the teacher would make this strategic connection clear to students. The same applies to introducing or progressing use of Ordnance Survey (OS) maps, for example. One unit introduces how to locate places using grid references on an OS map; a future unit progress this skill by locating places on an OS map and matching an aerial photograph, or two OS maps of different scales.

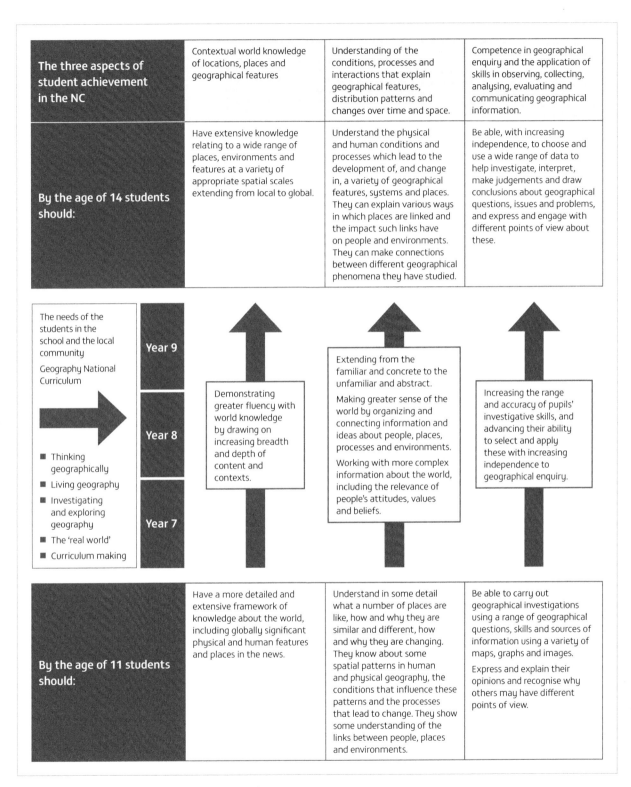

The three aspects of student achievement in the NC	Contextual world knowledge of locations, places and geographical features	Understanding of the conditions, processes and interactions that explain geographical features, distribution patterns and changes over time and space.	Competence in geographical enquiry and the application of skills in observing, collecting, analysing, evaluating and communicating geographical information.
By the age of 14 students should:	Have extensive knowledge relating to a wide range of places, environments and features at a variety of appropriate spatial scales extending from local to global.	Understand the physical and human conditions and processes which lead to the development of, and change in, a variety of geographical features, systems and places. They can explain various ways in which places are linked and the impact such links have on people and environments. They can make connections between different geographical phenomena they have studied.	Be able, with increasing independence, to choose and use a wide range of data to help investigate, interpret, make judgements and draw conclusions about geographical questions, issues and problems, and express and engage with different points of view about these.

The needs of the students in the school and the local community

Geography National Curriculum

- Thinking geographically
- Living geography
- Investigating and exploring geography
- The 'real world'
- Curriculum making

Year 9

Year 8

Year 7

Demonstrating greater fluency with world knowledge by drawing on increasing breadth and depth of content and contexts.

Extending from the familiar and concrete to the unfamiliar and abstract.

Making greater sense of the world by organizing and connecting information and ideas about people, places, processes and environments.

Working with more complex information about the world, including the relevance of people's attitudes, values and beliefs.

Increasing the range and accuracy of pupils' investigative skills, and advancing their ability to select and apply these with increasing independence to geographical enquiry.

| By the age of 11 students should: | Have a more detailed and extensive framework of knowledge about the world, including globally significant physical and human features and places in the news. | Understand in some detail what a number of places are like, how and why they are similar and different, how and why they are changing. They know about some spatial patterns in human and physical geography, the conditions that influence these patterns and the processes that lead to change. They show some understanding of the links between people, places and environments. | Be able to carry out geographical investigations using a range of geographical questions, skills and sources of information using a variety of maps, graphs and images. Express and explain their opinions and recognise why others may have different points of view. |

Figure 5.5: The curriculum as a progression framework. ⬇

A coast unit could involve students describing and explaining geographical patterns for a stretch of coast, using a range of geographical data including OS maps at different scales, historical OS maps, aerial and ground-level photos. All the responsibilities assigned to each unit of work can be plotted on a strategic grid or framework (Figure 5.6). This approach represents a key aspect of 'sequencing towards cumulatively sufficient knowledge and skills' (Ofsted, 2019a, p. 9). Each unit of work is composed of a series of sequenced lessons.

A lesson plan

This is one of a sequence of lessons that make up a unit. Each lesson requires a clear sequence of activities to support student progresses towards the aims of the lesson, and its assigned responsibil-

ities towards the aims and purpose of the medium-term plan. Each lesson is planned as a stepping stone of learning towards the assigned responsibilities of the unit of work.

Key stage 3 long-term plan as a progression planning grid

Typically, geography departments present the long-term plan as a mere list of topics for each year group, as we saw earlier in Figure 5.4. A more helpful and strategic way of developing this plan is by using a grid (Figure 5.6) that utilises the progression strands in the GA's progression framework Chapter 3, pages 43–6). This grid can be used to plot the progression of world contextual knowledge, geographical understanding and skills across the units of work to support planning for progress.

Figure 5.6: Curriculum planning grid to create key stage 3 long-term plan with progression in mind. ⬇

	The three aspects of student achievement in the NC	Contextual world knowledge of locations, places and geographical features.	Understand conditions processes and interactions that explain geographical features, distribution patterns and changes over time and space. Understand the physical and human conditions and processes which lead to the development of, and change in, a variety of geographical features, systems and places. They can explain various ways in which places are interdependent and interconnected. They can make connections between different geographical phenomena they have studied.			Competence in **geographical enquiry** and the application of skills in observing, collecting, analysing, evaluating and communicating geographical information. Be able, with increasing independence, to choose and use a wide range of data to help investigate, interpret, make judgements and draw conclusions about geographical questions, issues and problems, expressing and thinking critically about different points of view about these. Write at length their geographical ideas, using a wide-ranging geographical vocabulary.		Judgements could be expressed and recorded as **working towards, meeting** and **exceeding** the expectations for their age or whatever system is in place at your school.
	By the age of 14 students	Have extensive knowledge of a wide range of places, environments and features at a variety of scales extending from local to global including Russia, Asia, Africa and the Middle East.						
	Units of work		Physical geography	Human geography	Physical/ human interaction	Geographical skills	Fieldwork	Key assessment opportunity
15								
14								
13								
12	How will the curriculum support students to progressing towards the vision?				Where will you introduce and progress concepts and skills?			
11								
10								
9								
8				How will you make the intent and progress strands clear to students?				
7								
6								
5	How will you sequence units to support students towards cumulatively sufficient knowledge and skills?						How will you create a variety of assessment opportunities to ensure pupils are making progress towards the vision?	
4								
3								
2								
1								
	By the age of 11 students	Have a framework of knowledge about the world, including Europe, global North and South, and the local area, including significant physical and human features and places in the news.	Understand what a number of places are like, how and why they are similar and different, how and why they are changing. Know about some spatial patterns in human and physical geography, the conditions that influence these patterns and the processes that lead to change. Show some understanding of the links between people, places and environments.			Are able to carry out geographical investigations using a range of geographical questions, skills and sources of information using a variety of maps, graphs and images. Students can express and explain their opinions and recognise why others may have different points of view.		

The units of work that make up the plan are interconnected by the three progression strands. Figure 5.6 is a planning framework for you to use for your key stage 3 curriculum: it is a development of the principles shown in Figure 5.5. Figure 5.6 identifies key questions for you to consider as you create your plan using the grid. You can use this grid to bring together and plan for progression in understanding of the concepts and content of your curriculum, as well as the skills in the context of places around the world, at a variety of scales.

The age-related expectations for an 11-year-old from the GA's *A progression framework for geography* leaflet – world contextual knowledge, an understanding of geographical ideas, and geographical enquiry and skills – are provided for each progression strand or aspect of achievement at the bottom of the grid. The benchmark statements for a 14-year-old are placed at the top of the grid. You can adapt these statements to embed your vision of where your students should be in their learning at the end of key stage 3. Year 7 units begin at the bottom of the grid, and work upwards, planning progress towards the 14-year-old statements at the top. Schools are likely to be used to documents like this starting with year 7 at the top and working down; this grid is presented in this way intentionally, as a change of mindset with regard to the planning process, to emphasise that progress goes upwards towards the vision.

The left-hand column is provided for you write in the sequence of units you devised in the previous activities. For each unit you can begin to map out the contextual knowledge, understanding, and skills you plan to develop. As you do this, you will begin to build a progression map of your curriculum. Recording planning in this detail on one grid will allow you to see issues you perhaps had not considered in your initial planning. Subdividing the understanding strand into physical and human, for example, allows you to spot if there is an imbalance between physical and human geography in the sequence of units for a year group. You can also use different coloured fonts to plot and track where a concept, such as sustainability, is introduced and then progressed across the units.

Two of the case study schools have developed this long-term planning grid to present their key stage 3 curriculum.

Two examples of planning for progression

1 Planning for progress using OS maps

Learning to read and interpret different types of OS maps is a fundamental aspect of geography teaching, clearly identified in all the versions of the NC and GCSE geography. Often schools will teach an introductory unit to OS maps in key stage 3, in part to consolidate skills that we hope have already been developed, as part of geography in key stages 1 and 2. This unit often includes basic map skills such as direction, compass points, scale, measuring distance, map symbols, four- and six-figure grid references, representation of height on maps, spot heights, contours, and describing routes. Once established, these aspects of map use and interpretation can be developed studying different places and topics. It is not helpful if next time students use an OS map is as part of their GCSE course! Here students are often taught a skills unit, designed to refresh these map skills. Unfortunately, opportunities to develop these skills are often not embedded in the GCSE curriculum. In the run-up to the exam, year 11 students will undertake further revision of these map skills. Roberts (2013) reinforces this point:

'Many geography courses devote a lot of time when students start secondary school teaching map skills. ...What I find astonishing is that they emphasize the importance of these skills but then fail to make much use of them when investigating themes and places. ... If the skills are not used for several years, such as six-figure grid references, then students will forget how to use them. If skills are not applied in meaningful contexts students are less likely to perceive their value' (p. 58).

This issue has also been identified by Ofsted; Iwaskow (2013) noting:

'Mapwork skills continue to be poorly developed. It is not uncommon for students to be unfamiliar with Ordnance Survey maps. Maps are a basic tool of geography but few students admit to being comfortable reading or using maps. Students often inform inspectors that they rarely have the opportunity to use maps in lessons. They are expected to develop an understanding of places and issues without

being clear about where these places are, or knowing about the unique characteristics of their landscape. In far too many schools, map use is limited to specific examination requirements, rather than the progressive development of these specific geographical skills.' Ofsted (2013, pp. 53–4.)

Ofsted generic grade descriptors and supplementary subject-specific guidance for geography for inspectors stipulated that greater attention should be paid to the use of maps and, in particular, locational knowledge. Part of the 'outstanding' description for quality of teaching was:

'Maps, at a variety of scales, are used frequently as a matter of routine and are an intrinsic part of learning in geography. This ensures that students have good spatial awareness and are very secure in their ability to locate the places they are studying.' (Ofsted (2014)

This excellent statement could be incorporated into a strategic curriculum vision, forming a good starting point for planning for progress in map skills. The 'If/Then' strategy in the next column can be used to help you think through the implications of planning for progress in map skills across your curriculum.

If ... we want students who can use maps, at a variety of scales, as a matter of routine to develop good spatial awareness and become secure in their ability to locate the places they are studying.

Then ... we need to design a curriculum that introduces a range of map skills: a curriculum that provides opportunities for applying these skills in meaningful contexts, when investigating different themes and places across the units of work that make up our long-term plan. In this way students will come to see the value of these skills in helping them understand their world.

The map skills section of the Ofsted geography research and analysis review (2021) reinforces these earlier references from Ofsted and HMI:

'Integrating opportunities to develop these skills throughout the curriculum supports pupils' development of fluency and automaticity ... The more proficient a pupil is in using maps, the stronger their ability to relate to geographical concepts. For example, pupils are better able to interpret the spatial information and identify increasingly complex patterns, such as land use.'

Type of map	Year group	Topic/purpose
Climate maps	Year 8	Students analyse and create a global map showing world climate zones, and link to ocean currents.
Economic or resource maps	Year 7	Students analyse a resource map of Africa about which countries might be 'resource rich'
Physical maps	Year 7	Students analyse and use physical maps of the UK and Africa.
	Year 8	Students analyse physical maps of Brazil and Iraq.
Political maps	Year 7	All topics as introduction to and locations of, from national to international scale.
	Year 8	
OS maps	Year 7	Use 1:25,000 OS map of Pontefract area to complete a murder mystery task. Year 8 use 1:10,000 street view of Pontefract to create Ponte-opoly game.
	Year 8	
Topographic maps	Year 7	OS map, Pontefract maps and designing a car rally.
Topological maps	Year 8	Use of Worldmapper maps of World Military Expenditure for e.g. in 'The geography of conflict'.
Google Maps, Google Earth and atlases	Year 7	Use Google Maps and Google Earth on our IWB. Atlases are also used regularly.
	Year 8	

Figure 5.7: Use of maps in key stage 3 geography at The King's School. **Source:** Cook, K. (2014).

Starting from a clear vision of what a geography department is trying to achieve for students, and using a different mindset to planning with progression in mind, can lead to a more coherent approach to using maps. Cook (2014) responded to Iwaskow's comments about map skills when starting to plan her new key stage 3 curriculum. To clarify how her department could develop students' knowledge and confidence in handling a variety of maps, they produced a table (Figure 5.7). This helped them think about progression and developing students' abilities to interpret different maps at a variety of scales and in different contexts.

Aston and Renshaw (2014) explained how in their 2014 programme of study they included an enquiry into land use in Leicester, explicitly developing OS map skills during year 7. They hoped this would lay a solid foundation of OS map skills, but intended for map skills to be featured at every available opportunity in geography lessons. They subscribed to Digimap for Schools to assist with this process.

You can use the curriculum planning grid (Figure 5.6) to think through how you will progress opportunities for your students to apply these map skills. Gardner (2015) has produced a guidance booklet, published by the OS, that includes a planning grid for progressing map skills across key stage 3.

The GA website (2017) includes online guidance about planning for progress in OS map skills that would be useful to consider in your planning process.

2 Planning for progress in geographical understanding interweaving place-based units

The GNC (DfE, 2013) lists the content of world contextual knowledge for key stage 3 as follows:

Pupils should be taught:

Locational knowledge

- extend their locational knowledge and deepen their spatial awareness of the world's countries, using maps of the world to focus on Africa, Russia, Asia (including China and India), and the Middle East, focusing on their environmental regions, including polar and hot deserts, key physical and human characteristics, countries and major cities.

It is important to consider a clear rationale for teaching these specific places, beyond the fact they are in the list of content for the GNC:

- What is the significance, or the big ideas, behind teaching about the continents of Africa and Asia, the region of the Middle East, and the country Russia?

- Have these areas been selected for the GNC for a reason?

- What is the rationale for studying at a continental scale?

- What challenges and opportunities does this bring?

The continents of Africa and Asia are dynamic regions of diversity and change, and studying these regions at this continental scale can provide students with a foundation of contextual knowledge that can be built on at GCSE, when investigating case studies for the changing economic world, or urban issues. The Middle East is a highly significant region of the world, both historically and geographically, and is constantly in the news. It is a region of great oil wealth and conflict, a region often misrepresented and misunderstood in the media: all important reasons and opportunities to be part of a coherent geography curriculum. Look for possible curriculum links with history or RE. Russia is the world's largest country in terms of area, a fact that has had a major influence on the way the country has evolved. The way 'we' see Russia and the way 'they' see 'the West' may encourage a curriculum plan that introduces key stage 3 students to global politics. The point is the curriculum content is not set in stone, and is not 'given'. There is enormous flexibility.

Some indication of the official view of the potential significance for creating place-based units of work in a key stage 3 curriculum is given in the systematic content section of GNC. This statement probably disguises the opportunity that locational or contextual knowledge provides to aid the creation a coherent curriculum:

The systematic or propositional knowledge, identified as human and physical geography in the GNC (see the box on the next page), can be interconnected with the regional or contextual knowledge of the specified places and regions to study, in order to develop and progress students' understanding of human and physical processes and how they interact. Standish (2018) explains:

'Systematic geography focuses on one geographical phenomenon or 'layer' of the Earth's surface at a time and explores how it varies with respect to other geographical layers. Regional geography examines the totality of geographical phenomena or layers, and how they are related, at a given locale or region.' (p. 68)

He provides a helpful diagram, Figure 5.8, that demonstrates the potential of place-based units to progress student understanding of concepts and ideas introduced in prior units of study: in particular, progressing understanding of how these concepts interact and are interdependent.

The Ofsted geography research and analysis review (2021), reinforces Standish's view that key features of a high-quality geography curriculum include giving students:

' ... the knowledge they need to develop an increasingly complex understanding of place. Their understanding of place helps them to connect different aspects of geography. It also gives them different perspectives through which to consider the content studied.'

Enser (2020) explains how his department has developed this idea in planning their key stage 3 curriculum, 'interweaving' systematic and regional geography. He explains:

'This gives students opportunities to retrieve information and to apply it in new situations leading to meaningful learning. Our aim is not only to make what they learn more durable, but also to move from a culture of doing (where topics are studied in isolation, rarely to be
referred to again until it is revision time) to a culture of learning, where students build up the "big picture" of geography and see the synoptic links that underpin what can seem a disparate list of topics.' (p. 16)

Enser goes on to provide examples of how this has been developed. In a year 8 unit of work on Africa, students progress understanding of development studied in year 7, as well as world climate and biomes. They begin to look at how these elements interact in this continent. He explains that:

'This approach has allowed us to show our students that geography is a distinct discipline where different elements of the subject are studied for a purpose. They now know that what they study in one lesson will be important for what comes later and that there is an expectation that they remember it so that they can apply it again.'

Enser also explains how his department is now adopting a similar approach at GCSE. The first cohort for AQA GCSE in the school were taught the content of the specification – Urban Challenges as one large unit in year 10, and then Economic World as another large unit in year 11. Now, students are taught the UK's Changing Economy in year 10, and then investigate the urban challenges faced in London in light of these changes. He feels that this has led to students making much more meaningful connections between the topics, and starting to think synoptically. Similarly, year 11 students study Nigeria's changing economy and its implications in the context of the challenges facing Lagos: Enser explains that teachers encourage students to draw parallels with the UK and London studied a year before.

Human and physical geography

- understand, through the use of detailed **place-based exemplars at a variety of scales**, the key processes in:

- physical geography relating to: geological timescales and plate tectonics; rocks, weathering and soils; weather and climate, including the change in climate from the Ice Age to the present; and glaciation, hydrology and coasts

- human geography relating to: population and urbanisation; international development; economic activity in the primary, secondary, tertiary and quaternary sectors; and the use of natural resources

- understand how human and physical processes interact to influence, and change landscapes, environments and the climate; and how human activity relies on effective functioning of natural systems.

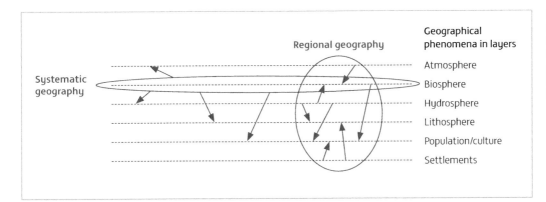

Figure 5.8:
Conceptualising
systematic
and regional
geography.
Source: Standish
(2018), p. 68.

This interweaving creates the interpretative narrative of the curriculum (Chapter 3). It brings to life Ofsted's key indicator for curriculum intent, identified at the beginning of this chapter. Interweaving systematic and regional units offers one approach to sequencing topics to develop a coherent curriculum. You can investigate further approaches developed by the five case study schools.

Key stage 4 long-term plan as a progression planning grid

The example provided by Enser for developing interweaving and sequencing at GCSE demonstrates that the principles of curriculum design outlined in this chapter for key stage 3 apply equally at GCSE. Chapter 3, pages 46–8 highlighted the built-in progression in the government curriculum documents 5–19. Chapter 4 shows how the aims of GCSE provide a strategic vision for a GCSE curriculum. The GCSE Assessment Objectives have developed from these aims, and form the progression strands for planning a GCSE curriculum. Figure 5.9 provides a similar progression planning grid for GCSE. The age-related benchmark expectations for a 14 year-old are now at the base of the grid; the expectations for a 16 year-old at the top. Figure 3.12 in Chapter 3 demonstrates the alignment between the progression strands for key stage 3 and the GCSE AOs, that form the progression strands for this GCSE progression planning grid. The three scales of curriculum planning, explained for key stage 3, apply equally for GCSE. This grid can be used to create a curriculum 'coherently planned and sequenced towards cumulatively sufficient knowledge and skills' (Ofsted (2019a), p. 9), using the GCSE specification to align the prescribed concepts, content and skills.

Activity 5.5 provides a way of developing a synoptic overview of the GCSE specification in the department; a necessary step before using the grid to plan the curriculum.

Using the curriculum planning grids to create key performance indicators

Initially you will use the curriculum grids to create your key stage 3 and/or key stage 4 curriculum, with statements or lists of content, concepts and skills for each unit, to think through and evolve the coherence and sequencing. As this becomes established, you can begin to replace the lists with key performance indicators (KPIs). In effect, these lists identify the key elements of world contextual knowledge, understanding and skills for each sequenced unit of work that, if mastered, demonstrate students' grasp of that facet of your emerging curriculum. The KPIs outline the learning that you hope **all** students should be able to demonstrate at the end of any given unit in the curriculum plan. As a result, the KPIs are specific to an enquiry question (and unit) and relate to the relevant propositional, contextual and procedural knowledge taught in the unit. In general terms, it is expected that at the end of each unit students will be able to select and deploy appropriate and detailed contextual knowledge, apply the unit's specific geographical concept or concepts (procedural knowledge), reach a supported judgement linked to the enquiry question, and communicate their findings effectively. These are essential building blocks in learning required in a curriculum, and form a prerequisite for future learning in the coherently planned and sequenced curriculum.

ACTIVITY 5.5: GETTING TO KNOW THE GCSE SPECIFICATION TO DEVELOP A SYNOPTIC OVERVIEW ⬇

TALKING POINT: What knowledge and skills form the GCSE specification?

In a department meeting, identify the core knowledge and skills of the GCSE specification, and how it links to the GCSE aims and AOs.

PRACTICAL ACTIVITY: Work together to create a mind map to provide a synoptic overview.

To begin the planning process you can use the GCSE specification to create your own planning mind map. This represents a useful way to begin the process of curriculum-making – planning holistically to develop students who have a synoptic understanding of geography; taught by teachers that have a holistic overview of the new specification. An example is provided below.'

PRACTICAL ACTIVITY: Sequencing card sort.

Using your mind map, identify emerging themes and create cards for each. In a department meeting, lay out the cards you have created on a sheet of paper. Spend time discussing:

- a logical sequence to this content: move the cards to create the sequence

- how the content and the key concepts you have identified will be brought together to form units of work

- how many units of work will make up your GCSE plan

- how these units will be sequenced

- what should be the focus of the units of work this content will form: themes, skills, places, issues, particular experiences (e.g. individual investigations), fieldwork, or a mixture of all

- how skills and fieldwork opportunities can be integrated across units to ensure students make progress in the skills.

Lay out the cards sorted into a final agreed sequence; take a photo of it as this will be important to begin to create a key stage plan.

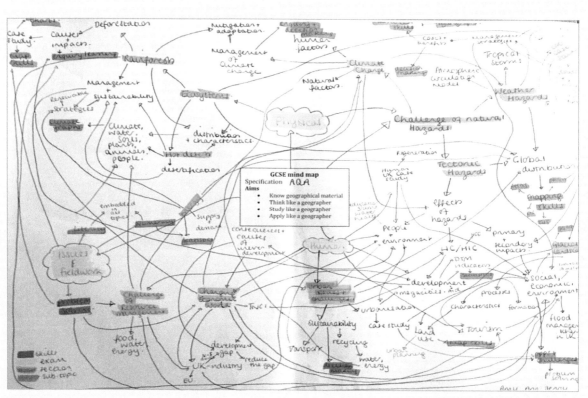

Key stage 4 plan	GCSE AOs	AO1 know geographical material. Demonstrate knowledge of locations, places, processes, environments and different scales. **15%**	AO2 think like a geographer. Demonstrate geographical understanding of concepts and how they are used in relation to places, environments and processes and the inter-relationships between places, environments and processes. **25%**		AO3 applying geography. Apply knowledge and understanding to interpret, analyse and evaluate geographical information and issues. **25%** AO4 study like a geographer. Select, adapt and use a variety of skills and techniques to investigate questions and issues and communicate findings and to make judgements. **35%**		
	GA age-related expectations. By age 16 students should:	Have a broader and deeper understanding of locational contexts, including greater awareness of the importance of scale and the concept of global.	Gain a deeper understanding of the processes that lead to geographical changes and the multi-variate nature of human-physical relationships and the interactions between them, with a stronger focus on forming valid generalisations and abstractions together with a growing awareness of the importance of theoretical perspectives and conceptual frameworks in geography.		Be able to plan and undertake independent enquiry in which skills, knowledge and understanding are applied to investigate geographical questions and show competence in a range of intellectual and communication skills, including the formulation of arguments, that include elements of synthesis and evaluation of material.		

Year	Term	Time	Units of work	Locational contexts	Physical geography process, landform	Human geography process	Physical/ human interaction	Interpret, analyse, evaluate	Geographical skills	Fieldwork
11										
10										
		GA age-related expectations. By age 14 students should:	Have extensive knowledge relating to a wide range of places, environments and features at a variety of scales, extending from local to global.	Understand the physical and human conditions and processes which lead to the development of, and change in, a variety of geographical systems, features and places. They can explain various ways in which places are linked and the impact such links have on people and environments. They can make connections between different geographical phenomena they have studied.			Be able, with increasing independence, to choose and use a wide range of data to help investigate, interpret, make judgements and draw conclusions about geographical questions, issues and problems and express and engage with different points of view about these.			

Figure 5.9: Curriculum planning grid to create a key stage 4 long-term plan with progression in mind. ⤓

Re-visiting a KPI can provide opportunities to:

■ demonstrate mastery *

■ address any gaps in learning

■ widen and deepen learning as students apply their knowledge in a different context or tackle more complex interconnections between concepts.

* Mastery means that students should be able to recall and apply what they have learnt in the future, rather than just at the time they first meet an idea or technique.

The removal of levels (a system of progression and assessment separate to the curriculum) allows for the planning of a curriculum with assessment more naturally placed at its heart. Using the curriculum planning grid to record KPIs forges a clear and coherent relationship between the 'what to teach' and designing the 'what of student achievement' (Figure 5.11 is an example). This makes assessment transparent to all stake-holders.

CURRICULUM (what to teach) → (Schemes, lesson plans and lessons in school) → KPIs (what to assess against)

Figure 5.10: Relationship between curriculum and KPIs.

No.	Unit	Contextual world knowledge	Understanding — Physical geography	Human geography	Physical-human interaction	Competence in geographical enquiry — Skills
8	Population	Know the global distribution of population, and location of the world's major cities		Demonstrate understanding of the geographical concepts and ideas – population distribution, change, growth, migration, urbanisation Appreciate that population change occurs at different rates and times in different countries Apply the Demographic Transition Model and a migration model in different contexts Identify how countries attempt to control population change Appreciate the decisions that people make to migrate Demonstrate how migration changes settlements Identify the interconnections between population change, use of natural resources and development		Interpret statistics, graphs, models, population density maps, population pyramids, to investigate population Consider decisions that people make to change Identify the latitude and longitude of cities Compare OS maps of different scales Use a range of historical data Identify change, comparing 1890 OS maps with a current OS map Identify and explain the world pattern of population distribution
7	Development	Identify global patterns of development, locating countries in different states of development Identify regional inequality in the UK		Demonstrate an understanding of the concept of development and appreciate different definitions of development Appreciate that development occurs at different rates and times in different countries Understand that there are regional disparities of development within countries Identify reasons for poverty, including gender inequality Explain how organisations work to support development Further develop understanding of the concept of sustainability, investigating sustainable development goals		Use a Development Compass Rose to classify indicators of development Interpret statistics, Dollar Street website and choropleth maps to investigate patterns of development at different scales Communicate understanding of development and use new terminology Apply understanding of causes of poverty to Nepal

Figure 5.11: Extract of a grid showing progression in terms of KPIs, across part of a key stage 3 curriculum plan. ⬇

Scheme of work/plan – unit title

This could be an enquiry question which captures the essence of what the unit is trying to achieve. A key aspect of the reflection phase of the unit can involve students answering this overarching unit enquiry question. This will demonstrate students' interconnected understanding of the sequence of lessons.

About the unit

This sets out the main focus of teaching and learning. It makes clear the responsibilities of the unit in terms of introducing and progressing contextual, propositional and procedural knowledge, the three progression strands.

Prior learning

The foundation of cumulative knowledge or schemata that this unit is planning to build upon for each progression strand. It is really important to clearly identify this knowledge. Teachers and students will work together in the implementation of this unit plan to make connections with this prior knowledge in order to integrate new knowledge into the students' long-term memory. This is a vital element in the process of becoming a geographer.

Links to 2014 National Curriculum

Identifies how the unit plan links to different sections of the geography national curriculum.

Eg locational knowledge, geographical skills and fieldwork

Key learning

Identifies the key learning objectives for the unit, to be shared with students.

Key geographical terminology

This sets out the relationship between students' developing understanding and use of language, and the knowledge and skills in the unit. It lists the key vocabulary and language concepts that students will be required to articulate and incorporate as they write at length. This vocabulary will build on that developed in prior learning. Students can be encouraged to develop their own glossary for each unit.

Geographical data

A key aspect of the plan is to establish and collect together, a wide range of geographical data, both primary and secondary sources, to use in each lesson in the sequence.

Future learning at key stage 3

It is important to be clear how the responsibilities for progress in a unit of work, are to be further progressed in future units. Sharing this with students is an important part of making clear the purpose of learning towards the end goal or destination of the curriculum journey.

Key aspects of student achievement

- **Contextual world knowledge**
  Details relating to the unit
- **Understanding of conditions, processes and environments**
  Details relating to the unit
- **Competence in geographical enquiry and skills**
  Details relating to the unit

These are broad descriptions of what most students will know and be able to do at the end of the unit, for each progression strand. They could be the KPIs copied across from the long-term plan. They also describe the range of responses that might be achieved by those attaining above or below the standard expected, related to the age-related benchmark statements

Assessment opportunities

The activities in each of the sequence of lessons, will provide opportunities for informal ongoing assessment as pupils make sense of geographical data. Each unit can also provide a more in depth more formal assessment that provides opportunity for pupils to demonstrate their understanding of the overarching objectives for the unit, linked to the unit enquiry question title.

Websites

Key resources to use in units are often online. This section of the unit plan provides a place to record the urls of these websites, and update where necessary.

Future learning at GCSE

The KS3 curriculum develops a foundation of knowledge, understanding and skills to prepare pupils for the next stage of learning at GCSE. Mapping this out and sharing this with pupils, again makes clear the purpose of learning.

Figure 5.12: A unit plan overview explaining the function of each element. A blank version of this scheme of work/plan is available to download. ⬇

Creating unit plans for learning towards the vision

QCA (2000) explained the function of a unit plan as:

'... medium-term plan, usually designed for a term or less. It identifies learning objectives derived from the programme of study, suggests activities to meet these and describes the outcomes of pupils' learning. The sequence of learning objectives and activities promotes progression within the unit. Each unit includes an estimate of the time it will take to teach.

The activities within a unit go some way towards setting out short-term plans. They will need supplementing with lesson plans to match individual class requirements, for example, pupils' different abilities and resources available.' (p. 5)

Long- and medium-term planning involves all staff in a department working together to ensure coherence and curriculum continuity. Short-term planning is the responsibility of individual teachers, who build on the medium-term plan, taking account of the needs of students.

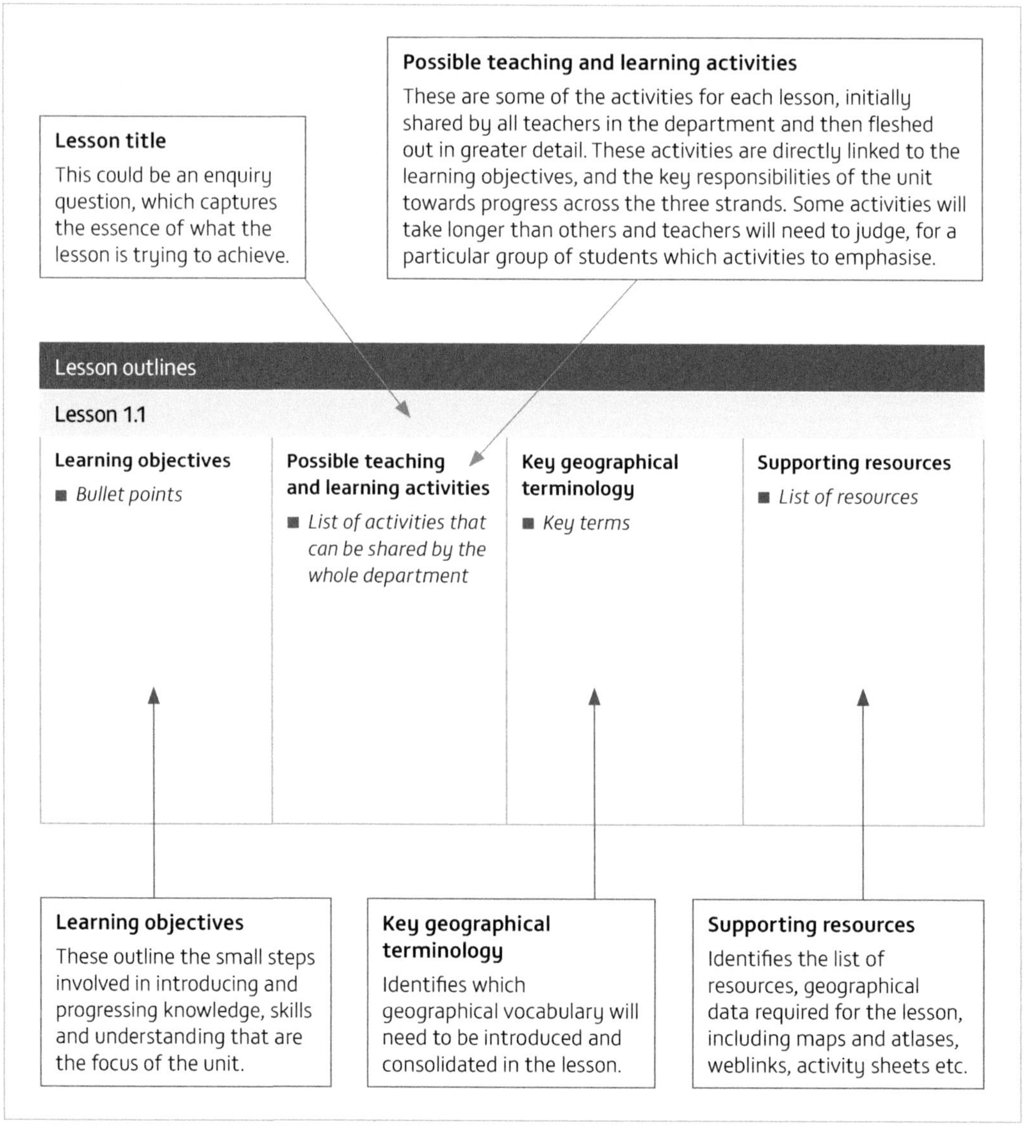

Lesson title
This could be an enquiry question, which captures the essence of what the lesson is trying to achieve.

Possible teaching and learning activities
These are some of the activities for each lesson, initially shared by all teachers in the department and then fleshed out in greater detail. These activities are directly linked to the learning objectives, and the key responsibilities of the unit towards progress across the three strands. Some activities will take longer than others and teachers will need to judge, for a particular group of students which activities to emphasise.

Lesson outlines

Lesson 1.1

Learning objectives
- Bullet points

Possible teaching and learning activities
- List of activities that can be shared by the whole department

Key geographical terminology
- Key terms

Supporting resources
- List of resources

Learning objectives
These outline the small steps involved in introducing and progressing knowledge, skills and understanding that are the focus of the unit.

Key geographical terminology
Identifies which geographical vocabulary will need to be introduced and consolidated in the lesson.

Supporting resources
Identifies the list of resources, geographical data required for the lesson, including maps and atlases, weblinks, activity sheets etc.

Figure 5.13:
Lesson outline – part of a unit plan. A blank version of this lesson outline is available to download. ⬇

The responsibilities assigned to each unit for providing the coherent curriculum 'narrative' should already have been established in the department's long-term plan. This should be a collaborative venture across the department. It would also be useful to collaborate on a sketch outline for each medium-term unit plan, including: an enquiry question; unit title; key learning; number and possible sequence of lesson; ideas for key resources – geographical data including maps and potential for using atlases, GIS and websites. Once established, different teachers can be given responsibility to flesh out this sketch in more detail. Each unit plan can be shared on the school network. Opportunities can be provided for all teachers in the department to make further contributions. The unit plan needs to be seen as an evolving document. It represents an excellent way to share and record ideas and resources, such as websites, perhaps with evaluation comments about what works, and ways the sequence of lessons could be amended in light of each experience in implementing the plan.

Conclusion

Once you have completed Stages 1–4 of the curriculum design process, the curriculum intent should be clear. You now know what you want your students to achieve, in the long- and medium-terms. You hope you have created coherent and sequenced plans, towards cumulatively sufficient knowledge and skills for future learning and employment.

The test of the plan is the next stage in the design process: its implementation, the way it is taught and experienced by students in the classroom. Inevitably you will need to evaluate and adapt the intended plan in light of this interaction in the classroom, as the next chapter shows. Before embarking on this stage, however, it is useful to consider how Ofsted will inspect curriculum intent, including the grade descriptors provided in the Ofsted School Inspection Handbook (2019b) in particular pages 41–8. You can use this to reflect on the progress you have made in establishing your curriculum intent.

What is clear from these statements is that Ofsted regard sequencing to be very significant in designing a coherent curriculum to support student progress.

ACTIVITY 5.6: REFLECTION ACTIVITY

You could present the Ofsted grade descriptors and the following extracts from school inspection reports in a department meeting for your colleagues to identify key points about designing a coherent curriculum.

The team could be encouraged to apply the statements to your curriculum intent – as a reflection process, before embarking on stage 5 curriculum implementation.

Extracts from a number of school inspection reports for the 2019 EIF provide a flavour of what inspectors are seeing and looking for in schools:

- Students' learning in some subjects is not sequenced coherently. Teachers should ensure that curriculum plans for all subjects contain the knowledge, understanding and skills that students should know in a logical order.

- Across the curriculum, students are not always able to remember or describe their learning well enough. Leaders should ensure that students can use subject-specific vocabulary to explain their thinking confidently and accurately.

- The school's curriculum in a few subjects, for example in business studies, modern foreign languages, mathematics and geography, is not as well sequenced as it is in English. The plans do not always help students to build securely on what they already know. Leaders need to ensure that the quality of planning across subjects matches that seen in English.

- Subject leaders make sure that teachers know how subjects should be taught and provide teachers with professional development, support and training. Leaders draw upon support from the trust, for example to help non-specialist teachers to develop their knowledge of the subjects that they teach.

References

All websites last accessed 27/07/2021.

Aston, R. and Renshaw, S. (2014) 'Planning a new key stage 3', *Teaching Geography*, 39, 2, pp. 64–5.

Cook, K. (2014) 'Planning a new key stage 3', *Teaching Geography*, 39, 1, pp. 16–17.

DfE (2013) 'National curriculum in England: Geography programmes of study: key stage 3'. Available at https://assets.publishing.service.gov.uk/government/uploads/system/uploads/attachment_data/file/239087/SECONDARY_national_curriculum_-_Geography.pdf

DfE (2014) *GCSE subject content for geography*. Available at www.gov.uk/government/publications/gcse-geography

Digimap for Schools. Available at https://digimapforschools.edina.ac.uk

Enser, M. (2020) 'Interweaving geography: retrieval, spacing and interleaving in the geography curriculum', *Teaching Geography*, 45, 1, pp. 15–17.

Gardner, D. (2015) *Key Stage 3: Planning for pupil progress*. Available at https://dfsresources.edina.ac.uk/resource/planning-pupil-progress-ks3-geography

Geographical Association website (2017) 'Maps and Mapping' online guidance on planning for progress in OS map skills. Available at www.geography.org.uk/Curriculum/Mapping

Geographical Association (2020) *A progression framework for geography*. Available at www.geography.org.uk/A-Progression-Framework-for-Geography

Gleen, J. (2020) 'Geography's intent: developing your curriculum', *Teaching Geography*, 45, 3, pp. 108–10.

Iwaskow, L. (2013) 'Geography: a fragile environment?', *Teaching Geography*, 38, 2, pp. 53–5.

Jankell, L.D., Sandahl, J. and Örbring, D.(2021) 'Organising concepts in geography education: a model', *Geography*, 106, 2, pp. 66–75. Available at https://doi.org/10.1080/00167487.2021.1919406

Lambert, D. and Morgan, J. (2010) *Teaching Geography 11–18: A conceptual approach*. Maidenhead: Open University Press.

Ofsted (2014) 'Geography survey visits: Supplementary subject-specific guidance for inspectors on making judgements during visits to schools'. Available at www.geography.org.uk/download/ga_ofsted%20subject-specific%20guidance%20for%20geography%20(dec%202013).pdf

Ofsted (2019a) Education Inspection Framework. Available at https://www.gov.uk/government/collections/education-inspection-framework

Ofsted (2019b) *School inspection handbook: Handbook for inspecting schools in England under section 5 of the Education Act 2005*. Available at https://www.gov.uk/government/publications/school-inspection-handbook-eif

Ofsted (2021) Research review: geography. Available at www.gov.uk/government/publications/research-review-series-geography/research-review-series-geography

QCA (2000) *Geography: A scheme of work for key stage 3 Teacher's guide*. Available at https://webarchive.nationalarchives.gov.uk/20100512134450/http://www.standards.dfes.gov.uk/schemes2/secondary_geography/?view=get

Roberts, M. (2013) *Geography Through Enquiry*. Sheffield: Geographical Association.

Standish, A. (2018) 'The place of regional geography' in Jones, M. and Lambert, D. (eds) *Debates in Secondary Geography* (2nd edition), pp. 62–74. Abingdon: Routledge.

Implementation: aligning curriculum, pedagogy and assessment

 IMPLEMENTATION   **5** Teach and assess pupil progress towards the curriculum intent

Ofsted explains implementation as 'the way the intended curriculum is taught and assessed'. Ofsted (2019a), p. 41. As teachers begin to implement a new curriculum, they need to be clear on the intent, and how it is planned to support student progress towards the vision, or end point, of the key stage. It is important to think carefully about the three main elements of curriculum making (see Chapter 2, p 24–5): this helps us align the most appropriate pedagogies, resources and approaches to assessment to support the implementation of the vision.

Drawing on the idea of 'curriculum making' in helping teachers prepare for the new inspection framework, Kinder and Owens (2019), point out that particular thought needs to be given to:

- how the intent for the subject helps steer the teaching and assessment

- why specific teaching approaches have been selected, and how they are appropriate for all students

- how specialist aspects, such as the provision of fieldwork across the curriculum, help build knowledge and skills

- the subject and specialist pedagogical knowledge of those teaching geography in the school – and what is being done to support them.

Reflection

As part of implementation strategy, it is important that your geography department reflects on quality approaches to teaching and learning. This provides a useful starting point to aligning curriculum, pedagogy and assessment to achieve your intended vision. A curriculum designed to develop students who can think geographically will embed powerful knowledge, enacting the ideas introduced in Chapter 2, pp. 25–9, and Chapter 3, pp. 36–43. In particular, it will require a well-structured curriculum underpinned by geographical concepts, engaging students in enquiry learning, fieldwork, use of a range of media and maps to investigate places, people and issues, at a variety of scales. Margaret Roberts in her article 'Geographical education is powerful if …' (2017a) emphasises the significance of what she calls 'powerful pedagogy': giving 'power' to your students to think geographically. She concludes:

'If geographical education is to be powerful, then it demands a powerful pedagogy. Pedagogy is influenced by what are considered to be the purposes of education and by ideas about learning. I consider that the key purposes of geographical education are to enable students to think geographically and to develop a critical understanding of the world.' (p. 8)

Your reflection process regarding this pedagogy can benefit from considering what quality geography teaching looks like, as well as how far your existing approaches to pedagogy are 'powerful'. Ofsted (2014) published subject-specific grade descriptors for each National Curriculum subject, including geography, to provide additional guidance for schools and inspectors. Although published before the latest curriculum review, these grade descriptors for outstanding quality of teaching still represent a useful starting point for this reflection process.

The activity below uses the principles from the Ofsted geography research review (2021) to support your thinking about curriculum implementation, to bring your intent to life for your students. You can use it to identify aspects of teaching that your department feels will be important to the implementation of your curriculum intent, together with aspects where the department may need professional development. The department will inevitably think of other aspects that they feel are significant in developing appropriate pedagogical approaches to support your students to achieve your vision.

ACTIVITY 6.1: THINKING ABOUT HOW TO IMPLEMENT THE CURRICULUM INTENT ⬇

TALKING POINT: What are the key aspects of our curriculum intent vision?

In order to implement your curriculum intent, teachers in the department will need consider the most appropriate pedagogical approaches to support students in the classroom to achieve your agreed vision or end point for students by the end of the key stage.

In a department meeting or training day session discuss current strategies used in the classroom, using the following questions:

- How do we need to improve our subject knowledge for our intended curriculum?

- How will our teaching embed secure understanding, and support the ability for our students to think geographically?

- How will our approaches to assessment support this understanding?

- What resources and specialist approaches will we need?

- Which teaching approaches will work best in different units, to achieve our goals?

PRACTICAL ACTION

The table on page 101 shows a sample from the Ofsted geography research review (2021) of the features of a high-quality geography curriculum. Download the table on the next page (see page 3 for details) and add more to it as you think relevant. Identify your department's priorities to successfully implement your curriculum intent, as well as the professional development needs, for each member of the department. The Ofsted review (2021) makes clear the importance of professional development: '... the most critical factor in ensuring a high-quality geographical education is teachers' subject knowledge... As geography is a dynamic subject, the need to maintain both up-to-date subject knowledge and also to engage in

discourse about the nature of the subject and pedagogy are key. Many authors identify the supportive role of the Geographical Association and the Royal Geographical Society (with the Institute of British Geographers) in this regard.'

PRACTICAL ACTION: Professional development

The Geographical Association offers a wide range of publications, resources and face-to-face and online training to support your professional development needs so you can implement your curriculum, including:

- **professional publications:** *The Handbook of Secondary Geography, Assessing your KS3 geography curriculum, Geography through Enquiry*

- **journals: Teaching Geography:** includes a wide range of articles by teachers about implementing the curriculum

- **practical teaching resources:** KS3 Teacher Toolkits; GCSE Geography Teacher's Toolkits, website Teaching Resources

- **Annual Conference:** www.geography.org.uk/GA-Annual-Conference-and-Exhibition

- **online CPD:** for example, planning for progress in using OS maps: www.geography.org.uk/Curriculum/Mapping

- **CPD training courses:** designing your curriculum, fieldwork, etc.

- **ITE section of GA website:** support for trainees and ECTs provides an array of material to use as a mentor of trainees, but can also be used to support ECTs and non-specialist teachers to understand how best to teach geography, particularly the 'Learning to teach geography' section: www.geography.org.uk/Learning-to-teach-geography

- **bespoke GA consultancy:** www.geography.org.uk/consultancy-services

Example features of a high quality geography curriculum taken from the Ofsted geography research review (2021) (add others to your own version of this table)	Which descriptors are most important to implementing our curriculum intent vision?	Which descriptors are important for professional development
■ In developing students' disciplinary knowledge, teachers' plans allow students to take a holistic view of the content studied and recognise the interconnectedness of different geographical content.		
■ Place knowledge is prioritised in the geography curriculum. It brings meaning to locations and processes studied.		
■ Students' procedural knowledge (geographical skills) allows them to gather, analyse, present and interpret spatial information. In doing so, they are adept at identifying patterns and trends.		
■ The experience of fieldwork draws together students' locational knowledge and that of human and physical processes. It supports students to appreciate the interplay between them.		

Key elements of implementing a coherent geography curriculum 11–16

The GA Manifesto *A Different View* (2009) is very clear about the significance of geographical enquiry and fieldwork in the implementation of a geography curriculum:

> 'The GA believes in geographical enquiry: that is, in students as active participants and investigators, not just the passive recipients of knowledge. ... Enquiry and investigation lie at the heart of geographical thinking... Fieldwork – that is, learning directly in the untidy real world outside the classroom – is an essential component of geography education. There is no substitute for "real world learning" – at least for some of the time. In geography this is manifest in a special way: we call it fieldwork, although it is not always conducted in fields!' (p. 19 and p. 23)

Weeden and Lambert (2006) make the point that good geography lessons should provide students with access to rich and varied resources of geographical data, opportunities for enquiry in the real world, and utilise the potential of technologies to support data handling, processing and communication. They maintain that formative assessment approaches should be shaped by these priorities; in other words, using formative assessment to determine how far learning in lessons is supporting students to progress towards the curriculum intent.

The rest of this chapter focuses on several key elements of the implementation of a coherent geography curriculum 11–16:

- ■ geographical enquiry
- ■ resources – integrating the use of a wide range of geographical data. The use of maps as a matter of routine was explained in the last chapter (pp. 87–89)
- ■ integrating and planning for progression in fieldwork opportunities
- ■ approaches to assessment.

For each element an introduction is provided, signposting ways you can dig deeper to improve your implementation strategy.

Geographical enquiry

Margaret Roberts (Roberts, 2012), in her lecture at the 2011 Annual Conference, identified three essential aspects of a good geography lesson. These were based on 30 years observing many geography lessons, both in her role as PGCE tutor at the University of Sheffield and as External Examiner for geography PGCE courses. They represent a holistic professional judgement of a lesson, rather than checking it against any external terminology or lists of standards. The following provides an overview of her perspective; a full read of the article will be very helpful to thinking through your approach to implementation.

1. There needs to be some geography in the lesson

The geography in a lesson will be represented by at least one of the following, and it may include all of them.

- **Geographical data**. This includes maps, visual data of all kinds, statistics, graphs, text, etc. It can be in textbooks, resource sheets, Power-Point presentations or on the internet. She maintains that students need to use geographical data to help them understand the complex world in which we live.

- **Geographical ideas**. These may be generalisations, concepts, theories; and they should underpin the lesson. 'I think that every geography lesson should introduce students to some geographical ideas. Geographers make sense of the world through their ideas ...' (p. 3)

- **Locational context**. Students should know the location of the places they are studying in a wider context. 'I think that what is studied in geography lessons should be located and placed within a wider context. Places, regions, countries and continents do not exist in isolation but are interconnected; the location of what is studied in relation to other places is significant. The contrast between the way that TV news programmes are generated and the geography lessons I have observed is striking. TV news programmes always locate the places which are being reported, starting with the globe, then moving in closer and then closer still. ... I have never seen geography teachers use PowerPoint to zoom in like this to what they are studying, to

place it in relation to other places or comment on the significance of a place's location. I rarely see atlases, globes or wall maps used.' (p. 4)

Regular use of Google Earth, initially focussed on the school location, typing the location to be studied in the lesson, and then allowing the software to zoom out from your school to a global view and then zoom in on the location, allows this to be done with ease. It can have a great impact on your students, connecting them with a new place to investigate.

2. There needs to be a connection with the learners' minds

'The emphasis of most planning and teaching is on getting students to know and understand what is in teachers' minds, to learn what they have planned for a unit of work. I think that it is equally important for teachers to get to know what is in students' minds. This is because if teachers are to plan for students to make progress in geography, then they need to know students' current capabilities: what they already know, understand and can do.' (p. 5)

The geography teacher should pay attention to:

- eliciting what students already know and understand about the geography

- checking and correcting misunderstandings

- finding out students' opinions and feelings

- supporting students' learning and progress.

3. There needs to be an opportunity for learners to make sense of new geographical knowledge for themselves

The geography teacher will:

- give students time to explore new geographical information and relate it to what they already know

- allow students to discuss ideas and geographical data with each other and the teacher

- ask for extended writing so that students need to sort out geographical information and ideas and make links between them.

The ideas Margaret presented relate geographical enquiry to constructivism and educational thinkers such as Piaget, Bruner and particularly Vygotsky – learners need to build on ideas they already have in order to understand new knowledge. Learning occurs through a process of actively constructing a world for the learner, by making sense of what happens during the process. The learner needs to be actively involved in their own learning. Ferretti (2018) explains that 'The role of the teacher is vital, by creating situations which will challenge young people and enable them to improve their understanding; providing information which has no connection with the learner's current view will soon be forgotten.' (p. 116) An enquiry approach can progress understanding, altering the long-term memory, as explained in Chapter 3, pages 50–51.

All five case study schools in Chapter 8 incorporate thinking geographically and enquiry into their vision statements, as well as referring to how an enquiry approach is embedded into the implementation of their intended curriculum.

Margaret Roberts' book *Geography through Enquiry* (2013) begins by outlining her thinking about enquiry. Most importantly, she states:

'I think of enquiry not simply as a set of skills but as an approach to teaching and learning geography ... when students are learning geography through enquiry, they extend their geographical knowledge and understanding at the same time as they learn skills. I think that what students learn and how they learn are inextricably related; I do not think that the curriculum can be separated from pedagogy. How students learn influences what they learn. When we plan an enquiry-based unit of work, we have to focus on both what is being invest-igated and how it is to be investigated.' (p. 8)

Roberts identifies four elements of an enquiry approach to learning geography (Figure 6.1):

1. Question-driven, to spark curiosity and create a need to know

2. To answer the key question students need study geographical data.

3. Opportunities need to be provided to make sense of this data, and make connections.

4. Students need to reflect on what they have learnt.

In Figure 6.2 the curriculum-making diagram has been aligned with geographical enquiry to help think through planning with an enquiry approach.

ACTIVITY 6.2: HOW DOES OUR CURRICULUM INTENT RELATE TO GEOGRAPHICAL ENQUIRY? ⬇

TALKING POINT: What are the key aspects of our curriculum intent vision?

Chapter 4 (pp. 65–68) explained the significance of critical think-ing in terms of creating a curriculum intent designed to develop students' geographical thinking capabilities. Geographical enquiry is fundamental to this thinking. Margaret Roberts makes it clear that adopting enquiry is much more than adding the odd one or two activities into unit plans; it is more a way of life.

In a department meeting or training day session discuss current strategies used in the classroom, using the following types of questions:

- What is our current understanding of geographical enquiry?

- How does our curriculum intent relate to geographical enquiry?

- How far do we currently embed an enquiry approach in the implementation of our curriculum? Is this enough?

- Do we have a culture of enquiry in our classrooms?

- Do our students actively engage in investigating geographical questions?

- What geographical data are they using?

- Does our curriculum plan for progress in geographical enquiry?

PRACTICAL ACTION: Professional development

The Geographical Association offers a wide range of publica-tions, resources and face-to-face and online training to support your thinking and understanding of geographical enquiry, and how it relates to your curriculum intent:

- Listen to Margaret Roberts talking to John Lyon about her career path as well as her views about the importance of enquiry learning in the GA's GeogPod Series 1, Episode 2 at https://www.geography.org.uk/GeogPod-The-GAs-Podcast

- The GA website provides online guidance and support about enquiry learning at https://www.geography.org.uk/Geographical-enquiry-in-the-classroom

- GA ITE guidance 'Why and how to teach geography' includes an excellent overview of geographical enquiry at https://www.geography.org.uk/Why-and-how-to-teach-geography

- Geography through Enquiry: Approaches to teaching and learning in the secondary school (Roberts, 2013) is the key resource to help all teachers of geography in a department to develop enquiry in their classroom, providing a wide range of practical approaches to enquiry learning.

Enquiry is question-driven	**Enquiry is supported by evidence**

Enquiry is question-driven
The teacher sparks curiosity, creating a need to know. Students:

- are curious
- speculate
- hypothesise
- use imagination
- generate ideas
- identify issues
- ask questions
- plan how to research

Enquiry is supported by evidence
The teacher enables students to use sources of geographical information as evidence. Students:

- search for information
- collect evidence
- select evidence
- sort information
- classify information

Enquiry requires thinking geographically
The teacher provides opportunities for students to make sense and exercise reasoning. Students:

- relate existing knowledge to new knowledge
- describe
- explain
- compare
- contrast
- analyse
- interpret
- recognise relationships
- analyse values
- clarify values
- reach conclusions

Enquiry is reflective
The teacher provides opportunities for both students and teacher to reflect on learning. Students are critical in relation to:

- sources of information
- skills and techniques used
- criteria for making judgements
- opinions
- what has been learnt
- how it has been learnt
- how the enquiry could be improved
- how the enquiry could be further developed
- the value of what has been learnt

Figure 6.1: Four elements of an enquiry approach to learning geography through enquiry. **Source:** Roberts (2013), p. 9.

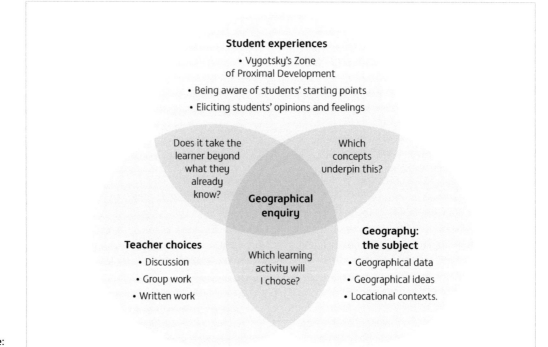

Figure 6.2: Enquiry and curriculum making. **Source:** R Kitchen.

Figure 6.2 brings to life Roberts' assertion that enquiry is more of a whole approach to teaching and learning rather than of a set of skills. This is an approach that should clearly link to your vision for your curriculum intent at key stage 3 and GCSE in working towards a coherent 11–16 geography curriculum.

The Ofsted research and analysis review (2021) highlights the significance of enquiry, stating that in a high-quality geography education:

■ Students are proficient in carrying out enquiries and decision-making exercises because they are secure in the prior knowledge they need for these.

■ The enquiry approach supports the development of students' disciplinary knowledge. For example, 'it increases their capacity to recognise and ask geographical questions, to critique sources, and to reflect on what they have learned, as well as the methods used'.

Enquiry in the NC and GCSE

The National Curriculum for Geography (2013) identifies enquiry in the aims and the geography statement and outline of content. At GCSE level, enquiry is evident in the aims for GCSE, progression statement, and in the subject content, scope of study and geographical skills listed.

Yet approaches to enquiry and using data at GCSE level can be confused, as illustrated by an analysis of key points from the 2019 Examiners' Reports to help improve student performance at GCSE. Different awarding bodies made comments about sources of information, such as '… when describing resources such as maps and graphs, candidates should make use of the information provided. Accurate reference to data, scale, compass directions will gain credit' (Eduqas A, 2020, p. 24). Rather worryingly, however, the following advice was provided for teachers in Examiners' Reports: 'Rehearsing how to respond to statistical data, different types of graph and a range of maps at different scales is important prior to taking the exam (AQA, 2020, p. 24). 'Teachers should practise using a variety of different graphs with candidates throughout the geography course' (Edexcel B, 2020, p. 24). This is very much a 'teaching to the test' mentality, seeing enquiry as a skill in a silo, to be 'rehearsed' and 'practised' for the exam. Rynne *et al.* make it clear

that enquiry and making sense of geographical data is a key element of curriculum design, linked to the aims of GCSE as the vision for the intent of a GCSE curriculum:

> *'However, practising for the exam should not take the place of designing a coherent GCSE geography curriculum. The curriculum should be planned at a strategic level to enable students to know geographical material, think like a geographer, study like a geographer and apply what they have learnt. In this curriculum experience, using geographical data is embedded and progressed in each unit of work, rather than rehearsed for the exam.'* (p. 24)

Embedding enquiry at the three scales of curriculum planning

Look back at Chapter 5, page 84, which refers to the three scales of curriculum planning. In effect your strategic long-term plan can be viewed as one large-scale enquiry, taking students towards the vision of your intent at the end of the key stage. Each unit of work or 'chunk' of the vision can be approached as an enquiry, with the unit title being an enquiry question, which students are ultimately empowered to answer in a reflective lesson at the end of the unit. Each lesson in the sequence that makes up the unit provides important stepping stones of geographical data, and opportunities to make sense of it. These can be carefully crafted into the unit plan to support students towards thinking geographically to support their capability to answer the unit enquiry question. Roberts (2017b) explains 'At the end of a unit of work, bringing together all aspects of the enquiry gives students opportunities to make connections between what they have learnt in each lesson and to reflect on their learning.' (p. 58). Roberts goes on to identify ten questions, though not necessarily in this order, to consider when planning lessons or units of work for enquiry:

1. What aspects of geography should be included?

Roberts set out a spider diagram with the categories she would recommend to help decide on these aspects (Figure 6.3).

2. What is your role to be?

The different roles are summarised in Figure 6.4.

3. What kind of questions should frame a unit of work?

Figure 6.3: Brainstorming ideas about what geography to include in a unit of work. **Source:** Roberts (2017b), p. 50.

Which of geography's big ideas could underpin this unit?

Place; space; scale; environment; landscape

Physical processes; human processes

Change and development; globalisation; sustainability; inequality

Interdependence

Which specialist concepts do students need to understand?

E.g. a unit of work on coasts might include: abrasion, attrition, hydraulic action, longshore drift, swash, backwash, etc.

What aspects of geography should be included?

Context and locational knowledge

What contexts (local, national, international) will be referred to?

What place names and locations will be referred to?

Which case studies might be used?

Taking into account:

- availability of source materials
- availability of up-to-date statistics
- risks of stereotyping places.

Figure 6.4: The role of the teacher in enquiry-based approaches to learning geography.

	Strongly guided	Framed	Negotiated
Role of teacher and student	More teacher guidance/less student self-direction	Some teacher guidance/some student self-direction	Less teacher guidance/more student self-direction
Enquiry is question-driven	Focus of enquiry and questions decided by teacher	Teacher devises activities to encourage students to identify questions or sub-questions	Students devise questions and sub-questions and negotiate them with teachers
Using geographical sources as evidence	Geographical sources chosen by teacher	Students select some sources or select relevant data from given sources	Students given support by teachers to find own sources
Thinking geographically	All activities devised by teacher	Teacher introduces students to techniques and conceptual frameworks, which they learn to use selectively	Students decide how to analyse and interpret data
Conclusions and reflections	Teacher checks conclusions reached	Students discuss conclusions they have reached	Students reach own conclusions and evaluate them critically
Summary	The teacher controls the construction of knowledge by making all decisions about content, data, activities and conclusions	Teacher inducts students into ways in which geographical knowledge is constructed. Students are made aware of choices and are encouraged to be critical	Students are enabled, with teacher guidance, to investigate questions of interest to themselves and to evaluate their conclusions critically

4. What knowledge and skills do students already have related to this unit of work?

5. What sources of geographical information can the students use as evidence?

6. Will students work as a class, in groups, or individually?

7. What kinds of classroom activities would be appropriate for this unit of work?

8. What are the students expected to learn?

9. How is learning to be assessed?

10. How can final activities and reflection help students learn through enquiry?

You can use the overview of geographical enquiry provided here together with the references to dig deeper into how your curriculum intent relates to enquiry by using Activity 6.2.

Resources – integrating the use of a wide range of geographical data

Using resources is an essential element of geographical enquiry. In *Geography Through Enquiry* (2013) Roberts identifies the wide variety of geographical information available (Figure 6.5). Geography is very fortunate in terms of the range and quality of resources it offers. Biddulph, Lambert and Balderstone (2015) provide a detailed overview of many of these resources in Chapter 6: Resources. Rayner (2017), in Chapter 12 of the *Handbook of Secondary Geography*, also provides an excellent critical overview of the resources available to the geography teacher. In Chapter 5 (pp. 87–9) of this book, planning for progress in using maps is explained. There is not the space in this book to provide more than a snapshot of how using a wide range of resources can significantly enhance the implementation of curriculum intent.

Figure 6.5:
Various forms of representation and sources of geographical information.
Source: Roberts (2013), p. 52.

Sources of information

Images
- Photographs
- Paintings and drawings
- Film
- Diagrams
- Cartoons
- TV advertisements
- Satellite images
- Google Street View

Words
- Textbook descriptions and accounts
- Magazine and journal articles
- Newspaper articles
- Letters
- Advertisements
- Fiction
- Poetry and lyrics of songs
- Non-fiction, e.g. travel writing
- Brochures
- Twitter

Sound
- Commentaries on film
- Recorded interviews
- Music
- Natural sounds, e.g. the Amazon rainforest soundscape

Multimedia
- Incorporating several forms of representation e.g. text, still images, animation, film, audio

Statistical data
- Tables of statistics
- Graphs (bar, pie, line, flood hydrographs, population pyramids, climate)
- Choropleth maps
- Flow line maps
- Gapminder

Maps
- Street maps, Google maps
- Topographical maps, e.g. OS maps

- Atlas maps (political, physical, thematic)
- Worldmapper
- Weather maps
- Gapminder
- Non-educational maps, e.g. in brochures, newspapers, football programmes etc.
- GIS maps

Personal knowledge
- Memories of place, including remembered images and events
- Mental maps
- Affective maps – mapping feelings about places

Objects
- Rocks
- Vegetation
- Artefacts and objects from other places
- Bags of rubbish
- Food

The Ofsted Research Review for geography (2021) highlights the importance of resources: 'Access to high-quality and up-to-date resources is an important factor in implementing the geography curriculum.'. One of the implementation indicators in the EIF makes specific reference to resources:

> '... teachers **create an environment** that allows the **learner to focus on learning**. The **resources and materials** that teachers select – in a way that does not create unnecessary workload for staff – reflect the provider's ambitious intentions for the course of study and **clearly support the intent of a coherently planned curriculum**, sequenced towards cumulatively sufficient knowledge and skills for future learning and employment.' (Ofsted, 2019a, p. 10)

As with Roberts, this indicator makes clear that teachers need to select resources with care, ensuring that they clearly link to the intent of the curriculum, and are appropriate to connect with students and where they are in their learning, to allow them to add to their knowledge towards the vision or end point of the phase of the curriculum.

The GNC (DfE 2013) content specifies the following resources in the skills section:

> ■ build on their knowledge of globes, maps and atlases and apply and develop this knowledge routinely in the classroom and in the field
>
> ■ interpret Ordnance Survey maps in the classroom and the field, including using grid references and scale, topographical and other thematic mapping, and aerial and satellite photographs
>
> ■ use Geographical Information Systems (GIS) to view, analyse and interpret places and data

The GCSE subject content emphasises maps and GIS in researching secondary evidence, including digital sources, as part of the aim to study like a geographer (p. 3):

> *Maps*
>
> *10. The use of a range of maps, atlases, Ordnance Survey maps, satellite imagery and other graphic and digital material, including the use of GIS, to obtain, illustrate, analyse and evaluate geographical information. To include making maps and sketches to present and interpret geographical information.*

Rayner (2017) makes the point that 'It isn't "what" resources you use but "how" you use them that has the greatest impact on both the teaching and the geographical learning.' (p. 150)

The ITE guidance on the GA's website for trainees and ECTs (https://www.geography.org.uk/Initial-Teacher-Education/Support-for-trainees-and-ECTs) explains the significance of using resources in the classroom:

> 'Good geography teaching very much depends on selecting the appropriate resources for the learning you want to achieve and then using them well. This means, to be a good geography teacher you must:
>
> ■ be aware of the range of resources that are available
>
> ■ be able to critically evaluate the potential of different resources as learning aids
>
> ■ know how to produce resources, or tailor existing ones, for your students' needs
>
> ■ be effective in using resources to bring about successful learning, thinking clearly about how a particular source will relate to the learning objectives for a lesson
>
> ■ be clear in what you are trying to achieve in the use of a resource.'

Resources selected by teachers present a particular view of the world. Some sources present a view or standpoint that can exhibit bias. A biased source is fine, if the point of using it is to develop students' critical thinking. Sometimes, however, it is possible to present an unfiltered news report or video clip, for example, that presents bias that is left unchallenged. The teacher needs to critically assess resources used in the classroom, but at the same time provide opportunities to develop students' critical thinking. Rayner (2017) explains:

> 'One of the most important messages that critical media literacy teaches us is "to take a second look". A "second look" can reveal bias, omissions, hidden messages and so on – students need to be taught that they are also responsible for taking a "second look" at any media presented by their teacher or researched as part of a project or homework task.' (p. 151)

These are important skills that students will need to think geographically, particularly in this technologically-driven world of mobile online 24-hour news and social media soundbites.

Technology has strengths and weaknesses. Its unfiltered nature, and often lack of provenance, does create problems such as bias, already highlighted. Technology does, however, allow the teacher to bring together a range of resources in order to facilitate more active learning. Teachers now have the opportunity to bring the outside world into the classroom, in ever more stimulating ways. Google Earth, for example, and its ability to zoom through the scales from local to global, can make an excellent contribution to building students' locational knowledge and understanding of the concept of scale. GIS and Gapminder further illustrate the potential of online resources in the geography classroom.

GIS and other geotechnologies

Using GIS is clearly identified in both the GNC and GCSE subject content, shown above. Fargher (2017) explores the options geography teachers have to support students to learn about GIS and other geotechnologies. Fargher defines geospatial technologies as 'technology that is used for the visualisation, measurement and analysis of features on the surface of Earth.' (p. 244) A true GIS, Fargher explains, is 'a geographical information system which has the capacity to analyse geographical data sets. "True GIS", such as ESRI's ArcGIS [ArcGIS Online for Schools – https://schools.esriuk.com], can be accessed via software packages and online, and are powerful tools for the visualisation and spatial analysis of geographical information.' (p. 244). She acknowledges that geotechnologies, most notably Earth viewers such as Google Earth, offer impressive ways of investigating places, as outlined earlier. Figure 6.6 provides a summary of the different geospatial technologies.

Mitchell (2010) outlines a year 7 investigation of rivers using Google Earth to create a structured enquiry. She discovered that the students developed a greater sense of place than they had through using video clips in previous lessons. Students were motivated and engaged in learning with the software, as well as being more open to independent learning. When writing end of lesson evaluations: 'As many as 71% of the class said they had learnt more GIS using Google Earth than by watching the video, giving reasons such as "Instead of watching it on TV and not going where you want, Google Earth can take you wherever you want to go" and "I like looking about where it is and facts about it."' (p. 19)

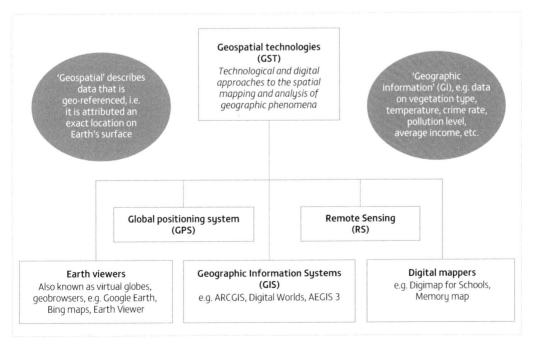

Figure 6.6: Geospatial technologies. **Source:** Fargher (2017), p. 245.

Fargher identifies the US company ESRI (originally the Environmental Systems Research Institute) as the main GIS provider used by schools. ArcGIS Online for Schools offers free teaching and learning resources for UK schools. which represents a very accessible and exciting place to start embedding GIS into your curriculum planning. The existing library of ESRI Storymaps represents an excellent resource to utilise across appropriate units of work to undertake geographical enquiries.

Harry West has written an excellent article (2021) full of ideas and advice about introducing and developing the use of GIS. One of the very important points he makes is 'the answer to the question as to how to "teach GIS" as well as subject content is simply – don't. You do not need to "teach GIS" as it is not, at school level, a topic in its own right (unlike in geography undergraduate study)'. (p. 14) He believes teachers are better integrating GIS into the curriculum and using it to introduce or reinforce content; for example, using ArcGIS Online to visualise spatial features and processes as part teaching different units of work.

Gapminder

'Gapminder is an independent Swedish foundation with no political, religious or economic affiliations. Gapminder fights devastating misconceptions and promotes a fact-based worldview everyone can understand. ('About' section, www.gapminder.org)

The foundation was co-founded by internationally renowned Professor Hans Rosling, a Swedish Professor of International Health. Gapminder presents important global data in clear 'bubble' charts that move dynamically through time so that the user can watch how the countries of the world have evolved. A series of excellent video clips, presented by Hans Rosling, are included in the tools section of the website, where he uses Gapminder tools and data to challenge and explain concepts such as population and development. Lang (2011) explained how Gapminder can support high-quality geographical enquiry:

'Gapminder World provides a means to challenge how people use terms such as "developed" and "developing"; it strengthens the idea that countries are on a constantly-changing development continuum, rather than in a "fixed" position.' (pp. 17–18)

The GA has published guidance on using Gapminder and teaching resources are available on its website (www.geography.org.uk/teaching-resources/gapminder-worldmapper).

Since Lang's article and the GA guidance, Gapminder has expanded considerably, most notably developing 'Dollar Street'. This web resource was developed by Anna Rosling Rönnlund. In the 'About' section of the Dollar Street website she explains how Dollar Street functions. Dollar Street uses photos as data to make the world more understandable by showing people, their homes and everyday items in their homes, organised as a street – poorest to left, richest to the right. This is an attempt to change the way people see the world.

Factfulness (Rosling *et al.*, 2018), a summation of the work of the Gapminder Foundation, became an international best-seller. The Foundation initiated the Ignorance Project to investigate and test what the public know and don't know about global patterns and macro-trends. These tests demonstrated a general ignorance; people tend to misinterpret statistical data about the world, developing a pessimistic, over-dramatic, biased worldview. The book explains that the over-dramatic worldview is related to how our brain functions, identifies ten instincts that make people jump to the wrong conclusions, and investigates each instinct in detail.

The way the Gapminder Foundation uses public data in the Ignorance Test clearly demonstrates a constructionist approach. Gapminder have gone into people's minds to discover their worldview, and then developed tools – statistics, graphs, photographs and the book – to help develop critical thinking skills to overcome the ten basic instincts to embrace a Factfulness view. The same process can form part of the implementation of your 11–16 curriculum. The Ignorance Project questionnaire can also be used with students, to gauge their worldview based on the knowledge they bring to the classroom. Students can investigate the resources of the Gapminder website and book to develop their critical thinking skills (Chapter 4, pp. 65–8), their capability to think geographically, making sense of concepts including development, population and change. Gapminder can be used across a range of units of work, and different key stages, as part of a coherent 11–16 curriculum. Teachers can decide which unit would be responsible for the introduction of Gapminder and Factfulness, within an appropriate context, and how its use will be progressed, in future units, leading to students interrogating data and charts independently, as part of geographical enquiries.

The Gapminder website includes a teacher area, with guidance on how to use the various tools. There is also a teacher guide about Factfulness, providing an overview of the book, as well as a series of lesson plans and activities with resources. A download section provides a range of PowerPoint slides, and posters for use in the classroom.

Alan Parkinson (2018) has developed an excellent collaborative key stage 3 unit of work using Factfulness and Gapminder, published on his blog Living Geography. This uses a wide range of geographical data from Gapminder and other sources. The unit fully embraces an enquiry approach, beginning with a challenge to student thinking by undertaking the Ignorance Test. The plan also suggests its use again, in a review lesson at the end of the unit, as a way of assessing student progress in geographical thinking: http://livinggeography.blogspot.com/2018/05/factfulness-collaborative-scheme-of-work.html

The potential of Gapminder as a resource has been explained in detail to demonstrate the importance of resources in planning geography lessons.

Integrating and planning for progression in fieldwork opportunities

The GA Manifesto *A Different View* (2009) identified fieldwork as an essential component of geography education. Fieldwork is also clearly identified as a requirement in both GNC and GCSE. Bonnett (2008) asserts that 'Geography wants to take children outside the schools and into the streets and fields ... and into the rain or the sunshine" (p. 80). Lambert and Reiss (2014) identify the significance of fieldwork in geography and science curriculums: 'Fieldwork is therefore more than a mere "signature pedagogy" in geography and the sciences. It brings conceptual, cognitive, procedural and social gains, much of which would be lost without the particular opportunities fieldwork provides.' (p. 8) Roberts (2013) identifies a number of advantages of investigation and enquiry through fieldwork: '... students can relate more easily to what they are studying because they can experience it directly with their senses; they can collect their own first-hand data; they can develop a deeper understanding of the data they are using because they know how they were collected ...' (p. 8).

The Ofsted Research Review for geography (2021) maintains that 'Fieldwork connects pupils with the complexities of the real world, making it both stimulating and fascinating and a valuable element of the subject. However, it also requires teachers to have sound subject knowledge so that they can confidently explore the uncertainties and ambiguities that come from moving geography from the classroom into real environments with pupils.'

Kinder (2018) identifies many of these potential gains, summarised in Figure 6.7.

Figure 6.7: The potential purposes and outcomes of geography fieldwork. **Source:** Kinder (2018), adapted from Job (1996), Caton (2006) and the DfES (2006).

Educational purpose	Geography fieldwork aim	Outcomes for learners
Conceptual	Developing knowledge and understanding of geographical processes, landforms, issues	■ Improved academic achievement ■ Opportunities for informal learning ■ A bridge to higher-order learning
Skills-related	Developing skills in data collection, presentation and analysis with real data	■ Skills and independence in a widening range of environments ■ The ability to deal with uncertainty
Aesthetic	Developing sensitivity to and appreciation of built and natural environments	■ Stimulation, inspiration and improved motivation ■ Nurture of creativity
Values-related	Developing empathy with views of others and care about/for the environment	■ Development of active citizens and stewards of the environment
Social and personal development	Personal, learning and thinking skills, such as independent enquiry, critical thinking, decision-making, team working	■ Engaging and relevant learning for young people ■ Challenge and the opportunity to take acceptable levels of risk ■ Improved attitudes to learning ■ Reduced behavioural problems and improved attendance

Planning for progress in fieldwork

The curriculum grids for key stage 3 and GCSE in Figures 5.6 and 5.9 (pages 86 and 93) to help you design your curriculum intent both include a column for fieldwork to help embed fieldwork opportunities as part of the curriculum journey for each key stage. Most of the schools showcased in Chapter 8 include fieldwork in their vision statements, and as a result plan for opportunities within their curriculum. Monk (2016), in making reference to the GA's progression framework, asserts: 'Fieldwork should be an explicit component of this planning: skills best developed outside the classroom must be integrated into a broader context to embed achievement and progression.' (p. 20)

Widdowson (2017) identifies opportunities for fieldwork at a variety of scales, which have been adapted with examples (Figure 6.8).

Widdowson provides an idea of what progression in geography fieldwork might look like in the secondary school. Ideas presented here can be used to help think through fieldwork opportunities and how they might be integrated into long-term curriculum planning.

You can investigate these ideas as part of Activity 6.3 and further in Chapter 8 – the case studies for Spalding Grammar School and the Harris Federation give examples of how schools have planned for progress in fieldwork, and embedded the process in their curriculum design.

ACTIVITY 6.3: EMBEDDING FIELDWORK OPPORTUNITIES INTO YOUR CURRICULUM

TALKING POINT: How does fieldwork help to bring our curriculum intent to life?

Consider the guidance offered in this book about fieldwork opportunities, the variety of scales, and principles of progression. It will also be useful to consider the fieldwork provision developed in the Harris MAT curriculum toolkit, as well as Spalding Grammar School (Chapter 8).

In a department meeting or training day session, discuss current classroom strategies using the following questions:

- What fieldwork opportunities do we currently offer to our 11–16 year-old students?

- Do these fieldwork opportunities support student learning towards our curriculum vision at key stage 3 and GCSE?

- How can we further develop fieldwork in our curriculum?

- Do we successfully utilise the school grounds and local area as a resource for fieldwork?

- Do we successfully integrate the enquiry process, use of OS maps and geographical data into our fieldwork?

- How can we use Figures 6.8 and 6.9 to plan for student progress in fieldwork skills?

PRACTICAL ACTION

Map your existing fieldwork opportunities onto your copies of the progression frameworks for key stages 3 and 4, using the fieldwork column (Chapter 5, Figures 5.6 and 5.9). Identify additional fieldwork opportunities you could integrate into your units of work, and add them to your long-term plan.

Research approaches to fieldwork to further develop your curriculum intent

The GA website provides detailed guidance about the benefits and impact of fieldwork, as well as ideas and resources on planning fieldwork from a variety of schools: www.geography.org.uk/Geography-fieldwork

The GA ITE guidance and support for Trainees and NQTs provides an extensive range of ideas and guidance about fieldwork: www.geography.org.uk/Planning-fieldwork

The Royal Geographical Society (with IBG) also provides extensive online support for fieldwork in geography: www.rgs.org/in-the-field/fieldwork-in-schools

The Field Studies Council provides excellent guidance about planning and implementing geography fieldwork in different environments: www.field-studies-council.org/resources/

School grounds: These types of fieldwork can be conducted during lesson time.	A lesson could be spent mapping the school or following a route around the school with a large-scale OS map of the school grounds and/or an aerial photo. This is an ideal first lesson for new year 7 students: it provides an immediate insight into the geographical skills developed in their primary schools, as well as demonstrating the significance of the subject in helping students find their way around a new place.
	As part of a unit of work on weather and climate students could study the microclimate of the school grounds, or spend time managing the school datalogging weather station.
Local environment: This can usually be done within a morning or afternoon.	The following ideas could be integrated into different units of work across a key stage:
	■ investigating different housing types in the locality of the school ■ testing ideas about the types of businesses that could be developed in the local area ■ an environmental survey, or evidence of sustainability in the area involving attempts to reduce the impact of climate change ■ the potential risk of flooding ■ how population is changing in the locality.
Further afield: Fieldwork can be undertaken as a one-day visit or a residential trip. Residential trips take longer and will be more expensive, so the costs have to be weighed against the potential benefits of taking students to new locations to study geography.	Coast, river, glacial landscapes can be investigated, or different types of towns and cities, with special functions such as market town, or tourist resort, or a rural landscape or farm.
	An external provider such as the Field Studies Council centres could be used for this fieldwork; the school will benefit not only from tailor-made specialist facilities, but also the expertise and local knowledge of the teaching staff at the centre.
Foreign, not to say exotic, locations – a noticeable trend for schools to organise fieldwork. This has happened over the past few years with the benefit of cheaper flights.	'Often geography departments use such trips to promote the subject within their schools. While any attempt to increase the uptake of geography is to be applauded, the increased use of overseas fieldwork locations does raise questions about sustainability and the extent to which opportunities for fieldwork in the UK are being missed.' (p. 231)

Figure 6.8: Fieldwork at a variety of scales. **Source:** adapted from Widdowson (2017).

Location Local ⟶ Distant	In general, progression will be from local to distant locations, though not necessarily in linear fashion. There may be good geographical reasons to return to the local area even for older students. It is advisable for students to build their confidence in the use of basic fieldwork techniques in a familiar environment. Sudden immersion of students in an unfamiliar environment for their first fieldwork experience could be counter-productive.
Scale Small ⟶ Large	There should be general progression in fieldwork from small- to large-scale, again with the proviso that there may be good reasons for older students to return to the smaller scale. So, for example, while younger students might study movement of material along a beach, older students could investigate large-scale coastal management strategies.
Skills and techniques Limited repertoire of basic techniques ⟶ wider repertoire including more sophisticated techniques	Students should build their repertoire of fieldwork techniques over time, starting with basic techniques such as measurement, mapping and questionnaires and graduating to more sophisticated techniques such as environmental impact assessment and in-depth interviews. They should also develop more sophisticated data presentation and analysis skills.
Independence Structured ⟶ Unstructured	Students should learn to carry out fieldwork with growing levels of independence. For example, younger students may be given an enquiry question to investigate and told what techniques to use, while older students would be expected to devise their own questions and sequences of enquiry.

Figure 6.9: Progression in secondary geography fieldwork. **Source:** Widdowson (2017).

Assessment

Chapter 5 identified the potential of using the age-related expectations in the GA's progression framework guidance to plan a curriculum with progress and assessment at its heart. The long-term curriculum plan can be used to identify KPIs that make assessment clear and transparent, planning a curriculum with assessment in mind (see Chapter 5, pages 91–94). The long-term curriculum plan can potentially provide a framework for assessment. In order to create a manageable planning and assessment system in your school it is helpful to consider the three levels of assessment thinking: short, medium and long term, shown in overview in Figure 6.10.

Scale/focus	Practice, for example	Progress and standards
Short term Day-to-day	Assessment for learning classroom practice, e.g. questioning, formative feedback/response, etc.	Evident in teaching and learning, in students' ongoing work, response to feedback, etc.
Frequent Basic knowledge/ skills	Short test, identified piece of homework; more in-depth marking	Progress check (confidence vs concern?) can give you a number
Half-termly Conceptual, procedural knowledge	Short research task, problem-solving exercise, etc. Access to work at particular standards, e.g. display Peer/self-assessment	Criterion marking and feedback Linked to pitch/age-related expectations
Long term (year/key stage) Substantial, conceptual development	A major piece of work, e.g. enquiry, decision-making exercise, extended writing End of year: perhaps synoptic, drawing learning together	As above, plus an opportunity to develop a portfolio of geography work exemplifying and sharing standards and illustrating progress

Figure 6.10:
Monitoring progress at different timescales.
Source: GA (2020).

1. A first principle of learning is to **start from where the student is**. Recognise that learning occurs when students have opportunities to connect their personal experiences of the world around them with the subject of geography and thus reconstruct their understanding. This can be achieved through classroom dialogue, which is two-way: student to teacher and teacher to student. If the teacher asks a question that enables students to identify their current thinking, this can be used as a starting point for the subsequent dialogue about learning and assessment.

2. The second principle of learning is for **students to take an active part** in the dialogue. The teacher's role is to create a learning environment where students are prepared to give a range of responses and be supported in clarifying inconsistencies so they can respond to challenges.

3. A third principle is that **students must know what they are trying to achieve**. They need to know what a good response might look like and how their work compares with it.

Figure 6.11: The four principles of learning in geography.
Source: Gardner, Weeden and Butt (eds) (2015) (Adapted from Weeden and Lambert (2006)

Short-term (day-to-day) assessment

An understanding of the progression shown in the GA's *A progression framework for geography*, (Chapter 3, pp. 43–5), is essential underpinning for assessment for learning practices. The benchmark expectations are of no use in making day-to-day assessments, and are not designed for sharing directly with students. Progress can be shown on a day-to-day basis, even if assessment information is more informal and ephemeral in nature. Rather than plan a series of activities to 'deliver content', planning should develop more active learning opportunities, that connect students to their prior learning. It can also be connected to future learning, making clear to students the significance of the current learning to the curriculum journey they are on. Weeden and Lambert (2006) explain four principles of learning in geography that demonstrate the process that underpins formative assessment (Figure 6.11).

Weeden and Lambert maintain that 'formative assessment opportunities used in day-to-day

Understanding the quality criteria helps students to reach a better understanding of what they need to do to achieve the desired standard of work. Also connecting students to the vision for the key stage periodically is important here, connecting the student to the vision of the end goal, in shorthand 'becoming a geographer'. This also enables students to take more responsibility for their learning and make better judgements about whether or not their work meets the criteria. Peer- and self-assessment are essential here, because the process of judging their own work and that of other students encourages active involvement and develops their understanding of the expected standards.

4. A fourth principle arises when students are given opportunities to **talk about geographical ideas**. Whether this takes place as a whole-class dialogue or in peer groups, students are learning to actively use the language of geography – its vocabulary and grammar – which allows them to explore their understanding and scaffolds their learning.

teaching can develop student's knowledge and understanding of the enquiry process' (p. 5). The teacher utilises a wide variety of carefully selected geographical data for students to interact with, make sense of, and connect with geographical ideas. The range of classroom activities that may also be seen as assessment opportunities are listed in Figure 6.12, indicating that assessment, teaching and learning are all part of the same circular and coherent process.

Oral evidence

Questioning
Listening
Discussing
Presentations
Interviews
Debates
Audio recordings
Video recordings
Role plays
Simulations

Written evidence

Questionnaires Diaries
Reports Essays
Notes Stories
Newspaper articles
Scripts
Short answers
Bullet point lists
Poems
Descriptions

Graphic evidence

Diagrams
Sketches
Drawings
Graphs
Printouts
Overlays

Products

Models
Artefacts
Games
Photographs
Web pages

Figure 6.12: Learning activities that present potential evidence on which to base assessment. **Source:** Gardner, Weeden and Butt (eds) (2015), p. 28 (adapted from Lambert and Lines (2000), p. 131).

Medium-term assessment

At the beginning of year 7 you can determine how far your new students are working at the age 11 benchmark statements for geography with an initial unit of work designed as a transitional assessment. Students can be provided with opportunities to demonstrate their achievement throughout the key stage, through more formal periodic assessment, typically towards the end of a unit of work. Where units of work have embedded enquiry, this more formal periodic assessment could take the form of a review of the unit, where students can answer a unit of work's overarching enquiry question, designed to capture what the unit is trying to achieve. Here, assessing using the criteria for the unit can be used formatively, to identify broad progress, strengths and weaknesses and to identify curriculum targets, as well as summatively to monitor progress towards the benchmark expectations. A 'mixed economy' of assessment opportunities can be established (Figure 6.13). This might include short tests of specific knowledge, more developed enquiries to assess conceptual

- Geographical enquiries
- Decision-making activities
- Extended or shorter, more focused pieces of writing in a variety of different forms and for a range of purposes
- Analysis and interpretation of a variety of maps at different scales as well as other geographical data
- Text annotation or visual organisers, such as thought mapping, storyboards, concept mapping or timelines
- Oral work, including student presentations to the class, contributions to class discussions, drama activities or discussions with teachers
- Drawing of sketch maps, diagrams, field sketches
- Students' self- and peer-assessment

Figure 6.13: Different types of geographical assessment evidence. **Source:** Gardner, Weeden and Butt (eds) (2015), p. 15.

understanding and skills, and perhaps occasional synoptic assessment, such as problem-solving or decision-making exercises at the end of a year or key stage. These can focus on the extent to which students can apply skills, link ideas together and move from the particular to the general, so demonstrating their progress as geographical thinkers. These assessment opportunities will draw upon the benchmark expectations, and the intent vision for your curriculum.

Long-term assessment

The benchmark expectations help set a national standard so that schools can be secure in their judgement for monitoring and reporting purposes.

They can be used with transitional summative assessments at the end of each year in a key stage, as well as the end of the key stage. This end of key stage assessment could take the form of a unit of study that provides opportunities to demonstrate the vision for the intended curriculum: opportunities for students to demonstrate that they have become a geographer, and can see, understand and communicate the interconnections between the concepts and ideas they have investigated. The whole process of using benchmark expectations to assess student progress towards the curriculum vision or end point, supporting students on their curriculum journey, is summarised in Figures 6.14 and 6.15.

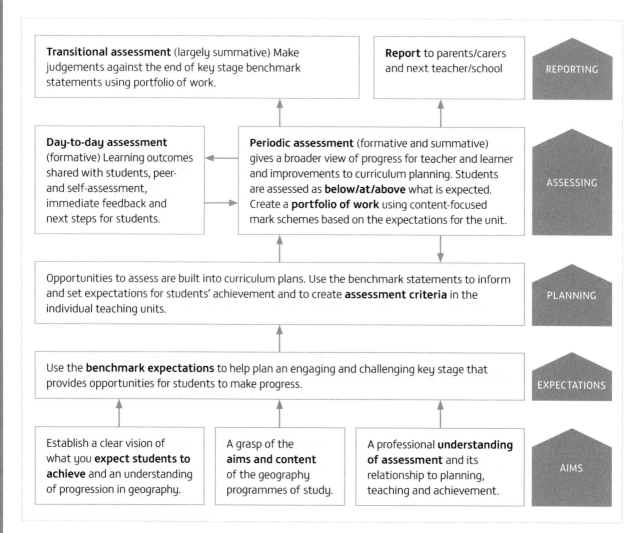

Figure 6.14: Using the benchmark expectations to plan for progression and assessment. **Source**: Geographical Association (2020), p. 6 .

The three aspects of student achievement in the NC	Contextual world knowledge of locations, places and geographical features	Understanding of the conditions, processes and interactions that explain geographical features, distribution patterns and changes over time and space.	Competence in geographical enquiry and the application of skills in observing, collecting, analysing, evaluating and communicating geographical information.
Benchmark expectations for students at age 14	Have extensive knowledge relating to a wide range of places, environments and features at a variety of appropriate spatial scales extending from local to global.	Understand the physical and human conditions and processes which lead to the development of, and change in, a variety of geographical features, systems and places. They can explain various ways in which places are linked and the impact such links have on people and environments. They can make connections between different geographical phenomena they have studied.	Be able, with increasing independence, to choose and use a wide range of data to help investigate, interpret, make judgements and draw conclusions about geographical questions, issues and problems, and express and engage with different points of view about these.

Day-to-day assessment – in each lesson linked to learning objectives. The benchmark expectations are not relevant for day-to-day assessment.

Key stage 3 plan

End of key stage – where are we now?

Year 9 Content units 1-6

Year 8 Content units 1-6

Year 7 Content units 1-6

Transitional assessment – occasional synoptic assessment such as problem-solving or decision-making exercises at the end of a year or key stage.

Periodic assessment – students should have the chance to demonstrate their achievement through more formal periodic assessment – a major piece of work, typically towards the end of a unit of work.

Transitional assessment – baseline new year 7, to identify if your new students have achieved the expectations for 11-year-olds so you can begin to develop a framework and key stage 3 plan to assess the progress they make later.

| Benchmark expectations for students at age 11 | Have a more detailed and extensive framework of knowledge about the world, including globally significant physical and human features and places in the news. | Understand in some detail what a number of places are like, how and why they are similar and different, how and why they are changing. They know about some spatial patterns in human and physical geography, the conditions that influence these patterns and the processes that lead to change. They show some understanding of the links between people, places and environments. | Be able to carry out geographical investigations using a range of geographical questions, skills and sources of information using a variety of maps, graphs and images. Express and explain their opinions and recognise why others may have different points of view. |

Figure 6.15: Levels of assessment within the curriculum plan.

Ofsted view of assessment

Ofsted have tried to overcome a number of myths regarding the use of assessment (Activity 6.4).

These views on assessment are reinforced in the Ofsted Geography Research Review (2021):

'Although summative tests and exams at the end of a course serve these purposes, they also pose risks if they are used throughout a course, or if the assessment criteria are extrapolated to progress measures.

First, they typically assess a broad body of knowledge. It is not until the end of the course of study that pupils have the breadth of knowledge, depth of understanding, appreciation of the interconnectedness of components from each form of substantive knowledge, and disciplinary knowledge to attempt these assessments. Therefore, they are not so useful for diagnostic purposes and are likely to be used infrequently.

Second, the criteria were not written to be broken down into milestones. Consequently, using GCSE criteria to evaluate progress from years 7 to 11 in a secondary school presents a flawed picture.

Finally, fixing attention on a terminal assessment or exam runs the risk of narrowing the curriculum. If particular geographical concepts are omitted from the curriculum, for example weather and climate, then pupils will struggle to comprehend the systems that lie behind many geographical processes. As a result, pupils' responses will lack a detailed understanding and full appreciation of phenomena and their impact.'

Ofsted are, therefore, suggesting an approach to assessment rooted in the curriculum for each subject. The approach to assessment outlined in this book is clearly about assessing the geography, and students' curriculum journey towards a clear end point, an approach which is very much in tune with Ofsted.

The GA's progression framework is central to the curriculum design process outlined in this book. It is founded in the subject discipline and ideas about how students learn in geography.

ACTIVITY 6.4

Watch the video clip which shows Sean Harford, National Director Education, Ofsted, 2016: www.youtube.com/watch?v=H7whb8dOk5Q

Here he explains what Ofsted want to see during inspections regarding assessment. This was recorded in 2016, as part of his work with the government Commission on Assessment without Levels, and before Ofsted embarked on their research into curriculum, which led to the new EIF. His comments, however, are consistent with the views expressed by Ofsted in their Phase 3 research report on curriculum:

'The evidence forms for the secondary schools visited identified some weaknesses in how curriculum assessment was being applied. A common finding for the secondary schools in band 2 or 3 for curriculum quality was that they were assessing students in key stage 3 using GCSE grades 1 to 9 from the beginning of year 7. This is problematic as this type of assessment is not focused on the key stage 3 curriculum being delivered and what students actually knew and understood.

Furthermore, evidence from the HMI focus group showed that in some schools a homogeneity of approach was found across all subjects. In these cases, leaders had established a whole-school assessment approach that used exam models to structure their notions of progress, but had not considered what progression looked like in individual subjects. This indicated that the specific progression of knowledge, including disciplinary knowledge of the subject, was not being considered by leaders.' (Ofsted (2019b), p. 45)

Read the quotes that further demonstrate the views of Ofsted about assessment. How does this compare with approaches to assessment in your school?

Discuss the implications of these views to your curriculum intent and the department and school approach to assessment.

There are a number of significant principles to stick to if you are to effectively support and plan for your students' progress in geography. As this chapter demonstrates, you need to have a clear understanding of the standard you are trying to reach, where your students are now in their geographical learning, and how best to help them bridge the gap. The DfE have clearly stated that:

'Schools will be able to introduce their own approaches to formative assessment, to support pupil attainment and progression. The assessment framework should be built into the school curriculum, so that schools can check what pupils have learned and whether they are on track to meet expectations at the end of the key stage, and so that they can report regularly to parents.' (DfE, 2013).

Many schools, misinterpreting this statement from the DfE and clinging to old ways of thinking about progression and assessment, created flight paths towards GCSE or progression ladders that in effect recreate levels, and the detachment of assessment from the curriculum. The Ofsted Research review (2021) makes clear the unsuitability of whole-school tracking systems to subjects such as geography:

'These [systems] have often identified specific points that a pupil, having reached a particular level of attainment in English and/or mathematics at the age of 11, should reach each term as they progress through key stage 3.

The nature of the geography curriculum, being cumulative, means that knowledge of complexity is often not reached until pupils are nearing the end of the key stage. In fact, many concepts are not properly appreciated until key stage 4 or even sixth-form study. Linear progress ladders therefore do not serve the subject well.'

The focus on curriculum in the new EIF has provided an important opportunity to achieve a common understanding of progression in a school where the curriculum is planned with progression and assessment at its heart, and, therefore, the focus for classroom teaching.

Conclusion

As your curriculum is implemented – 'the curriculum as taught and experienced' (Ofsted, 2019c, p. 3) – it is important that the intent is clear, throughout.

ACTIVITY 6.5: CURRICULUM IMPLEMENTATION REFLECTION

It is useful to consider how Ofsted will inspect curriculum implementation, including the grade descriptors they have developed, provided in the Ofsted School Inspection Handbook, in particular pages 41–8. You can consider these, in relation to your curriculum implementation, to reflect on the progress you intend to make in the implementation of your curriculum.

Ofsted (2019a) School inspection handbook: Handbook for inspecting schools in England under section 5 of the Education Act 2005 available at: https://www.gov.uk/government/publications/school-inspection-handbook-eif

This chapter has demonstrated that an enquiry process is pivotal in bringing together pedagogy, assessment and progress. The implementation of a coherent and sequenced curriculum plan supports your students towards cumulatively sufficient knowledge and skills for future learning and employment, through an enquiry process. The approach utilises a wide range of geographical data and fieldwork opportunities for students to make sense of, as they develop their geographical thinking.

References

All websites last accessed 27/07/2021.

Bonnett, A. (2008) *What is geography?* London: Sage.

Biddulph, M., Lambert, D. and Balderstone, D. (2015) *Learning to Teach Geography in the Secondary School: A Companion to School Experience*. Abingdon: Routledge.

DfE (2013) *Assessing without levels*. London: DfE.

DfE (2014) *Geography GCSE subject content*. Available at https://assets.publishing.service.gov.uk/government/uploads/system/uploads/attachment_data/file/301253/GCSE_geography.pdf

DfE (2016) Report of the Independent Teacher Workload Review Group, *Eliminating unnecessary workload around planning and teaching resources* (2016). Available at https://assets.publishing.service.gov.uk/government/uploads/system/uploads/attachment_data/file/511257/Eliminating-unnecessary-workload-around-planning-and-teaching-resources.pdf

Fargher, M. (2017) 'GIS and other geospatial technologies' in Jones, M. (ed) *The Handbook of Secondary Geography*. Sheffield: Geographical Association. pp. 244–59.

Ferretti, J. (2018) 'The enquiry approach in geography' in Jones, M. and Lambert, D. (eds) *Debates in Secondary Geography* (2nd edition). pp. 115–26. Abingdon: Routledge.

Gardner, D., Weeden, P. and Butt, G. (eds) (2015) *Assessing progress in your KS3 geography curriculum*. Sheffield: Geographical Association

Geographical Association (2009) *A Different View: A Manifesto from the Geographical Association*. Sheffield: Geographical Association. Available at www.geography.org.uk/GA-Manifesto-for-geography

Geographical Association (2020) *A progression framework for geography*. Available at www.geography.org.uk/eBooks-detail/71c435a8-c548-4e38-80db-2305275fbee5

Geographical Association (2020-21) GeogPod at https://www.geography.org.uk/GeogPod-The-GAs-Podcast

Geographical Association website ITE support: www.geography.org.uk/Initial-Teacher-Education/Support-for-trainees-and-ECTs

Kinder, A. (2018) 'Acquiring geographical knowledge and understanding through fieldwork', *Teaching Geography*, 43, 3, pp. 109–12.

Kinder, A. and Owens, P. (2019) 'The new Education Inspection Framework – through a geographical lens', *Teaching Geography*, 44, 3, pp. 97–100.

Lambert, D. and Reiss, M. (2014) *The place of fieldwork in geography and science qualifications*. London: UCL IoE Press.

Lang, D. (2011) 'Gapminder: bringing statistics to life', *Teaching Geography*, 36, 1, pp. 17–19.

Mitchell, L. (2010) 'Why use GIS?', *Teaching Geography*, 35, 1, pp. 18–20.

Monk, P. (2016) 'Progression in fieldwork', *Teaching Geography*, 41, 1, pp. 20–21.

National Curriculum for Geography (2013) *KS3 Programme of Study*. Available at https://assets.publishing.service.gov.uk/government/uploads/system/uploads/attachment_data/file/239087/SECONDARY_national_curriculum_-_Geography.pdf

Ofsted (2019a) *School inspection handbook: Handbook for inspecting schools in England under section 5 of the Education Act 2005*. Available at https://www.gov.uk/government/publications/school-inspection-handbook-eif

Ofsted (2019b) *The education inspection framework*. Available at https://www.gov.uk/government/collections/education-inspection-framework

Ofsted (2019c) *Inspecting the curriculum: revising inspection methodology to support the education inspection frame-work*. Available at https://assets.publishing.service.gov.uk/government/uploads/system/uploads/attachment_data/file/814685/Inspecting_the_curriculum.pdf

Ofsted (2021) *Research review series: geography*. Available at https://www.gov.uk/government/publications/research-review-series-geography/research-review-series-geography

Parkinson, A. (2018) *Factfulness scheme of work*. Living Geography blog post. Available at http://livinggeography.blogspot.com/2018/05/factfulness-collaborative-scheme-of-work.html

Rayner, D. (2017) in Jones, M. (ed) *The Handbook of Secondary Geography*. Sheffield: Geographical Association. pp. 150–65.

Roberts, M. (2012) *What makes a geography lesson good?* Available at www.geography.org.uk/write/MediaUploads/Teacher%20education/GA_PRMGHWhatMakesAGeographyLessonGood.pdf

Roberts, M. (2013) *Geography Through Enquiry: Approaches to teaching and learning in the secondary school*. Sheffield: Geographical Association.

Roberts, M. (2017a) 'Geographical education is powerful if ...', *Teaching Geography*, 42, 1, pp. 6–9.

Roberts, M. (2017b) in Jones, M. (ed) *The Handbook of Secondary Geography*. Sheffield: Geographical Association. pp 48–61.

Rosling, H., Rosling, O., Rosling Ronnlund, A. (2019) *Factfulness*. London: Hodder and Stoughton.

Rynne, E., Hinchliffe, L., Hopkins, J., Gardner, D. and Pilkinton, E. (2020) 'Using examiners' reports from GCSE 2019 to improve future performance', *Teaching Geography*, 45, 1, pp. 22–5.

Weeden, P. and Lambert, D. (2006) *Geography Inside the Black Box*. London: NFER Nelson.

West, H (2021) 'Taking the first steps towards bringing GIS into the classroom' *Teaching Geography*, 46, 1, pp. 14–16.

Widdowson, J. (2017) in Jones, M. (ed) *The Handbook of Secondary Geography*. Sheffield: Geographical Association. pp. 232–8.

Impact of the curriculum

 IMPACT   **6** Evaluate and record the impact   **7** Maintain, change or move on

There are two stages in this impact phase of the curriculum design process:

- 6 Evaluate and record the impact
- 7 Maintain, change or move on.

Each stage is supported by guidance, resources and tools.

Stage 6: Evaluation and recording impact

The curriculum design process diagram, Figure 5 (p. 62) is presented as a circle, to demonstrate that the curriculum should be seen as being in a state of continuous development. The curriculum needs to evolve in response to ever-changing internal needs, such as new cohorts of students with different learning needs, or teaching staff turnover leading to differences in expertise in the classroom. There are also externally imposed factors, such as new exam specifications, or new and evolving ideas in geography education, as well as the dynamically changing world that is the focus of geographical study.

Evaluation and assessment, although often used interchangeably, operate at different scales. **Evaluation** is concerned at a macro or holistic level: in this case, considering how far the curriculum intent has been achieved. **Assessment** operates as a process at a micro level, supporting students to progress as geographers. Conducting regular evaluation of the school curriculum, and the effectiveness of its implementation, needs to be a priority. There is a close relationship between Stages 1–3 of the curriculum design process, and Stage 6: evaluation. This is an opportunity to report on the differences between your starting point and where

the implementation of a new curriculum has taken your students. This is why it is so important that you spend time carefully considering your curriculum intent and taking a baseline, as a starting point, to be able to successfully identify how effective your curriculum design process has been. There are a number of key questions to consider, for example:

- is the curriculum actually leading to the intended impact?
- how do we know?
- what are the perceptions of students?
- do students appreciate how the geography curriculum has prepared them for the next stage education, employment or training?

Evaluation is a fundamental element of the annual school improvement cycle – a process of goal setting, monitoring, evidence collecting and evaluation – your school will have no doubt developed their own evaluation tools for this process. Effective schools can be defined as those that progress the learning and development of all of their students, regardless of intake characteristics, so that they demonstrate progress. To achieve this effectiveness, subject departments and school leaders need to work together to monitor and evaluate the evolution of the school curriculum.

Within the implementation of the curriculum, you will use assessment to monitor your students' progress towards the end point or vision you identified for the key stage. The transitional assessments, identified in the assessment section of the last chapter, represent reflection points, where you assess the progress students have made towards meeting the curriculum vision. Where students are not achieving, intervention strategies and amendments to the curriculum can be devised to support them. In a sense, this is part of an evaluation process, but evaluation also needs to be considered more widely. It needs to include the development of a range of different metrics, to measure and determine the successful impact of the curriculum. This will lead to a review, and possible adaptation, of the curriculum.

Monitoring student progress is more straightforward than evaluation of the curriculum: its principal focus is to understand whether students are achieving mastery of the curriculum and demonstrating the capability to think like a geographer. Either the student demonstrates mastery and understanding, or not. Monitoring progress through regular assessment points is a familiar process in most schools.

Evaluation is different: it is a process that leads to a judgment on how effective something has been. Evaluation of the curriculum considers the processes involved in conceiving, teaching, and experiencing the curriculum. Curriculum evaluation aims to examine the impact of the implemented curriculum on student (learning) achievement. As a result, if necessary the intended curriculum, and teaching and learning processes in the classroom, can be revised. Evaluation requires decisions about which stakeholders to collect data from, the nature of the data, and its analysis to determine impact and what to do next. Activity 7.1 will help you determine which stakeholders to consider to evaluate the impact of your curriculum on your students.

Look at the school case study for Spalding Grammar School (Chapter 8, page 146) that identifies a wide range of evaluation approaches you can use to consider if their curriculum is working.

Evaluating the impact of the curriculum on students

Periodically a geography department can evaluate and record the impact of the intended curriculum. It is at this evaluation stage that you fully realise the importance of thinking in depth about Stage 1 of the design process – your intent, what you want your students to achieve. The more thought you have given to visualising what success looks like, the easier it is not only to implement, but also

to evaluate. Again, the more in-depth the thinking about Stage 2, your starting point, what your students were like as geographers before your curriculum changes, the easier it is to identify changes as a result of your new curriculum. Consider whether your students' ability to think geographically has evolved in the new curriculum. Are students making connections in their learning, demonstrating understanding of the geographical concepts you identified in your intent? This is clearly focussed on your vision, but you may also be able to identify other changes in your students in terms of engagement, behaviour, curiosity, motivation, commitment and enthusiasm for geographical learning, as shown in Figure 7.1. The same considerations can also be made for the teachers of geography in your department. How have they changed, not only in terms of the way they teach, but how they consider the subject, their pedagogical approaches in the classroom, their enthusiasm, their commitment to planning and researching the subject and approaches to teaching and learning, and lessons? Most importantly, how have their interactions with students in the classroom developed; their commitment to supporting and monitoring student learning and progress, the quality of feedback they provide to support next steps in learning?

The indicators for behaviour and attitudes in the EIF are a good starting point for considering how far a new geography curriculum has led to an improvement (see pages 10–11 of the EIF (Ofsted, 2019a)).

Evaluating the curriculum – the significance of student voice

Evaluation can also involve your students in a much deeper way. A central theme of this book is the significance of enquiry learning, and the curriculum-making process. These are both underpinned by the energy and experiences of students, their thinking and life experiences. Student voice can be used as a natural extension of this, in terms of evaluating your curriculum. The basic premise of 'student voice' is that listening and responding to what students say about their experiences as learners can be a powerful tool in helping teachers to investigate and improve their own practice. Your curriculum has been planned by the teachers in your school, it has an intent articulated and planned by these teachers. The evaluation of this curriculum should engage with your students,

ACTIVITY 7.1: IS YOUR CURRICULUM WORKING? HOW DO YOU KNOW? ⬇

Is your curriculum helping your students to develop all of the geographical knowledge, understanding and skills that you want to achieve – to think like a geographer? How do you know?

GCSE results and assessments help you to recognise achievement in some important aspects of the curriculum. However, many schools want to have a much broader set of measures in place that reflects the intent of their curriculum. They want to measure what they value, not just value what they measure.

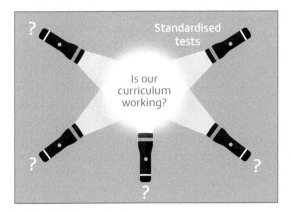

TALKING POINT: Do you measure what you value?

Reflect on the knowledge, understanding and skills that you identified were important for your students in your intent vision. How do you collect evidence to show that your curriculum is helping your students to develop as geographers?

If you think of standardised tests and GCSE results as a torch that highlights a specific part of your curriculum, what other torches do you have in place?

What other torches would you like to add to highlight different aspects of your curriculum and reflect your aims?

TALKING POINT: Who is worth asking?

Members of your department might have a slightly different perspective on what is working well in terms of the curriculum. Learners are at the heart of your curriculum and should be central to any evaluation. Who else is important in the context of your school community? How about in the wider education network?

Talk with colleagues about whose views might help you to get a clear picture of the impact of your curriculum. You might think about the following groups:

School Leadership Team	Schools with whom you network	Subject Associations
Learners	Local employers	Ofsted
Governors	Academy Trust	Parents

Are there any other groups who would be able to contribute useful views?

Each of the groups of people you identify is likely to encompass a range of views; for example, not all learners and parents are going to feel the same about the geography curriculum. How could you go about capturing these different perspectives?

PRACTICAL ACTIVITY: Identify your metrics

On a copy of the torches diagram, identify the key sources of evidence you want to shine on your curriculum.

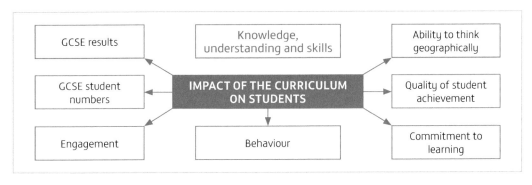

Figure 7.1: Indicators of the impact of the curriculum on students.

as they have experienced this curriculum. This is a key element of a process-praxis curriculum model (Chapter 2, pp. 23–5). Capturing their views of the geography they have experienced is vitally important; it is for them you have planned the curriculum. Their views are invaluable to continually evolve your curriculum.

The GA's *A Different View: A Manifesto from the Geographical Association* (2009) states 'Young people themselves, working with their teachers and drawing from their own experiences and curiosity, should be encouraged to help shape the geography curriculum.' (p. 15) The manifesto introduces the Young People's Geographies Project (YPG; www.geography.org.uk/Young-Peoples-Geographies) which began in 2006, exploring ways for young people's interests, experiences, aspirations and curiosity to influence the geography curriculum. 'A YPG curriculum results when teachers are responsive to what students *make of* what they get in geography lessons.' (online) – thus fully embracing Roberts' vision of enquiry learning. The manifesto identified 'conversation' as the characteristic of YPG. Conversation between teacher and students, pedagogies encouraging communication and exchange of ideas, utilising young people's everyday experiences, built upon by teachers, as a starting point to take them beyond their immediate horizon to develop powerful knowledge.

Biddulph (2010), in an editorial in *Teaching Geography* identified that students 'experience a wide range of personal geographies before they reached the geography classroom door.' She concludes 'Acknowledging and valuing what young people bring to the curriculum is one way of ensuring that the geography they learn is both meaningful and connected to their everyday lives.' (p. 46) Not only should this ongoing conversation between teacher and student be embedded in the implementation of the curriculum as part of geographical enquiry, but it can also be utilised as part of an evaluation process.

The GA website page for the Young People's Geographies project includes two evaluator reports (Hopwood, 2007) about the project. The example above includes conversations with students that clearly indicate student progress and understanding of the subject as a discipline. After a fieldwork visit in Leicester, using picture frames, students articulated comments including:

> *'Most pupils think geography is about maps and stuff. But I know it's about how you live and how you affect other people and stuff. This has changed my view of geography. It helps me think about the deeper meanings, like why war started and stuff. Not just changed my ideas of geography, but made my learning better as well'.*
>
> *'Now I see that geography is all around, it affects us all. Me, I am geography. It's about us as a community'*
>
> *'You realise that your own lives are related to geography'*
>
> *'It's like your life and what you do.'*

You could have similar conversations with your students, capturing their ideas and thoughts as evidence demonstrating the effectiveness of your curriculum implementation.

One geography teacher, Daniel Whittall (2019), asked eleven year 12 students and seven year 13 students their opinions on what makes the knowledge that they are taught in geography powerful:

> *'It emerged from discussion that students use geographical ideas, such as climate change, sustainability and globalisation, to interpret issues beyond their everyday experience. Students made comments such as 'ideas that we are taught in our geography classes are very useful as they have a lot of real-world application and help us to understand the world around us better', and 'students then feel empowered that they can make a difference, motivating them to make world-changing decisions in the future'. Students commented on the importance of explanations provided by their teacher, and the usefulness of high-quality lesson resources such as images, maps and video clips, in learning about specific places. Fieldwork was also identified as being significant by students, who felt that the experience of learning about a place is enhanced by visiting it, and that they found it easier to interpret geographical terminology when engaging with it in the field.'*

Such examples demonstrate how these students are beginning to understand how geography contributes to their lives, both now and in the future. This is an important stepping stone in their appreciation of how the subject prepares them for the next stage of their education, employment or training. Capturing student comments about your curriculum in this way provides deep insights into the successes, or areas for further development, in your curriculum. It is important that a geography department celebrates and acts upon such comments. The views of students and the actions they initiate should be shared with teachers and students both in the department and across the school. In other words, as stated in the GA manifesto, the views of young people help to shape the curriculum. Sharing these student views about the curriculum with other students can help develop a learning culture, where students begin to feel ownership of the curriculum and their own learning. Part of the methodology of the Ofsted inspection process involves talking to students about their learning (Ofsted (2019), p. 24).

Evaluation – when is the right time?

You need to be realistic about how long it will take for your curriculum changes to have an impact. You are looking for significant, long-term changes and these will often take time to emerge. For example, if your priority is to increase the quality and extent of independent geographical enquiry, and you start with years 7 and 8, you will be unlikely to see the impact in less than two years; however, it is possible to monitor the implementation of change across units of work, using the methods outlined, more regularly.

Recording the impact

There are many ways to record the impact of curriculum developments on learners. Some schools use grids and matrices like Figure 7.2 to evaluate each of their priorities.

Portfolio of evidence

As you begin to collect evidence about your curriculum, you can keep data together in an evaluation portfolio. Activity 7.2 supports this process.

The GA Geography Quality Marks

The GA has created a ready-made template for creating an evaluation portfolio. The Geography Quality Marks (www.geography.org.uk/quality-marks) are awards that recognise and promote quality and progress in geography leadership, curriculum development and learning and teaching in schools. This Quality Mark Framework has been constructed from the new EIF, and it can be used to support the evaluation process outlined in this chapter.

Figure 7.2: Grid to record impact of curriculum intent as a result of evaluation. **Source:** QCA (2008), p. 10.

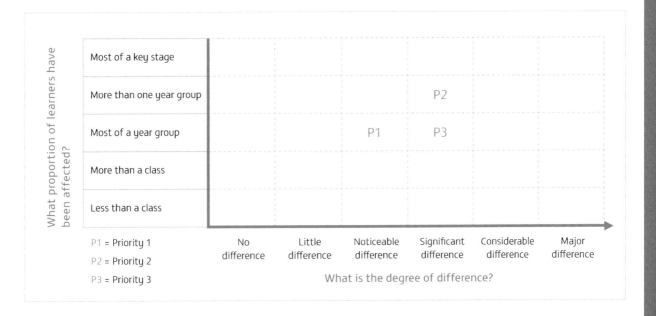

ACTIVITY 7.2: PUTTING TOGETHER AN EVALUATION PORTFOLIO ⬇

One way to become a better self-advocate for your geography curriculum is to develop an evaluation portfolio.

A good evaluation portfolio will:

- encourage you to collect evidence regularly
- focus on outcomes rather than activities
- include contributions from all stakeholders involved
- be a source of information for internal reviews, peer reviews and reporting, as well as external reviews and inspections
- become a permanent record of achievement.

TALKING POINT: What should you include?
The evidence you collect should be related to this overarching question:

How far does the geographical learning flow from intention, to implementation, to impact, in lessons across the department?

The evidence you are planning to collect will use the methods identified by Ofsted for the new EIF, in particular in the 'deep dive'.

Things to consider:

- what evidence of achievement are you planning to collect?
- what format will this evidence be in?
- how could you best present it in your portfolio?

PRACTICAL ACTION: Starting an evaluation portfolio
It makes sense to structure the evaluation framework using the Ofsted definition of curriculum, built around intent, implementation and impact. The guidance provided in this chapter should provide the basis for building your portfolio.

Make sure that your portfolio is brief, clear and supported by evidence, including students' work. It is a record of achievement rather than a formal report. You will probably find it invaluable when you do need to report findings to audiences such as the school leadership team, governors, parents, and Ofsted.

As a department works through the process, evidence can be collected in an online evaluation portfolio managed by the GA. This evidence is eventually submitted to the GA for external evaluation and feedback.

Successful Quality Mark schools have identified how the Secondary Geography Quality Mark (SGQM) process has supported their curriculum work:

'Engaging with the SGQM process has given the department a real drive and focus in order to develop the quality geography curriculum we provide even further. We have been able to evaluate our strengths and weaknesses as a department and the focus we have been given has enabled us to progress in specific areas.'

'The SGQM has encouraged us all to think carefully about what we do with reference to our department's definition of excellent geography.

Refreshing our minds in terms of what we mean by excellent geography has caused us to rethink how we work towards it. This has benefited our students and they are well on the way to achieving our high expectations.'

'The SGQM process is embedded in the way our department works, as we have been involved in this scheme for a while. Engaging in the process as a core team helps us maintain a shared vision and drive the department forward.'

Using the Ofsted inspection methodology to evaluate your curriculum

Ofsted's EIF provides an external evaluation of the strengths and achievements of your curriculum. Kinder and Owens (2019), utilising the EIF, identify three key questions to consider in terms of curriculum impact:

- To what extent have students progressed towards curriculum 'goals' and evidenced what they can remember about the content studied?

- How do geographical knowledge and skills prepare all students for the next stage of education?

- What do student outcomes tell us about the appropriateness of the curriculum intent? (p. 100, Figure 3)

They explain that:

'The new framework quite rightly continues to place great importance on learning outcomes and assessment and inspectors will continue to make use of national performance information. However, it also makes clear that learning must build towards a goal and that pupils are expected to acquire knowledge and skills progressively.' (p. 98)

Ofsted make it clear that the end result of a good, well-taught curriculum is that students know more and are able to do more. The positive results of students' learning can then be seen in the standards they achieve. This makes work scrutiny an important part of the inspection process as it is here, in particular, that student progress will be evident.

The impact indicators in the EIF (Ofsted, 2019a) are:

- *learners develop detailed knowledge and skills across the curriculum and, as a result, achieve well. Where relevant, this is reflected in results from national tests and examinations that meet government expectations, or in the qualifications obtained*

- *learners are ready for the next stage of education, employment or training. Where relevant, they gain qualifications that allow them to go on to destinations that meet their interests, aspirations and the intention of their course of study. They read widely and often, with fluency and comprehension.*

The self-evaluation undertaken by a geography department to determine whether these indicators are achieved is a matter of professional judgment. The ideas and tools provided so far in this chapter have been designed to support this process. Ofsted inspections are a significant part of this evaluation process. You can also utilise the methodology of inspection; not to ensure you are doing what Ofsted want, but to ensure that your curriculum is successfully supporting your students to progress. The Ofsted methodologies are explained in 'Inspecting the curriculum: Revising inspection methodology to support the education inspection framework' (2019b). A key element of this methodology is what Ofsted call 'deep dives'. Leadership teams in many schools are involving their subject departments in using this guidance to conduct their own 'deep dives'. Often, the main focus of this is to practise the process in preparation for inspection; but this is underplaying the main advantages of adopting Ofsted methodologies, which is to evaluate the curriculum as part of an ongoing process of curriculum design.

Developing an inspection method to assess 'quality of education'

This method has three elements:

- top-level view

- deep dive

- bringing it together.

The process is explained here (Ofsted, 2019b, p. 4) and summarized in the diagram overleaf (Figure 7.3).

You can utilise the three main elements of the inspection method to develop a similar interconnected approach to evaluating the curriculum.

This is about a whole school overview; this can, however, be adapted to a geography department for purposes of evaluation:

'Identify the current strengths and weaknesses of the 11–16 geography curriculum, in the way teaching supports students to learn the curriculum, the standards that students achieve, students' behaviour and attitudes, and personal development' Ofsted (2019b): adapted headteacher's assessment of whole-school curriculum to geography. Section 15, p. 5.

The purpose of a **deep dive** approach is 'to gather the evidence necessary to form an accurate evaluation of how education flows from intention to implementation to impact within a school.' (Ofsted, 2019b, p. 6) In secondary schools, they will typically focus on a sample of four to six subjects, looking at a wide variety of students in different year groups across that sample. The deep dive includes the elements shown in Figure 7.3, overleaf.

- *evaluation of **senior leaders'** intent for the curriculum in this subject or area, and their understanding of its implementation and impact*

- *evaluation of **curriculum leaders'** long- and medium-term thinking and planning, including the rationale for content choices and curriculum sequencing*

- *visits to a deliberately and explicitly connected **sample of lessons***

- *work **scrutiny** of books or other kinds of work produced by pupils who are part of classes that have also been (or will also be) observed by inspectors*

- *discussion with **teachers** to understand how the curriculum informs their choices about content and sequencing to support effective learning*

- *discussions with a group of **pupils** from the lessons observed*

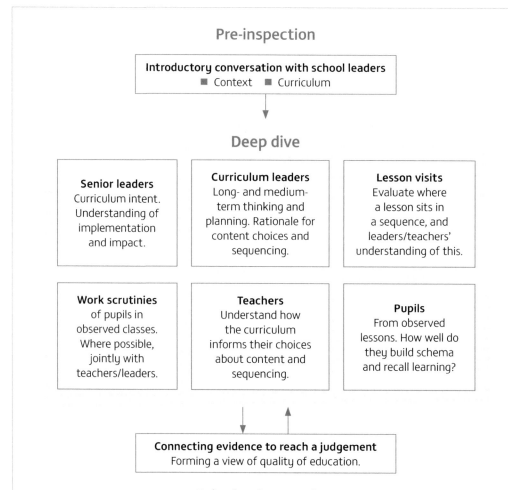

Figure 7.3: Developing an inspection method to assess quality of education. **Source:** Ofsted (2019b), p. 8.

Kinder and Owens (2019) report that Ofsted published two pilot-phase research exercises about approaches to work scrutiny (Ofsted, 2019c) and lesson observation (Ofsted, 2019d), and provide a table summarising indicators developed by Ofsted for these two methods. This research can be used to develop these methods for the purpose of evaluating your curriculum.

An overarching question to consider in using all these methods is: How far does the geographical learning flow from intention, to implementation, to impact, in lessons across the department?

ACTIVITY 7.3: THE OFSTED 'DEEP DIVE' AND HOW IT CAN HELP

TALKING POINT: What is the Ofsted 'deep dive' and how can we use the process to evaluate our curriculum?

Research phase

A useful overview of the inspection methodologies can be found by watching Matthew Purves, HMI, explaining 'deep dives': www.youtube.com/watch?v=byqlQ9nxshg

You can arrive at a more detailed analysis by reading about the Ofsted methodologies, particularly the 'deep dive' process explained in 'Inspecting the curriculum: Revising inspection methodology to support the education inspection framework' (2019b), pp. 3–10, in conjunction with Figures 7.3 and 7.4 in this chapter.

A practical geography-specific perspective of the 'deep dive' process is offered by Rachel Kay, Head of Geography in a Huddersfield school, inspected by Ofsted using this process in 2019. She has helpfully recorded the experience, and its benefits for the geography curriculum in her school (Kay, 2021). Her article includes four very useful additional downloads, demonstrating how Rachel informed inspectors about the thinking behind the school's curriculum plans for geography, as well as a list of the questions asked by inspectors.

Rachel has explained her experience of the 'deep dive' in conversation with John Lyon in GeogPod, Series 6, Episode 36: www.geography.org.uk/GeogPod-The-GAs-Podcast

PRACTICAL ACTION: Using the deep dive process to evaluate your curriculum

■ Identify key elements of the 'deep dive' process you think you can use to evaluate your curriculum.

An overarching question to consider in using all these methods is:

How far does the geographical learning flow from intention, to implementation, to impact, in lessons across the department?

You can use the key elements of the deep dive to answer the following questions:

■ What is the rationale and sequencing for your long- and medium-term planning?

■ How far do a sample of lessons, student's work, and discussions with students and teachers in your department, demonstrate the curriculum intent and decisions made about sequencing learning?

■ How does the intended and implemented curriculum impact on student progress?

The geography subject lead can use the methods of the deep dive, in particular lesson observations, work scrutiny, and ongoing discussions with teacher and students, for a dual purpose. Most importantly, to evaluate the geography curriculum: to identify what is, and what might not be, working; but also it provides a way of preparing a geography department to experience the process in an actual Ofsted inspection, as in Rachel Kay's school.

A good starting point would be to develop a range of questions to form the basis of evaluating student work, and lessons, using the indicators in Figure 7.4 overleaf.

Figure 7.4:
EIF pilot-phase work scrutiny and lesson observation research indicators.
Source: Kinder and Owens, taken from Ofsted, 2019c; 2019d.

Book scrutiny research indicators	Lesson observation research indicators
■ Building on previous learning – consistent, coherent and logically sequenced knowledge development ■ Depth of coverage – suitably broad range of topics within a subject ■ Depth of coverage – independent thinking, subject-specific concepts and connections to prior knowledge ■ Student progress – acquisition of knowledge and understanding appropriate to starting points ■ Practice – opportunities to revisit, deepen and solidify subject understanding and to demonstrate this.	**Curriculum** ■ subject expertise and skills to provide learning opportunities ■ equality of opportunity – lesson as building block to the wider curriculum ■ strategies to support reading/vocabulary/numeracy ■ suitably demanding content ■ logical sequence ■ recall and practise previously learned skills and knowledge ■ assessment of the current skills and knowledge of learners. **Teaching** ■ good communication skills ■ students build knowledge and make connections ■ relevant and appropriate resources to clarify meaning ■ good questioning skills and effective checks for understanding ■ explicit, detailed and constructive feedback. **Behaviour** ■ supportive classrooms focused on learning ■ focused classrooms through high expectations for students ■ clear and consistent expectations that are understood and followed ■ students' behaviour contributes to the focus on learning.

Stage 7: Maintain, change or move on

So far, evaluation has focussed on identifying the impact of the curriculum on student progress. Stage 7 of the curriculum process is to consider what actions are necessary to enhance the curriculum offer. The actions in this stage stem from the third question identified by Kinder and Owens:

■ What do student outcomes tell us about the appropriateness of the curriculum intent?

This stage is driven by another series of questions related to this effectiveness, using evidence compiled during the implementation of the curriculum and strategies outlined in the deep dive:

■ Do you maintain the curriculum and all its elements?

■ Do you change aspects of the curriculum intent to further develop student impact?

■ How do you move on?

A number of important sub-questions need to be considered to determine appropriate responses to these overarching questions, linked to the 'three energies' – the discipline of geography, subject specialist teaching, and the students themselves – in the curriculum-making process. The following provide an overview; you will no doubt identify others.

The key stage 3 curriculum

■ Is the curriculum coherent?

■ Does it offer a sufficiently broad and balanced understanding of the world to provide for the needs of all students, regardless of whether they go on to study geography at GCSE?

- Does it provide a coherent foundation for GCSE geography?
- Is the curriculum suitably ambitious to provide all our students with the knowledge they need to succeed in life?
- Are the units of work correctly sequenced to create clear stepping stones of progress for the curriculum journey?

The subject

- Does our curriculum sufficiently embrace the ideas of curriculum, pedagogy and assessment prevalent in the geography education community?
- How do we ensure our curriculum continues to provide a relevant understanding of our interconnected and dynamic world?

The teacher

- Is the curriculum vision appropriate?
- How can the subject knowledge and pedagogical expertise of each teacher be further developed to suit the needs of all students?
- How can we develop approaches to key elements within the curriculum, such as the integration of fieldwork, progressive use of OS and other maps and GIS to develop the spatial awareness of students?
- Are the approaches to teaching and learning appropriate to support the curriculum vision?
- Is students' understanding checked systematically?
- Are the approaches to assessment sufficiently wide to provide students with the opportunities to demonstrate their understanding and progress towards the vision?
- How do teachers ensure their subject, curriculum and pedagogical knowledge is up-to-date and influences the curriculum and its implementation towards our vision of student achievement?

The students

- Is the curriculum intent appropriate to the needs of all students at the school?
- Are our students thinking geographically, and how do we evidence this?
- Can changes be made to better support the progress of all students?
- Do we promote student engagement and discussion in the geography?
- Do our students have a positive and well-motivated attitude to studying geography?
- In the long term, do students remember the content they have been taught?
- Do students demonstrate understanding of the key concepts and ideas we have identified in the curriculum intent?
- Have our students progressed from our starting point, identified in Stage 2 of the process?
- How can the views and ideas of our students influence modifications to the curriculum and pedagogy?

Conclusion

Curriculum design is an ongoing process. Regularly evaluating and developing your curriculum will help ensure your changes have an impact on learners' achievements, lives and prospects. It is very easy to become so immersed in the process in your own department that you become blinkered to alternative views and approaches. Sharing with and listening to how other subjects and schools have approached curriculum design is invaluable, whether working with other departments in your own school, or across a MAT; using social media; or involvement in CPD.

The next chapter in this book provides case studies of how five different schools have approached the process of curriculum design.

References

All websites last accessed 27/07/2021.

Biddulph, M. (2010) 'Editorial: Valuing young people's geographies', *Teaching Geography*, 35, 2, p. 45.

Geographical Association (2009) *A Different View: A Manifesto from the Geographical Association*. Sheffield: Geographical Association. Available at www.geography.org.uk/GA-Manifesto-for-geography

Hopwood, N. (2007) *The Young People's Geographies Evaluator's Report*. Available at www.geography.org.uk/Young-Peoples-Geographies

Kay. R. (2021) 'The deep dive geography experience: intent, implementation and impact', *Teaching Geography*, 46, 1, pp. 11–13.

Kinder, A. and Owens, P. (2019) 'The new Education Inspection Framework – through a geographical lens', *Teaching Geography*, 44, 3, p. 98.

Ofsted (2019a) *The education inspection framework*. Available at www.gov.uk/government/publications/education-inspection-framework

Ofsted (2019b) *Inspecting the curriculum: Revising inspection methodology to support the education inspection framework*. Available at https://assets.publishing.service.gov.uk/government/uploads/system/uploads/attachment_data/file/814685/Inspecting_the_curriculum.pdf

Ofsted (2019c) *Workbook scrutiny: Ensuring validity and reliability in inspections*. Available at https://assets.publishing.service.gov.uk/government/uploads/system/uploads/attachment_data/file/936240/Inspecting_education_quality_workbook_scrutiny_report.pdf

Ofsted (2019d) *How valid and reliable is the use of lesson observation in supporting judgements on the quality of education?* Available at https://assets.publishing.service.gov.uk/government/uploads/system/uploads/attachment_data/file/936246/Inspecting_education_quality_Lesson_observation_report.pdf

QCA (2008) *Disciplined curriculum innovation: Making a difference*. Available at http://archive.teachfind.com/qcda/www.qcda.gov.uk/resources/publicationdf21.html

Whittall, D. (2019) 'Learning powerful knowledge successfully: perspectives from sixth form geography students', Impact: Journal of the Chartered College of Teaching. Available at https://impact.chartered.college/article/learning-powerful-knowledge-successfully-perspectives-sixth-form-geography-students/

Curriculum design in practice

As you have discovered, curriculum making is a complicated, collaborative process. Curriculum making and design are at the heart of the professional role of a teacher. In the day-to-day intensity of teaching, we can easily be pulled into the detail of what to teach next lesson. This is an urgent necessity, but this book has provided a range of key questions, examples and tools – the why, what and how of teaching – to help you keep in mind the bigger picture. As a matter of classroom routine, the teacher can share elements of this big picture with students, so they are clear on the purpose of learning, how it connects with prior and future learning, and how they are progressing towards the shared vision – the curriculum intent.

Curriculum making in practice is not a linear endeavour, and there is no one right way to create a curriculum plan. The enacted curriculum is more a series of interactions between teachers, students and the knowledge to be imparted, and understood. The subject knowledge and experiences of a group of geography teachers in a department are unique, as are the life experiences and ambitions of students, as well as the ethos and ambitions in each school. Curriculum design involves the interaction of all these variables and more, leading to the creation of a bespoke curriculum in each school. What is of great importance is that you are clear on the curriculum intent decisions you make, and can justify the choices in sequencing the curriculum to best support student progress towards this intent.

In this chapter we showcase examples of how five schools have approached their geography curriculum – and what they have learnt and achieved so far. Each is a snapshot in time of an ongoing design process. Extensive reference has been made to examples of practice in these schools throughout the guidance chapters of this book.

These case studies have been developed collaboratively over a ten-month period, in 2019–20. Each school has used the writing template or tool to help them tell their curriculum story (Activity 8.1). This template integrates all the key curriculum questions introduced in the guidance section of this book, thus providing an overview of the curriculum making process. It can be linked to the tool in Chapter 7 about developing an evaluation portfolio (Activity 7.2, p. 126).

ACTIVITY 8.1: THE CURRICULUM STORY TEMPLATE

You can use this template to write up your curriculum story as part of your portfolio. This is an invaluable way of focussing your geography department on the big picture of your curriculum, which can be shared with others, including your senior leadership team, the teachers within the geography department, parents, the governing body, even Ofsted. Your responses to the questions represent a coherent and evolving statement of what you are trying to achieve, how you have organised the learning and how you have identified its impact.

Key curriculum questions to consider in writing your curriculum story

Curriculum intent

Vision (Stages 1–3)

What are you trying to achieve for students by the end of the key stage?

What geography will your students know, understand and be able to do by the end of the key stage that they couldn't do at the beginning?

What big ideas and concepts will be introduced, and progressed across the key stage?

What important geographical skills will be introduced and progressed?

What is the starting point for your students as they begin this key stage?

Which aspects of your vision are currently weaknesses in your students?

How does your existing curriculum support progress towards the vision?

What are the strengths and weaknesses of your existing curriculum?

What changes do you need to make to the existing curriculum?

Which aspects of your vision do you need to develop into new units of work, ideas, resources?

How will students make progress in their geographical learning during the key stage?

How will the department share the vision with key stakeholders, most importantly the students?

What thinking/research and professional development led to your vision for students and their progress in geography?

How did the department team work together on creating the vision?

Curriculum design (Stage 4)

This is a copy of your strategic key stage plan, developed to demonstrate the integration of content with progression strands for geographical knowledge, concepts and skills.

The following questions help to explain the thinking behind this plan:

How have you planned for student progress across the whole key stage, each unit, and lessons?

What professional development was required to help teachers design your curriculum?

How have you selected and sequenced curriculum content to reflect and support student progress towards your vision?

How do the units of work interconnect to support

a holistic view of the world?

How does your curriculum develop an understanding of geographical concepts?

What contributions do different units of work make towards the strategic vision for the key stage, in terms of introducing or progressing geography concepts and skills?

How have you embedded your end goals and vision clearly into your curriculum?

Have you maintained, modified or rejected units of work used previously?

What is the planned focus of the units: themes, places, issues, skills, particular experiences (e.g. individual investigations), fieldwork or a mixture of all?

What opportunities are there for liaising or cross-curricular working with other subjects?

Curriculum implementation (Stage 5)

How has your curriculum intent influenced approaches to pedagogy and assessment?

What specific teaching approaches have been selected, e.g. enquiry or fieldwork?

What is the ethos of those teaching geography in your school?

What subject specialist and pedagogical knowledge professional development was required to implement your curriculum intent?

How will you know students are making progress towards your vision?

What different approaches to assessment evidenced your students' progress towards the vision?

How are geographical concepts and skills progressed through different units of work?

How has the sequencing of content helped to build student knowledge, understanding and skills in geography over time?

How is teaching helping students remember the geography content in the long term?

What types of resources and approaches have you utilised to support students in progressing towards the vision?

Curriculum impact (Stage 6)

How are you evaluating your curriculum?

How far have your students progressed towards the vision for your curriculum?

What impact has your curriculum had on student learning?

How are your students different now from the starting point you initially identified?

How has your new geography curriculum prepared your students for the next stage of education?

What challenges have you experienced in changing your curriculum?

How have you overcome them?

What key things have you learnt as a result of your curriculum development work?

Next steps (Stage 7)

What would you do differently next time?

How can you further improve/develop your curriculum?

What do you need to do next?

Figure 8.1: Curriculum journey template. ⬇

SCHOOL CASE STUDIES

A snapshot from each of the five school case studies, or curriculum stories, follow with a focus on a specific aspect of their story that relates to intent, implementation or impact. The full case studies can be downloaded from the area of the GA website dedicated to this book (see page 3 for details). **The continuous nature of curriculum development, means each case study will have moved on from this snapshot in time.**

School case study 1: Graveney School, London
Caiti Walter, Deputy Head of Geography until 2021.

Planning a coherent key stage 3 geography curriculum

School context
Graveney School is an 11–18 co-educational academy based in Tooting, inner London. The school is semi-selective (extension band students are awarded places based upon the Wandsworth test results) and is the top-performing school in the borough. 51% of students achieved the EBacc in 2019 and the Student Progress score was 0.51. The school offers a three-year key stage three and a two-year GCSE.

Focus of the case study extract – curriculum intent

Geography curriculum vision
The vision for geography study in our school aims to support the school's context, given that we are a large inner-city state school with a diverse intake. We want to prepare students for the realities of urban living, to reflect their own experiences, while also contextualising their experiences in the wider global community. We want them to be able to think in a geographically rigorous manner.

To ensure this vision is realised for every Graveney student, we set out the following three aims, which we hope every student will be able to achieve by the end of year nine:

- **AIM 1:** Apply knowledge to be able to **explore complex geographical issues** at a **range of scales**, including Tooting, greater London, the UK, Europe, and globally.

- **AIM 2: Think geographically through enquiry-based thinking**, emphasising **criticality** as a key skill.

- **AIM 3:** Demonstrate a comprehensive **range of geographically rigorous skills**, including geographical numeracy, geographical literacy, geographical oracy, and mapping skills.

This vision has not yet been shared with students, although we are considering this for next year so students gain more insight into the logic behind helping them to 'think geographically'.

Key stage 3 curriculum framework
Our geography department sets out to meet our three aims by exploring our curriculum through the geographical 'lenses' of place, space and scale. Our first topic at the start of key stage 3 intends to 'set

the scene' for our curriculum, by affording students exposure to both the spatial and temporal dimensions of geography from the outset. We do this through asking the 'fertile question' – in this case, 'What makes the perfect geographer?'

This topic lays the foundation for our curriculum, enthusing students about the concept of geography itself, by:

a) challenging them to develop complex geographical skills from the very beginning

b) exploring the key concepts that underpin the subject to appreciate the multifaceted nature of the subject

c) introducing small 'case studies' after a handful of lessons, to help them appreciate the value of deep geographical understanding as early as possible.

Beyond the first topic, in terms of curriculum selection, we have structured the key stage 3 schemes of learning using the two branches of geography – systematic geography and regional geography (Gersmehl, 2008). While most of our topics, as outlined in Figure 1, adopt the **systematic** conceptual structure, one topic in each year phase of key stage 3 adopts the **regional** approach, focusing on Africa, Asia and China, and Russia in years 7, 8, and 9 respectively. We feel that these approaches offer both procedural and contextual geographical knowledge to students, and that by exposing them to both approaches they will be able to 'appreciate and comprehend how the two complement one another' (Standish, 2017, p. 7).

The curriculum is mapped out using a topic framework, such that overarching topic themes pervade the entire key stage three curriculum, with the following geographical 'spheres' or 'worlds' revisited in each year of the key stage:

1. Our world to investigate

2. Our world with potential

3. Our world at risk

4. Our world of diversity

5. Our world to dispute.

We have not yet explicitly applied ideas behind these 'worlds' within topics, but students are shown this spiral and so are aware of the various worlds that we are exploring with them.

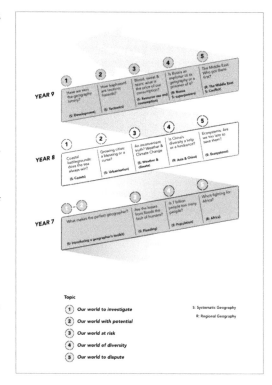

Figure 8.2: The Graveney geography key stage 3 'spiral of progression'.

Content sequencing

Topics have been sequenced with the following considerations in mind.

Sensible sequencing to account for prior knowledge. We want students to be able to make progress by increasingly identifying links in their geographical studies. We therefore carefully consider the order of all topics such that these 'linked learning' opportunities are maximised.

■ *Exemplar 1*: It makes sense to teach development before tectonics, since exploration of responses to a tectonic event in a high-income country compared to those in a low-income country requires a foundation knowledge about varying economic development to appreciate the nuances.

■ *Exemplar 2*: When teaching the regional geography topics we depend upon the students having prior knowledge of many of the geographical issues that we explore *in the context of the region in question*. For example, when we teach Russia in year 9 (see the Scheme of Work in full in the complete case study download) the lessons are taught with a view to retrieving knowledge from previous topics but in a new locational context.

For example, in lesson one of this scheme of work a key question is 'How old are the Ural mountains and how were they made?' Students would be unable to appreciate the collision of the Kazakhstania plate with the Euramerica plate 300 million years ago during the formation of Pangaea if they had no prior knowledge of the theories of continental drift and plate tectonics. With this in mind, our regional knowledge topics always feature towards the end of each academic year. Preceding specific place studies with theoretical knowledge provides the opportunity to apply the complex interactions of such knowledge that are bound within that given space.

■ *Exemplar 3*: The department continually reviews the appropriate place for dynamic topics like climate change and sustainability – these are core principles, but can include complex processes that may be better suited to older year groups. We currently introduce sustainability in the first topic in year 7. We introduce the issues associated with climate change in topics like flooding and Africa in year 7, but a full exploration of climate change mechanisms is not taught until part-way through year 8. Discussions of the placement of these topics are ongoing.

■ *Exemplar 4*: We are aware that some students are simply swayed towards the traditionally 'physical' topics rather than 'human' topics, and vice versa. While we try to ensure that every topic we teach touches on both of these classic branches of geography, we have alternated the predominantly physical and predominantly human units, such that we avoid switching off an entire section of students for any extended period of time.

■ *Exemplar 5*: Another reason for us placing region-based topics towards the end of each academic year is that we find that regional topics lend themselves towards long projects, where students are afforded an opportunity to create work of the highest quality – what Myatt (2018) dubs 'beautiful work'. The idea that work of the highest quality should be conceptualised

towards the end of the academic year makes sense; this is when students should be demonstrating that they have made the most progress.

Overview of the whole case study ⤓

1. School context
2. Geography department context
3. Geography curriculum vision
4. Our curriculum in the context of our school
5. How did the department work together to create the vision?
6. What is the starting point for our students as they begin this key stage?
7. Key stage three curriculum framework
8. Content sequencing
9. Building expectations and end goals into the curriculum
10. Curriculum implementation
11. How do different approaches to assessment evidence progress?
12. Curriculum impact
13. How do we know whether our department aims have been met?
14. What do we need to do next?

School case study 2: Trinity Academy Grammar, Sowerby Bridge

Andy Freer, Head of Humanities, Trinity Academy Grammar and Daniel Whittall, Geography Subject Lead and Head of Year 13, Trinity Sixth Form Academy.

Planning a coherent curriculum at GCSE – the curriculum is more than the exam specification

School and department context

Halifax, West Yorkshire, is a deprived area that has suffered badly at the hands of deindustrialisation but is undergoing post-industrial regeneration. This has a significant impact on our catchment areas, which show high levels of economic and social disadvantage. Trinity Academy, Sowerby Bridge's main catchment area is central Halifax and Sowerby Bridge, though not the more affluent surrounding villages. Currently, 57% of students are disadvantaged and 49% of students have English as an additional language.

Our two schools are both part of a multi-academy trust (MAT). We began working together on this curriculum planning when we were colleagues at a third school within the trust, Trinity Academy Halifax, but we are now both geography leads in our schools – Andy at Trinity Academy, Sowerby Bridge, and Dan at Trinity Sixth Form Academy.

Focus of the case study extract– curriculum intent

What process did we go through to create this curriculum?

In our thinking about curriculum, we have been especially struck by the work of Michael Young, and his suggestion that 'for children from disadvantaged homes, active participation in school may be the only opportunity that they have to acquire powerful knowledge and be able to move, intellectually at least, beyond their local and particular circumstances' (Young, 2011, p. 152).

Young's work prompted us to consider the role that a curriculum explicitly planned around providing opportunities for students to encounter powerful knowledge might play in supporting and overcoming the disadvantage gap. As a consequence, we began to think about how our curriculum might be planned and structured to put geography's powerful knowledge at its centre.

Dan had been inspired early in his geography teaching career by the GA's manifesto *A different view* (GA, 2009), and the work of David Lambert and John Morgan (2010), both of whom had argued for a concept-driven approach to geographical curriculum-making. We were also struck by the usefulness of Alaric Maude's (2016) five-fold typology for powerful knowledge in geography in helping us consider what powerful geographical knowledge actually is. Meanwhile, reading Charles Rawding's *Effective Innovation in the Secondary Geography Curriculum* (2013) helped us think about how to engage with concepts in our curriculum in such a way as to leave them open to multiple potential meanings, and to use them as tools through which students could interrogate the world and expand their horizons. The work of Clare Brooks (2016) prompted us to focus on the vital role that the individual teacher plays when it comes to making decisions about how the curriculum is understood, interpreted and put into practice locally. Finally, the work of Nick Hopwood

motivated us to consider how to 'take students' ideas seriously' because 'their interpretations of classroom experiences and subject conceptions matter, and … vary in striking ways' (Hopwood, 2012, p. 2).

Within our MAT we have sought to develop an all-through 11–16 curriculum across key stages 3 and 4 at Trinity Academy Grammar, Sowerby Bridge, that enables students to develop their understanding of geography as a subject. In doing so we have also drawn on our understanding of the post-16 curriculum at Trinity Sixth Form Academy, in an effort to ensure that students can see the subject in the round, and understand their progression through the subject as a journey towards a higher level of geographical thought.

To achieve this we focus our curriculum around seven conceptual golden threads that are interwoven across the key stage 3 and 4 curricula. After much thought, we settled on the following seven core concepts:

- Place
- Space
- Scale
- Global geography
- Interdependence
- Sustainable development
- Human and physical interactions.

Five of these concepts – place, space, scale, interdependence and sustainable development – were drawn from disciplinary geography and constituted what we considered to be the key concepts for the discipline of geography as it exists today. The other two – global geography and human and physical interactions – were chosen because they chimed with our sense of what makes geography as a school subject distinct from other school subjects, and also because these were aspects of the subject that researchers had found to be important for students elsewhere (Hopwood, 2012). These concepts are developed initially through the key stage 3 curriculum, and then feed directly into key stage 4. Drawing on concepts from the discipline of geography and integrating them into our GCSE teaching in ways that would enable students to understand and improve their knowledge of the world while also engaging with major debates at a local and global scale. We hoped to plan a curriculum that put into practice some of Maude's insights into types of powerful knowledge in geography, and Rawding's arguments about how concepts should cut across a curriculum rather than be taught once and then left behind.

Curriculum intent

Early on in the process of drawing up our curriculum it became clear to us that the way that the exam specification was framed offered opportunities to make links between our 'golden threads', or key concepts, in a variety of ways. However, a linear reading of the curriculum would, we thought, restrict these opportunities. We follow the AQA GCSE course, but we have come to understand the exam board specification as a list of content, rather than a curriculum. As subject-specialist teachers with expertise from across the discipline of geography, we were able to see clear links between different topic areas that were structured separately in the specification. An example of this is that in the Unit 2 section B – 'Changing economic world' – part of the specification there is a substantial element entitled 'The changing UK economy'.

Meanwhile, in Unit 2 section A there is a substantial element entitled 'Urban change in the UK'. We felt that those two sections, though kept separate in the specification, were too closely linked for us to separate them in our curriculum. We were especially keen to emphasise the ways in which the changing UK economy, and especially the processes of deindustrialisation, regeneration and the drive to a post-industrial economy, had been fundamental in shaping urban areas in the UK. This was particularly evident in our local area, Halifax, and in other nearby urban areas including Leeds and Manchester. By teaching these topic areas together we felt that the power of the geographical knowledge we taught would be increased, as it would take students beyond their everyday intellectual understandings of local and global places and processes in just the way that Young (2011) argues for.

In order to frame our overall curriculum we collectively drafted an intent statement (Figure 8.3) as part of our whole-school policy. We decided to use this statement as an opportunity to establish what we felt that our geography curriculum would do. The statement represents our shared vision as staff – it animates our work as teachers and drives the work that we do in planning our curriculum:

Figure 8.3:
Trinity Academy Grammar curriculum intent.

Curriculum intent

The geography curriculum at Trinity Academy Grammar, Sowerby Bridge, provides students with new ways of thinking about the world. Our curriculum will give students powerful ways of analysing, explaining and understanding different aspects of our world. Our curriculum will develop their knowledge of the world through the geographical themes of place, space, scale, interdependence, sustainable development and interactions between the human and physical world. Geography enables students to learn about thousands of years of discoveries about how the world works and develops the skills to add to this learning in the future.

Our lessons and curriculum are planned by subject specialists with interests in the relevant areas of geography, and teaching staff are constantly looking to engage with the wider profession through membership of professional bodies, such as the Geographical Association, and improve our subject knowledge using external agencies, such as the United Nations and the Royal Meteorological Society.

New knowledge in geography builds upon previous key content and/or themes and the curriculum is specifically structured for that reason. We aim to contribute to the development of students' perceptions and understandings of the world around them so that they can engage with contemporary issues. We aim also to support students in locating themselves and finding their way in an increasingly interconnected and, some have argued, placeless world.

Built into the geography curriculum are opportunities to explore the local area, such as the study of the microclimate of Sowerby Bridge. Central to GCSE geography are the field trips that allow the students to investigate a human and a physical environment, to see and understand how powerful concepts and processes from the classroom both inform and, at times, are challenged by the world around them. Fieldwork is central to the spirit and practice of enquiry, and we aim for our curriculum to support students in their ability to ask questions of the world around them and have the skills and knowledge to formulate intelligent answers to these questions.

Overview of whole case study ⬇

1. School context

2. Curriculum intent

3. Principles of sequencing the curriculum at GCSE

4. Key stage 4 curriculum map – explaining the embedding and planning for progression in understanding the 'golden threads'

5. Curriculum implementation to achieve the intent

6. Impact

7. Next steps.

This curriculum has been developed across different schools in a MAT. The overall intent is for the curriculum at key stage 4 to feed into an all-through 11–19 geography curriculum that promotes high levels of subject-specific conceptual literacy. The golden threads developed in the curriculum outlined here are therefore further developed and expanded upon across the key stage 5 curriculum for A level geography, and a process of ongoing review between the schools will continue in order to refine and develop this curriculum (see Figure 9.4, p. 145, Dan's A level curriculum intent statement.)

The full case study can be downloaded from this book's dedicated password-protected website.

School case study 3: Fortismere School

Kirsty Holder, Senior Leader responsible for implementation of the ECF and ITT.

School context

Fortismere School is an 11–18 mixed, comprehensive, foundation secondary school and sixth form, in Haringey, Greater London, with 1767 students on role (2019). It is a high-attaining school and was ranked 12th best comprehensive in *The Times* in 2016.

Students at Fortismere follow a three-year key stage 3 curriculum, with three hours of geography a fortnight. Students make their option choices for key stage 4 in the February of year 9. Geography is a strong department in the school community and the subject has continued to rise in popularity as a GCSE option over the last fourteen years.

The geography department consists of five teachers who solely teach geography. These are: myself (head of department), a teacher of 20 years and at Fortismere since 2004; our key stage 5 post-holder who has been at the school since 2001; an established main-scale teacher of 15 years who has been at the school since 2007; a Teach First-trained teacher who started with us in 2019 and is in their third year of teaching, and an NQT who also joined us in 2019.

Focus of the case study extract – curriculum implementation

Sharing the vision

At present our curriculum intent statement and an outline of the curriculum is shared with parents on the school website. We have also agreed the following approaches to making the vision of our intended curriculum more transparent with all parties. Some of these plans have not been fully implemented in 2021, in part due to COVID-19 restrictions.

- We planned to ensure all topics have a student summary sheet to stick in their book at the start of the topic. This sheet will share the learning objectives of each lesson within the scheme of work and highlight the links with other topics in the curriculum. It will also indicate to students which elements of contextual world knowledge, conceptual geographical understanding and geographical enquiry and skills the topic is working on. Students will return to this sheet through the topic.

- Displays of our summary tables in every classroom and the corridor.

- Development of a more student-friendly version of the tables into a curriculum map or pathway poster that students can stick into their books.

- We will routinely remind students of our vision at the start and end of topics – highlight to students where we are in our geography learning journey and to demonstrate links to prior and sometimes future learning – the 'thinking geographically webs' aim to support students in starting to do this independently.

- In schemes of work, teachers will flag up the interconnections, and highlight the contribution the particular unit is making to support student progress towards the end goal for the key stage.

How do we assess?

This year for all subjects we are launching a new and exciting assessment policy where the curriculum *is* the progression model, following the principle that students make progress if they learn the curriculum. As such we have an assessment system that aims to measure how much of the curriculum has been learnt.

Students in key stage 3 will have two summative assessments in each year. These will sample from the whole curriculum content that has been taught to that date, not just the most recent, and assessment design will respect subject differences by individual departments.

The current thinking for us in geography is that these assessments will combine geographical conceptual understanding and skills that have been taught to that point in the child's education – this will mean that it will incorporate a mix of topics and skills. There will also be low-stakes 'hinge' assessments in between these summative assessments that will support teachers and heads of department in gauging where students are in their learning and thus help teachers to respond to their needs to ensure student progression through the curriculum.

At the heart of our policy is a strong emphasis on formative assessment and high-quality classroom practice. The ultimate purpose of teaching that focuses on formative assessment is to create self-regulated learners who can leave school able and confident to continue learning throughout their lives. This responsive way of teaching and assessing is an approach that creates feedback, which is then used to improve students' performance. Students become more involved in the learning process and from this they gain confidence in what they are expected to learn and to what standard. We believe that the progress a student makes is the most important measure, and as such the curricula we all design in our subject areas are the progression models: students will have made progress if they have learnt the curriculum. This element of the policy is very much influenced by Barak Rosenshine's '10 Principles of Instruction' (Rosenshine, 2012) – in particular principle 6 – 'Check for understanding frequently and correct errors'.

In geography we have been increasingly building on our formative assessment in lessons, through such practices as 'Geog your memory' at the start of each lesson. This involves a set of five questions for students to work through at the start of the lesson – three questions from the previous lesson, one question from earlier in the topic and a further question related to a prior topic. We have also been developing the use of 'knowledge checker quizzes' – here we use online platforms such as Seneca and Google Quizzes, as well as written quizzes in lessons. Many classroom tasks are followed (or started) with shared success criteria (students often help to build these criteria), self-assessment and model answers. As a school and a department we will be exploring many more ways to develop and 'build in' our formative assessment practices, so students do not leave the classroom with misconceptions that would limit their progression to the next stage of the curriculum. This is a key part of Schema Theory and Rosenshine's 'Principles of Instruction'.

Overview of the whole case study ⬇

1. How the geography department approached redesigning the key stage 3 curriculum in 2020

2. Curriculum intent vision

3. How do we approach geographical knowledge and understanding? Includes an explanation of the five themes the geography curriculum explores

4. Embedding geographical skills

5. Approach to sequencing content

6. Curriculum implementation – approaches to sharing the vision – and assessment

7. What training have we received to help design the curriculum?

8. Next steps in the process.

School case study 4: The Harris Federation
Lizzie Butler, Lead Geography Consultant for the Harris Federation.

School context

The Harris Federation is a MAT in London, with 50 academies in total – 28 secondaries and 22 primaries. Despite covering a relatively small geographic area compared to other MATs, each has a unique context both in terms of the demographic intake and their approach to whole-school curricula and systems.

Geography departments across the Federation are comprised mainly of subject specialists; a small proportion of geography lessons across the Federation are taught by non-specialists, but this varies significantly by department and from year to year within each department. Across the Federation, each core subject is supported by a team of subject specialist consultants who work from the infrastructure of the central team and carry out three main roles in respect to school support:

1. To have oversight over the curriculum and assessment models within our subjects.

2. To support schools on a day-to-day basis with enacting the curriculum, teaching and learning, mentoring and coaching of teachers and heads of department, and supporting outcomes for exam classes.

3. To provide or co-ordinate subject-specific CPD and training in a series of centralised events, including schools' direct trainees, ECTs and more experienced teachers.

The first geography consultant within the Harris Federation was appointed from Easter 2014. One of their first priorities was the curriculum. The team expanded to two in September 2016 and has now grown to seven full time geography consultants.

Before 2014, there were very different approaches to geography teaching across the Federation and no common approach at key stage 3 or key stage 4. Prior to the formal introduction of the geography consultant role, a core group of heads of department from within the Federation had already started discussing the value of and possibilities for a shared curriculum. As such, from its inception, the 'Federation Common Curriculum' was a collaborative, bottom-up initiative, and its subsequent evolution ever since has continued in that spirit. The introduction of the new National Curriculum in 2014, the creation of the consultant role to formalise the cross-Federation collaboration at key stages 3 and 4, and the publication of 'KS3: The wasted years?' (Ofsted, 2015) were the catalysts needed to introduce this new, standardised and coherent geography curriculum across the Federation. At key stage 3 the Harris Federation geography curriculum has been created to provide an outline of the core content to be taught. Each individual department then undertakes their own curriculum-making

process to ensure the enacted curriculum their students receive reflects their unique context.

Following the introduction of the 2016 GCSE and A levels, the majority of schools adopted the same exam specification at key stage 4 (OCR B) and key stage 5 (OCR). OCR B was chosen at key stage 4 because of its focus on enquiring minds, which aligned with our intent of embedding enquiry to support geographical thinking. We preferred the way that skills and the UK components are integrated throughout the assessment structure rather than being included in separate papers. The enquiry focus of the Unit 3 paper also aligns with our intent to embed enquiry in key stage 3. Advising that Academies within the Federation follow the same exam specification at key stage 4 and curriculum at key stage 3 allows specialist support for schools from both the consultant team and external CPD. It also allows for common assessments and mock exams to take place across the Federation, which gives reliable data on student performance and progress.

Focus of the case study extract– curriculum intent, implementation and next steps

Intent

The Harris Federation geography intent covers three core areas:

1. The importance of geography in the curriculum; this is self-explanatory for geographers, so is not described here.

2. The evolving geography curriculum, with an emphasis on powerful disciplinary knowledge and geographical enquiry, to encourage students to *think geographically*. Access to powerful geographical knowledge is an entitlement for all students and through teaching it we help achieve social justice.

3. Geography teachers as curriculum makers; we believe that geography teachers have specialist knowledge, and through our curriculum we attempt to empower our teachers to make decisions for the particular needs of their students.

Within the context of 'powerful geographical knowledge' we were influenced by Alex Standish's (2017) work, in which he identifies the three types of geographical knowledge – contextual (knowledge of places), propositional (knowledge of

AO1 25%	AO2 50%	AO3 25%
Contextual knowledge	**Propositional knowledge**	**Procedural knowledge**
They have extensive knowledge relating to a wide range of places, environments and features at a variety of appropriate spatial scales, extending from local to global.	They understand the physical and human conditions and processes that lead to the development of, and change in, a variety of geographical features, systems and places. They can explain various ways in which places are linked and the impact such links have on places and environments. They make connections between different geographical phenomena they have studied with the use of geographical theories and laws.	They ask informative questions that promote geographical enquiry.

They use geographical enquiry to select and analyse a wide range of data to make judgements and draw conclusions about geographical issues and problems. |

systems) and procedural (knowledge of skills) – which informed our approach to structuring the curriculum. We developed three assessment objectives in key stage 3 to ensure that we were addressing each area of knowledge consistently, both in our curriculum and assessments. These are similar to the progression strands identified by the GA in their progression framework.

Intended curriculum plan

We call the core curriculum document for key stage 3 geography the 'Toolkit', and make the following statement on the front page to explain its purpose to all relevant stakeholders:

The term 'Toolkit' has been used intentionally instead of, say, scheme of work, short-term plan or other more familiar terms to describe curricula documents. This is because it has been designed in a way that allows geography departments from within the Harris Federation to engage critically with it through a process known as curriculum making.

Simply put, the Toolkit outlines the geographical knowledge deemed necessary for a key stage 3 student to end year 9 with. However, such knowledge only gains power when married with the choices of the teacher (pedagogy) and the experiences of the student in the classroom. It is the responsibility of individual geography departments within the Harris Federation to develop this Toolkit into a meaningful scheme of work and series of lessons so that their students may develop their ability to think geographically about the world.

The topics and sequence of the curriculum is outlined in Figure 8.5 (showing the September 2020 version), having gone through an annual process of evaluation, review and editing.

These topics were chosen to ensure a balance between systematic and regional topics (Standish, 2017), and human and physical geography. They also reflect the powerful knowledge that we felt was fundamental for students to acquire before the end of key stage 3 – to ready them to continue the subject in key stage 4, but more for the intrinsic value of that geographical knowledge. Each unit of work is developed with the three spheres of geographical knowledge (contextual, propositional and procedural) in mind, and while some units may lean more heavily in one direction, we have attempted to achieve a balance between regional and contextual knowledge, systematic and theoretical knowledge, and geographical skills.

'Big ideas'

Every year the curriculum undergoes a process of review. During the 2017 review, it became apparent that teachers across the Federation were having difficulty implementing one of the original units, on geology. This problem led to a restructure of the curriculum so that rather than form a discrete unit, all the key knowledge from this geology unit was woven into other topics throughout the curriculum where relevant and necessary for students to make sense of the knowledge that was coming next. Thus, the 'big ideas' were born and interwoven throughout the curriculum. Groups of geography teachers discussed and identified all the core 'ideas' which underpinned

Year 7

Topic	Topic title	Enquiry question
Topic 1	Geography: my passport to the world	How can geography help me understand the world?
Topic 2	Amazing environments	What are the world's main biomes and how do humans interact with them?
Topic 3	Behind the brand	What is the human and environmental cost of buying an iPhone?
Topic 4	Contemporary issues in the UK	What is the human and physical geography of the UK like?
Topic 5	Land ho!	How and why are the UK's rivers changing the landscape?

Year 8

Topic	Topic title	Enquiry question
Topic 6	From Cairo to Cape Town	What is Africa like and how it is changing?
Topic 7	Angry Earth	What are tectonic processes and how do they impact humans and environments?
Topic 8	How many is too many?	How are global population issues and resources causing challenges in the 21st century?
Topic 9	Borders	What are borders and how do they impact people and the environment?
Topic 10	Fieldwork skills	How can geographers study the world?

Year 9

Topic	Topic title	Enquiry question
Topic 11	The UK	What makes the UK so dynamic?
Topic 12	Gazing at glaciers	How does glaciation change the world?
Topic 13	Earth's biggest challenge?	Why is climate change a significant global challenge in the 21st century?
GCSE unit	Dynamic development (see key stage 4 MTPs)	Why are some countries more developed than others?

Figure 8.5: The Harris Federation key stage 3 long-term plan, 2020.

each topic in the key stage 3 curriculum. These conversations went through several cycles of reducing the 'big ideas' to fewer, more abstract hierarchical concepts, reminiscent of Maude's work (2020) on geographical key concepts.

Brooks' (2018) discussion of concepts, and their place in the geography curriculum helped further refine our thinking on the place we wanted these 'big ideas' to occupy in our curriculum. Of the abstract, hierarchical concepts such as place, space and environment she says 'they are helpful in determining the "ends" or outcomes of the curriculum, but not necessarily the process or

the "means" of how to achieve that end' (p106). Brooks also quotes Rawling's work on developing concepts in geography curricula which states that the hierarchical concepts should not be the starting point for curriculum design, but 'more of a skeleton on which to hang the more detailed curriculum flesh' (Rawling, 2007 p. 17 in Brooks, 2018 p. 106). The 'big ideas' we ended up with are organisational concepts which are the means to achieving understanding, over the course of the curriculum, of the hierarchical concepts which are omnipresent at key stage 3. We ended up with the five identified in Figure 8.6.

Climate	Geomorphology	Development	Sustainability	Human/physical interactions

Curriculum implementation

Our intention is that departments take ownership of their curriculum as 'curriculum makers'. If schools are to be able to do this, guidance in the Toolkit, in terms of implementing the curriculum needs to be flexible, as explained by Jessica Chapman, Head of Geography at Harris Girls' Academy East Dulwich:

The points in the Toolkit are broken down in a way that means they are broad enough that you can implement them in a range of ways to complement the context and intent of your school. Our school is based in south east London, with high levels of deprivation; we can use the topics throughout the Toolkit and adapt them to local geography. Students can access them, and use them to help access the bigger, broader concepts that they find difficult; also we can choose our own case studies and global examples to give students a love of geography and learning outside of their own community.

Next steps (Summer 2021)

This has already been a six-year journey of curriculum development; each year adds a new layer of deeper thinking, better resourcing, updating of knowledge and content and tweaks to sequencing. Through our involvement with the Fawcett Fellowship Programme at the Institute of Education this year we hope to produce empirical evidence of the success of the curriculum.

At the time of first writing (July 2020), globally a spotlight is being shone on issues of race, diversity and equity, representation and colonialism in all sections of society including education. The RGS (with IBG) statement in support of #BLM, and other articles, research and engagement with speakers have given us pause to reflect on geography's historical contribution to colonialism and the structural inequity that exists in academic geography nationally.

We are currently applying this to our curriculum model. There are two strands to this work; firstly, the content that is written into the 'Toolkit' which schools are explicitly required to teach and secondly, the pedagogy and choices of place, resources and approaches to teaching taken by each individual department.

Our ongoing curriculum consultation and review occurs with a very conscious lens on these issues. This includes careful consideration of the language used; the way topics are taught; the plurality of voices that are represented within the curriculum and opportunities for students to explore places that have meaning to them through a geographical lens. We were particularly inspired by the article by Milner *et al* (2021) in *Teaching Geography* which says 'The power of diversity in geography serves to tackle stereotypes, dismantle dominant narratives, improve representation of places and people, and empower students from all backgrounds through developing a multifaceted view of the world and their place within it.' (p. 59). We have updated our 'Intent' to ensure that the principles of equality, diversity and inclusion are embedded at the outset and reject a tokenistic or 'add on' approach. We are including within our key curriculum document a focus on equality, diversity and inclusive pedagogies to signpost to teachers where different approaches could be taken. We are engaging with academics who are publishing research in this field, and arranging CPD and training for teachers in the classroom. A key shift in our curriculum narrative, which we will look to embed in our curriculum documents, resources and teaching and learning has been to learn *from* other people rather than about them (Radcliffe, 2017); to hear directly from the people, places and communities, rather than through a recontextualised resource from a western perspective.

This work is ongoing and because it's not a 'box-to-tick' will never be finished. It is a continual presence in our thinking when continuing the evolution of the curriculum.

Overview of the whole case study ⬇

1. Introduction to the curriculum toolkit
2. Curriculum intent
3. Key stage 3 curriculum plan
4. Big ideas
5. Core content
6. Rationale for sequencing units in the plan
7. Curriculum implementation – the importance of enquiry and fieldwork
8. Evidence of impact
9. Curriculum review – a MAT-wide evaluation process
10. Next steps.

School case study 5: Spalding Grammar School, South Lincolnshire

Aidan Hesslewood, Head of Geography.

School context

Spalding Grammar School (SGS) is a relatively large (approx. 1000 on roll) selective boys' school in South Lincolnshire. Aspirations in this area are not high, and many adjacent areas are listed as TLIF (Teaching and Learning Innovation Fund) category 5 and category 6 Local Area Districts (areas identified by the DfE of social deprivation and limited social mobility). It is an old school with a rich history and is well-liked in the local community. In geography, students study a full three-year key stage 3 curriculum and can opt to study a two-year GCSE, currently examined by AQA. A level is also offered. Uptake for both is healthy and stable. The school recently appointed a new head of geography – Aidan Hesslewood –- to lead the department of experienced geography specialists. In the 2019–20 academic year the department has sought to reinvigorate the geography key stage 3 curriculum. After initial discussions, the department concluded that the existing curriculum lacked sufficient potential to engage and motivate students, and seemed out-of-date, lacking contemporary geographical topics and case studies.

The team, therefore, embarked on quite a challenging process: first, to establish a vision for the team and department; second, the influences through which a new key stage 3 curriculum could be made; and third, to write and implement a new curriculum with a view to progression in geographical thinking.

Focus of this case study extract – curriculum impact

Impact: Evaluating the efficacy of curriculum change

While significant time and effort has been invested into the vision and intent – and indeed the day-to-day implementation – it is now time to shift the focus onto the impact this curriculum change has had on the students. The fundamental question about impact for the team at SGS is *'how well do we achieve the aims and ambitions of our curriculum?'* The purposes of answering such a question are quite simply departmental development and accountability (this isn't a school that makes decisions based on the threat of inspection, but it does help to always be ready). This is not an easy question to answer, though, and requires comprehensive and sustained searching. The plan so far has been threefold. First, to ask the right questions about impact – to get forensic and examine impact from different perspectives. Second, to figure out how to investigate impact and identify methods that will yield the evidence. Third, to predict what this evidence will look like and what it will 'say' about the student-curriculum dyad. Anecdotal evidence so far suggests that classroom progress – especially the students' capacity to interpret data and enquire – is already demonstrable. Their extended writing is improving, and they are beginning to make links across the geography curriculum, using their previous learning to contextualise what they are currently studying. However, having just embarked on this part of the journey, a more robust action plan will help the team build on this evidence to help highlight the direction in which our next steps need to go. This is summarised in the table (Figure 8.7), with the caveat that each of the data collection methods needs its own methodology suited to the context of the students, the department, and the school.

The questions are certainly not exhaustive, but to the team at SGS they are a useful starting point from which to discuss and evaluate impact.

Key question	Methods	Evidence
Evaluating how the curriculum is designed		
1. Is the planned SGS geography curriculum ambitious enough, covering the necessary breadth and depth of geographical thinking that provides all students with greater capabilities later in life?	■ Cross-reference with key stage 3 National Curriculum ■ Compare with leading textbooks for 'pitch' ■ Curriculum audit pre-teaching and review post-teaching ■ SGQM	■ School leaders, department heads and geography teachers use expertise and experience to confirm level of challenge and ambition ■ Powerful disciplinary knowledge is clear
2. Does planning for progression (and sequencing) enable both high-performing students to be stretched and lower-performing students to be supported and included?	■ Curriculum audit pre-teaching and review post-teaching ■ Lesson study	■ Short-, medium-, and long-term plans for teaching within the curriculum incorporate challenging material and tasks while also including structure and scaffolding
3. Does the curriculum provide opportunities to build cultural capital?	■ Curriculum audit pre-teaching and review post-teaching ■ Lesson study ■ Student focus groups ■ Student review questionnaires	■ Powerful disciplinary knowledge (PDK –the basis of cultural capital) is woven throughout the curriculum ■ Lesson study illustrates that students understand PDK and can use it fluently
4. Does the key stage 3 curriculum prepare students for GCSE geography?	■ Curriculum audit pre-teaching and review post-teaching ■ Uptake analysis ■ GCSE examination results	■ No repetition of topics, yet GCSE students can recall and use PDK that underpins GCSE study ■ More and more students will choose to study geography as a result of good attainment and understanding at KS3 ■ Sustainably high or improving results
5. Does the GCSE curriculum (and teaching) prepare students for A level geography?	■ Curriculum audit pre-teaching and review post-teaching ■ Uptake analysis ■ A level examination results ■ Student focus groups	■ A level students use excellent GCSE attainment as a strong foundation for their course ■ More and more students will choose to study geography as a result of good attainment and understanding at GCSE ■ Sustainably high or improving results
6. Does the A level curriculum (and teaching) prepare students for life beyond SGS?	■ Destinations to which students progress when they leave school ■ A level examination results	■ More and more students will choose to study geography as a result of good attainment and understanding at A level ■ Sustainably high or improving results
Evaluating how the curriculum is taught		
7. Is the teaching of the curriculum consistent, and how does the department work collaboratively to ensure this?	■ Work scrutiny – student work across teachers ■ Lesson observations	■ Consistency in material in books ■ Consistency in teaching – identification of big geographical ideas (PDK)
8. What is the quality of teaching like? Do teachers stretch the most capable while supporting those who need it?	■ Lesson observations ■ Lesson study ■ Student focus groups	■ Students are engaged in lessons, ask pertinent questions, and challenged to understand PDK ■ Teachers are pedagogically fluent with PDK
9. Do teachers have good geographical knowledge and do they present subject matter clearly?	■ Lesson observations ■ Lesson study	■ Students are engaged in lessons, ask pertinent questions, and challenged to understand PDK ■ Teachers are pedagogically fluent with PDK

Figure 8.7: Evaluating the impact of the curriculum (continued overleaf).

10.	Do teachers check understanding for misconceptions and provide feedback? As a result, do teachers adapt their teaching as necessary?	■ Lesson observations ■ Lesson study	■ Teachers respond clearly to student understanding, ensuring that students are able to acquire PDK
11.	Are teaching resources high-quality?	■ Lesson observations ■ Lesson study ■ Student focus groups	■ Teaching resources are tailored to students and based on latest thinking/data, not regurgitated from old textbooks
12.	To what extent are members of the department supported in adapting to curriculum change?	■ Staff surveys/meetings	■ Staff are confident in teaching the curriculum and actively contribute towards it ■ Leaders provide necessary support

Evaluating student progress, outcomes, and preparedness for their next steps

13.	To what extent is students' work high quality?	■ Work scrutiny ■ Lesson observations ■ Lesson study	■ Student work is clear and shows understanding of PDK and key geographical ideas
14.	To what extent does assessment show student progression, and how does it help us identify whether our students are ready for the next stage in their education?	■ Internal data analysis	■ Overall trends indicate that students know, understand, and can do more over time, meeting personal targets and fulfilling GA benchmark expectations [from the progression framework (2020)]
15.	To what extent do students know more over time, and can they remember more of it?	■ Lesson observations ■ Lesson study ■ Work scrutiny – student work over time ■ Student focus groups ■ Student review questionnaires	■ Students are observed to build on their previous PDK in lessons ■ Student work shows that previously-learnt PDK is used to contextualise new knowledge ■ Students state that they know more over time and can remember it
16.	To what extent do the most disadvantaged students at SGS – as well as students with SEND – learn the knowledge and cultural capital they need to succeed in life?	■ Lesson observations ■ Lesson study ■ Work scrutiny – student work over time ■ Student focus groups ■ Internal data analysis	■ Disadvantaged and SEND students work as well as others in class, and book work is of as high quality ■ Disadvantaged and SEND students state that they feel they learn valuable and powerful knowledge ■ Internal data shows no gaps
17.	How do public examination results reflect the knowledge and skills students have gained over time?	■ Public examination results analysis	■ Examination results are consistently high or rapidly improving, and are above the national average

Figure 8.7: Evaluating the impact of the curriculum.

A similar framework that could be used is the GA's Secondary Geography Quality Mark, which similarly questions the efficacy of different elements of a departments' work, and allows for the collation of evidence and critical reflection that undoubtedly leads to improved outcomes. I was fortunate enough, several years ago, to lead the department in which I worked to SGQM Centre of Excellence. As a participant in the past, and now as a moderator for the GA's SGQM team, I would highly recommend any department go through the process, but especially as part of an impact evaluation.

This is our first step in the evaluation process, and now the really difficult work starts. Action planning is next, identifying month-by-month the evidence that needs to be collected and *how* it will be collected; for example, organising student focus groups and writing the question schedules that will underpin them. Indeed, student voice is an important part of any department/curriculum evaluation and it is imperative that this perspective is included. Students have a unique and very different view of their education from that of the teachers who construct it for them.

Following that, the team will collect the evidence (this should now remind you of the process of geographical enquiry!). This might mean keeping records of student work and comparing them, analysing internal data trends, conducting focus groups and lesson observations. Later in the year, the team will discuss and analyse the evidence, assessing where the strengths and weaknesses lie. With the input of senior leadership advice, this will form the basis of modifications to our department development plan (DDP) that details the 5-year strategy of improvement and evaluation: in short, the 'plan–do–review'. A brand-new curriculum and wholesale change are always risky enterprises and not without their challenges, one of which being time (or the lack of it). GIS, for example, has yet to be *fully* integrated into the curriculum, and 'careers in geography' needs a lot of attention, but we are now working on those. The idea of 'marginal gains' – smaller, incremental gains on *every* aspect of geography education at SGS, rather than focusing energy into single areas – is now the method of addressing the longer-term DDP (trying to 'finish' a DDP in one year and then creating another for the next seems nonsensical, hence the *5-year* plan). Many development items take years to fully address and there is nothing unprofessional about letting them 'roll over' into the next year if sufficient improvement has not been achieved.

Overview of the whole case study ⬇

1. Context

2. Intent: Vision, Influences and Inspiration

3. From intent to implementation: Progression framework and curriculum sequencing. This section includes a copy of the progression framework – 'The geographical journey on which our students embark is mapped around this framework, that sets out a model of progression of geographical knowledge, concepts and skills'.

4. Assessment

5. Rationale for sequencing the units in the curriculum

6. Integration of fieldwork

7. Impact: Evaluating the efficacy of curriculum change

References

All websites last accessed 27/07/2021.

Brooks, C. (2016) *Teacher subject identity in professional practice: Teaching with a professional compass*. Abingdon: Routledge.

Geographical Association (2009) *A Different View: A Manifesto from the Geographical Association*. Sheffield: Geographical Association. Available at www.geography.org.uk/GA-Manifesto-for-geography

GA (2012) *Thinking geographically* Available at https://www.geography.org.uk/write/mediauploads/download/ga_ginconsultation%20thinkinggeographically%20nc%202012.pdf

Geographical Association (2020) *A progression framework for geography*. Available at https://www.geography.org.uk/eBooks-detail/71c435a8-c548-4e38-80db-2305275fbee5

Gersmehl, P.J. (2008) *Teaching Geography*. New York: Guilford Press.

Hopwood, N. (2012) *Geography in secondary schools: Researching students' classroom experiences*. London: Bloomsbury.

Lambert, D. and Morgan, J. (2010) *Teaching Geography 11–18: A Conceptual Approach*. Maidenhead: Open University Press.

Maude, A. (2016) 'What might powerful geographical knowledge look like?', *Geography*, 101, 2, pp. 70–76.

Maude, A. (2020) 'The role of geography's concepts and powerful knowledge in a Future 3 curriculum', *International Research in Geographical and Environmental Education*, 29, 3, pp. 232–43.

Milner, C., Garcia, H. and Robinson, H. (2021) 'How to start a conversation about diversity in education' *Teaching Geography*, 46, 2. pp. 59–60

Myatt, M. (2018) *The Curriculum: Gallimaufry to coherence*. Woodbridge, Suffolk: John Catt Educational Ltd.

Ofsted (2015) *KS3: The wasted years?* Available at https://assets.publishing.service.gov.uk/government/uploads/system/uploads/attachment_data/file/459830/Key_Stage_3_the_wasted_years.pdf

Radcliffe, S. A. (2017) 'Decolonising geographical knowledges' *Transactions of the Institute of British Geographers*, 42, 3, pp. 323–33.

Rawding, C. (2013) *Effective innovation in the secondary geography curriculum: A practical guide*. Abingdon: Routledge.

Rosenshine, B. (2012) 'Principles of Instruction: Research-based strategies that all teachers should know', *American Educator*, Spring 2012, pp. 12–19.

Standish, A. (ed) (2017) *What should schools teach?* London: UCL Press.

Whittall, D. (2019) 'Learning powerful knowledge successfully: Perspectives from sixth form geography students', *Impact: The journal of the Chartered College of Teaching*. Available at https://impact.chartered.college/article/learning-powerful-knowledge-successfully-perspectives-sixth-form-geography-students

Young, M. (2011) 'What are schools for?', *Educação Sociedade & Culturas*, 32, pp. 145–55.

CHAPTER 9

Where next?

Hopefully this book has demonstrated what an exciting time it is to be a geography teacher! Ofsted's focus on curriculum in its Education Inspection Framework has had an impact, aligning the controls on the curriculum identified by Tim Oates (see Chapter 2, pp. 19–20). This change has led to a refocus on the curriculum in schools. This book has been written to support geography teachers, in this new era of curriculum design, to become what the GA Manifesto referred to as 'curriculum makers' (p. 27). Chapter 8 demonstrates the progress a number of geography departments have already made towards this.

The Ofsted research into the curriculum in schools, and the resultant EIF, has culminated in a systems view of a subject knowledge-based curriculum, passing through different states of intent, implementation and impact, all focussed on student progress. This book has highlighted this view, underpinned by the theories and ideas of the geography subject community, to provide a practical toolkit to support your curriculum development.

Curriculum designed to progress your students' capabilities to think geographically

Figure 9.1 – the Big Picture – summarises the process of designing a coherent geography curriculum. The diagram has been adapted from the QCA 'Big Picture' of the curriculum (2010) (Chapter, 1 Figure 1.2, p. 13); the three curriculum questions have been replaced by Ofsted's 'three I's': intent, implementation and impact. Figure 9.1 is a strategic tool to aid discussion about designing a coherent geography curriculum; it demonstrates the interconnections between the curriculum intent, implementation and impact. It provides an overview of the guidance section of this book. You can use this strategic view of the geography curriculum, in conjunction with the steps identified in the curriculum process diagram (Figure 9.2). This diagram demonstrates the key curriculum design tools integrated throughout the book, available to access on the GA website (see p. 3 for details).

The importance of specialist subject knowledge and ongoing professional development

What hopefully emerges from this book is that your main strength as a geography department, including any non-specialists, is the specialist subject knowledge, understanding, and skills that you collectively possess. At every stage from key stage 3 to key stage 5 this collective expertise is required to identify the geographical concepts, processes and skills to be progressed; make appropriate selections of content, sequenced in a coherent key stage curriculum plan; designed to have a positive impact on your students' progress towards your curriculum intent.

The GA Manifesto points out the challenge geography teachers face as curriculum makers, related to the dynamic nature of the world we study, and how we investigate it (pp. 28–9). The Manifesto explains that geography teachers 'need to have a productive and ongoing relationship with the subject' (p. 28). Teachers have a responsibility to keep up-to-date, maintain and develop their professional expertise, in terms of subject and curriculum; this is what Teacher Standard 3 identifies as 'demonstrate good subject and curriculum knowledge'. The Teachers' Standards (DfE, 2013) place the emphasis on the individual, requiring teachers to take responsibility for their own professional development, maintaining their knowledge and skills, remaining self-critical. Biddulph, Lambert and Balderstone, in a concluding chapter about ongoing professional development, (2015, p. 305), acknowledge the importance of support within schools, but argue that a reliance on 'in-school support' 'runs the risk of being very inward looking, and in order to sustain your professional development you need to look outwards too'. Alan Kinder, Chief Executive of the Geographical Association, opens up an important discussion in the final chapter of the GA's *Handbook of Secondary Geography* (2017, pp. 330–44) about the role of the teaching professional, and the relationship between individual

INTENT

Chapter 4 — What are we trying to achieve?

The national curriculum and GCSE aims for geography to ensure that all students:

NC Curriculum & GCSE aims	Develop contextual 'world knowledge': continents, oceans, countries, regions and location of places **know geographical material**	Understand the processes that give rise to key physical and human geographical features of the world **think like a geographer**	Are competent in the geographical skills **Study like a geographer/ applying geography**

Thinking geographically	A Future 3, progressive, powerful-knowledge-led curriculum, adopting a coherent and sequenced approach, planning for progression in understanding geographical concepts and skills, designed to develop students' capabilities to think creatively, critically and carefully Chapter 2 pp. 25–29, chapter 3 pp. 36–43, chapter 4 pp. 65–68

INTENT

Chapter 5 — Designing a coherent and sequenced curriculum planned for student progress

Turning the vision into a curriculum plan with assessment and progress at its heart

Towards coherence	Concepts	Knowledge	Skills
Three scales of planning for coherence	Long-term plan	Medium-term plan	Lesson plan

Chapter 5 pp. 84–86

IMPLEMENTATION

Chapter 6 — Enquiry-led approach to pedagogy, assessment integral

Approaches to pedagogy that support the curriculum intent – enquiry-led

Pedagogy	A range of approaches e.g. enquiry, active learning, practical and constructive	Students make sense of a wide range of geographical data as a matter of routine	Students use maps as a matter of routine	Fieldwork embedded	Living geography: ensuring that studies include more than a single perspective and are real and truly representative

Teachers use a variety of assessment approaches to check students understand systematically

Assessment fit for purpose Chapter 6, pp. 113–119	Is integral to effective teaching and learning	Day-to-day	Frequent – basic knowledge/skills	Half-termly – conceptual, procedural
	Long term – substantial, conceptual development	Helps identify clear targets for improvement	Links to the school's progression framework for geography which is consistently interpreted	Informs future planning and teaching

IMPACT

Chapter 7 — How well are we achieving our aims?

Impact – so that students have progressed and are ready for their next stage of education, employment or training

Fascination about the world, with capability to think geographically	Understand geographical phenomena at different scales local to global	Acquired a locational framework	Understand a range of the interactions and relationships between the physical and human world	Describe and explain geographical patterns	Use a range of geographical skills and enquiry independently

Evaluation process – Chapter 7 pp. 121–131

Figure 9.1: A big picture of designing your 11–16 curriculum. ⬇

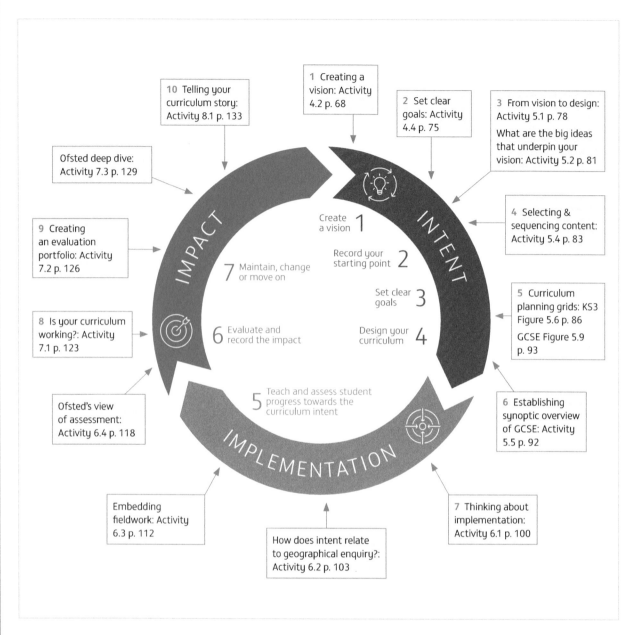

Figure 9.2: Steps in the curriculum design process. ⬇

10 Telling your curriculum story: Activity 8.1 p. 133

1 Creating a vision: Activity 4.2 p. 68

2 Set clear goals: Activity 4.4 p. 75

3 From vision to design: Activity 5.1 p. 78

What are the big ideas that underpin your vision: Activity 5.2 p. 81

Ofsted deep dive: Activity 7.3 p. 129

4 Selecting & sequencing content: Activity 5.4 p. 83

9 Creating an evaluation portfolio: Activity 7.2 p. 126

5 Curriculum planning grids: KS3 Figure 5.6 p. 86

GCSE Figure 5.9 p. 93

8 Is your curriculum working?: Activity 7.1 p. 123

6 Establishing synoptic overview of GCSE: Activity 5.5 p. 92

Ofsted's view of assessment: Activity 6.4 p. 118

7 Thinking about implementation: Activity 6.1 p. 100

Embedding fieldwork: Activity 6.3 p. 112

How does intent relate to geographical enquiry?: Activity 6.2 p. 103

IMPACT · INTENT · IMPLEMENTATION

1 Create a vision
2 Record your starting point
3 Set clear goals
4 Design your curriculum
5 Teach and assess student progress towards the curriculum intent
6 Evaluate and record the impact
7 Maintain, change or move on

teachers, their subject community and the wider environment. He explains the importance of such a community network to a geography teacher's ongoing professional development. The GA's strategy and vision 2020–25 aims for 'a vibrant and diverse subject community, inspiring high-quality geographical teaching and learning.'

The Ofsted Geography Research Review (2021) highlights the importance of ongoing professional development:

'Perhaps the most critical factor in ensuring a high-quality geographical education is teachers' subject knowledge ... If "good geographical subject knowledge is a prerequisite for good teaching", then subject-specific training becomes critical. Teachers need to have the knowledge to successfully plan and revise the geography curriculum, as well as to consider their own teaching and the impact that it has on pupils' learning ... As geography is a dynamic

subject, the need to maintain both up-to-date subject knowledge and also to engage in discourse about the nature of the subject and pedagogy are key. Many authors identify the supportive role of the Geographical Association and the Royal Geographical Society (with the Institute of British Geographers) in this regard.'

This GA publication is designed to pull together, in one place, a wide range of theories and ideas about curriculum development from the subject community, as well as provide practical guidance and tools to support curriculum design, alongside examples of school practice. The GA offers a wide range of publications, projects and processes, events, and professional development, that complement the guidance provided in this book. These opportunities for further development and even active involvement in the Association are summarised in Figure 9.3.

You can find out more about the Association and what it has to offer your geography department in the 'About' section of the GA website: www.geography.org.uk/About-the-GA

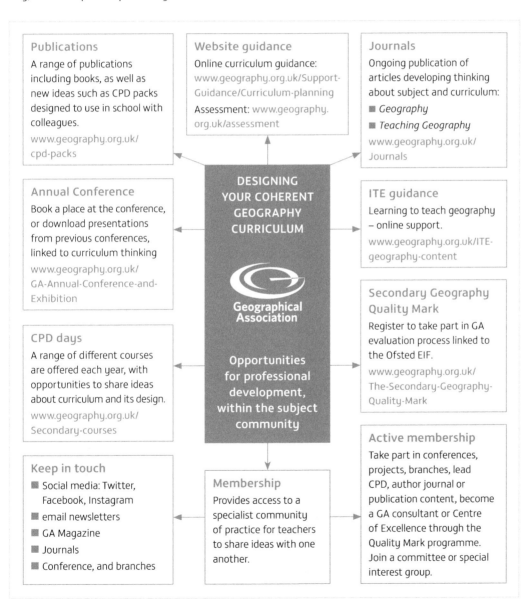

Figure 9.3: A summary of GA activities, support and services. ⬇

Action research

A Futures 3 curriculum (Chapter 2, p. 27), underpinned by a curriculum making process, involves teachers in deep thinking about curriculum intent. It involves an ongoing process of evaluation of the impact of this intent on students' progress, and how it is implemented in the classroom. This evaluation is central to the curriculum design process used in this book (Figure 9.2). In effect, this is action research; in developing your curriculum you are asking important questions along the way:

- what are we trying to achieve? (a research question)

- how do we organise the learning to achieve our intent?

- how do we know we have been successful?

- how can we improve our intent and implementation to increase impact?

Action research comprises posing a research question, embedding this in practice, and evaluating impact. It is useful to write up this research as a summary of your curriculum story; in effect your approach to curriculum. This can be shared with others, most importantly your senior management, but also all colleagues teaching geography in your department, so they are clear on the what, why, how and the intended impact of their teaching. The five case study schools have told their curriculum stories to share their ideas and practice to support the subject community. Figure 9.3 demonstrates how you can develop from being a member of the GA community, simply using resources like these case studies to develop your practice, to becoming an active member – sharing

what you learn about curriculum design by writing up your action research as a journal article, or leading a session at the Annual Conference, or a CPD day. The GA's Quality Mark provides a framework and an online portfolio to support this action research, with formal feedback on your actions.

The introduction to the case studies in Chapter 8 (Activity 8.1, pp. 133–5), provides a template of key questions which you could also use to tell your curriculum story.

The GA has developed an online portfolio, the GA Professional Passport, to support your deep thinking about curriculum as part of your professional development.

The passport and associated awards enable a focus on learning, process and impact rather than simply 'doing CPD'. You can find out more about the opportunities this can provide to support your curriculum action research at www.geography.org.uk/GA-Professional-Passport-and-Award.

What next – thinking strategically

As your experience and curriculum evolve, it is important you think more strategically. Many schools have initially focussed their attention on the key stage 3 curriculum, but as this book suggests, the principles of curriculum design are just as important at GCSE. Chapter 3 (pp. 46–8) and Figure 1 (p. 57) in the introduction to the guidance section of this book, highlight the progression built into the government geography curriculum documents 5–19. These can be used as a starting point to consider a 5–19 coherent geography curriculum. It may be possible to collaborate with your feeder primary school teachers to establish curriculum progression

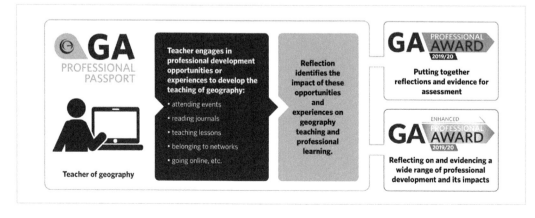

Figure 9.4:
The Geographical Association's Professional Passport and Awards.

and continuity across key stages 1–3. You should also think this through 11–16 using the tools provided in this book. It is also possible to develop coherence from key stage 3 to 5; an 11–16 school could collaborate with a sixth form college to achieve this, as Andy Freer and Daniel Whittall have in their case study (Chapter 8, pp. 137–40). This case study has focused on GCSE, but does explain how this curriculum builds on a foundation established at key stage 3. Daniel has further developed the approach at A level from a statement of intent (Figure 9.5). His work to evaluate the impact of this curriculum, with its focus on powerful knowledge, using student voice, is highlighted in Chapter 7 (p. 124).

At the end of each chapter in the book there is an extensive list of references for you to dig deeper in researching the ideas introduced in this book.

There are a number of key GA publications that you can use extensively with this book to design your coherent 11–16 geography curriculum:

- **Geography Through Enquiry** – Margaret Roberts
- **The Handbook of Secondary Geography** – Edited by Mark Jones
- **A Different View: A Manifesto from the Geographical Association** – a statement of beliefs and priorities. This is an excellent starting point for establishing your curriculum intent, as well as an overview of the curriculum making process.
- **A progression framework for geography** – (eBook – digital download) by John Hopkin with David Gardner, Alan Kinder, Ruth Totterdell and the GA Assessment and Examinations Special Interest Group. Provides key thinking about progression in geography 5–16, providing age-related benchmark statements within a progression framework. Referenced in Chapter 3: Progression.
- **GA website – support and guidance – curriculum planning** – www.geography.org. uk/Support-Guidance/Curriculum-planning

Geography curriculum mission statement

Never has there been a more important time to teach geography. It is essential in an age of climate change and geopolitical ferment that young people are equipped with the knowledge and skills required to understand Earth as the home of humankind and to value our more than human dependencies and relationalities. Teaching geography in the Anthropocene – the geological 'human epoch' in which human activity re-shapes physical systems on Earth – demands a rigorous approach to curriculum design and requires teachers to actively embrace their role as curriculum makers.

We take seriously Michael Young's assertion that 'For children from disadvantaged homes, active participation in school may be the only opportunity that they have to acquire powerful knowledge and be able to move, intellectually at least, beyond their local and particular circumstances' (Young, 2011, p. 152). Consequently, we believe that it is the responsibility of all geography teachers to regard themselves as curriculum makers whose task it is to promote the active participation of all our students in a powerful geographical education that is engaging, rigorous, intellectually stimulating and promotes critical thinking.

However, we also recognise that powerful knowledge is itself an insufficient framework for understanding the value of a geographical education. Powerful knowledge is defined by Young as knowledge drawn from specialised academic disciplines. We take seriously the critiques of this idea that have argued that academic knowledge is itself structured by hierarchies and inequalities, and that to put too much emphasis on academic disciplinary knowledge risks neglecting other forms of knowledge that are an essential element of a broad and diverse geographical education, including indigenous knowledges and students' own 'ethno-knowledges'. We recognise that as curriculum-makers we bring to this task our own privileges and we are open to, and mindful of, potential criticisms that could be made of our curriculum. Our curriculum is 'made' in such a way as to always be mindful of these risks, and actively seeks to overcome the 'danger of a single story', including the single story of powerful knowledge.

Figure 9.5:
A level geography curriculum intent – Daniel Whittall, Trinity Sixth Form Academy, Halifax (continued overleaf).

Mary Myatt has argued that when it comes to curriculum making 'coherence comes from paying attention to the big ideas that underpin each curriculum area' (Myatt, 2018, p.11). The A level geography curriculum at TSFA thus engages students in a narrative with what we consider to be geography's big ideas. Across our curriculum, students will encounter these big ideas and will explore their meaning in a diverse range of geographical contexts and at a range of spatial scales. We take an Earth systems perspective to the subject of geography and encourage students to interrogate the world through the conceptual lens provided by our subject's big ideas, such as place, space, interdependence and power geometries. Through these concepts students will come to better understand questions of sustainability, of Earth's physical processes, of urbanisation, globalisation and cultural diversity.

Geographical knowledge consists of far more than the accumulation of mere facts. We aim for a truthful understanding of the facts set within a critical conceptual framework. In building our curriculum we have therefore adopted the following six key principles, derived in part from Alaric Maude's (2015) research into powerful knowledge in geography:

1. Our curriculum will provide students with new ways of thinking about the world and will promote critical thought throughout.

2. Our curriculum will provide students with powerful ways of analyzing, explaining and understanding different aspects of our world.

3. Our curriculum will provide students with power over their own geographical knowledge. Students will be equipped with an understanding of what makes geographical knowledge distinctive, will be able to appreciate different approaches to the study of geography and will understand that they, and the communities they are a part of, are themselves engaged in struggles over geographical knowledge.

4. Our curriculum will enable young people to follow and participate in debates on significant local, national and global issues.

5. Our curriculum will develop students' knowledge of the world.

6. Our curriculum will enable students to appreciate the variety and diversity of geographical knowledges. Students will be equipped with an understanding of what makes geographical knowledge distinctive, and we will support students in critically evaluating geographical arguments.

We work with outside institutions and organisations and we are a research-active department seeking to contribute to an improved understanding of the curriculum-making process. We commit to regularly reviewing our curriculum to ensure that it meets the above principles so that our students develop the critical geographical understanding that will enable them to understand and engage with their world and develop what Derek Gregory has termed their 'geographical imaginations'.

Figure 9.5:
A level geography curriculum intent – Daniel Whittall, Trinity Sixth Form Academy, Halifax.

References

All websites last accessed 27/07/2021.

Biddulph, M., Lambert, D. and Balderstone, D. (2015) *Learning to Teach Geography in the Secondary School: A companion to school experience*. Abingdon: Routledge.

DfE (2013) *Teachers Standards*. London: Department for Education.

Geographical Association (2009) *A Different View: A Manifesto from the Geographical Association*. Sheffield: Geographical Association. Available at www.geography.org.uk/GA-Manifesto-for-geography

Jones, M. (ed) (2017) *The Handbook of Secondary Geography*. Sheffield: Geographical Association.

Kinder, A (2017) 'Belonging to a subject community', Chapter 24 in Jones, M. (ed) *The Handbook of Secondary Geography* pp. 330–343

Maude, A. (2016) 'What might powerful geographical knowledge look like?', *Geography*, 101, 2, pp. 70–76.

Myatt, M. (2018) *The Curriculum: Gallimaufry to coherence*. Woodbridge, Suffolk: John Catt Educational Ltd.

Ofsted (2021) *Ofsted geography research review*. Available at www.gov.uk/government/news/ofsted-publishes-research-review-on-geography

Young, M. (2011) 'What are schools for?', *Educação Sociedade & Culturas*, 32, pp. 145–55.

Index

Planning your coherent 11–16 geography curriculum: a design toolkit